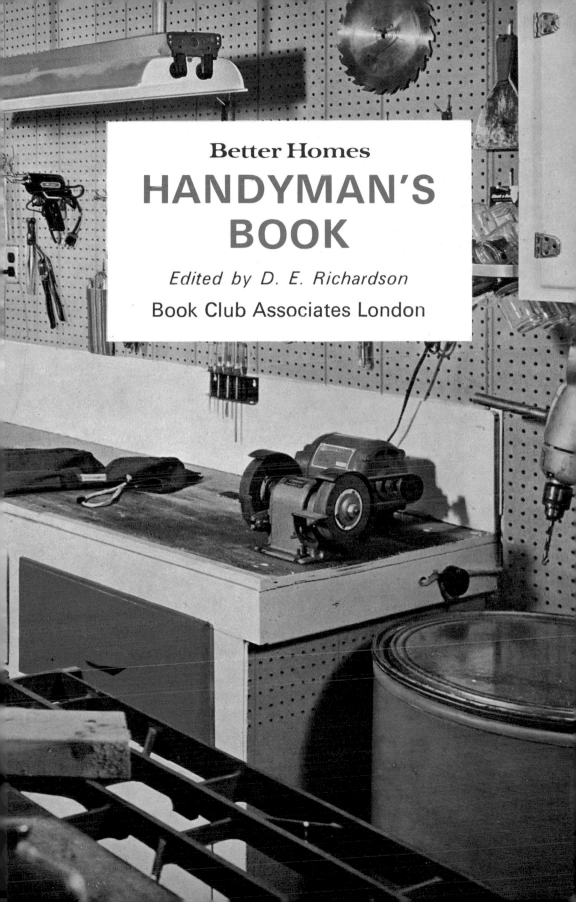

Better Homes

HANDYMAN'S BOOK

Edited by D. E. Richardson

Book Club Associates London

Contents

ISBN 0 00 435517 2

© Meredith Corporation 1969
Printed in Great Britain by Collins London and Glasgow

This edition published 1970 by
Book Club Associates
By arrangement with Messrs Wm. Collins Sons and Co. Ltd.

Reprinted 1971, 1972

Skill with tools and materials enables you to make home repairs and improvements.

To the handyman...

Although we are calling this the *Handyman's Book*, it might more aptly be called the *Unhandyman's Book*. Its purpose is to present, as clearly as possible, basic information on a wide range of subjects so that the uninitiated, unhandy man can cope with the many routine jobs around the house, as well as tackle confidently new projects of his own.

The book is also intended to serve as a source of reference for the handyman who is already competent to do many jobs. With it, he will be able to develop his skill and his technique for many jobs with which he is already familiar.

The experienced handyman will also benefit from this book by gaining insight into the use of new tools which may be able to do some jobs more efficiently than those he has been using. He will then be able to equip his workshop more wisely with the tools best suited to his needs.

In addition to the vast amount of basic information about jobs both inside and outside the home, there are complete sections on hand and power tools, furniture finishing techniques; modern interior and exterior paints; methods for fitting laminated plastic working surfaces and installing sliding doors; ideas for storage, room dividers, kitchen units; information about central heating and double glazing; and suggestions for the garden.

Tools and equipment

It will pay to acquire good tools, even if it means adding to your collection more slowly. Cheap ones are frustrating, sometimes dangerous—and false economy. Tools should be made of the best materials to do the job, should fit together properly, and have proper safety devices such as guards and correct wiring. Dangerous tools should be stored out of reach of children.

Care of tools

Once you obtain a good tool, give it the care it deserves. Keep cutting edges sharp—they are actually safer that way. The cutting edges of chisels or planes become blunt after about ten minutes work on hardwood.

Give your tools proper maintenance and lubrication—make a habit of cleaning them immediately after use. Prevent rust spots forming on chisels, saws and similar tools by greasing regularly. Do not wait to replace or repair damaged tools.

Space to work

Do-it-yourself projects need space—so try to have a particular room or shed where you can instal a work bench and store tools and equipment. You will also be able to leave a job without clearing up between sessions.

Saving money

One of the great advantages of being a competent handyman is the saving of money. So plan each project before you start work so that you can make the most of the saving. Make rough sketches, decide on the materials and quantities needed, which joints you intend to use, which wall fixings are required, etc. Then prepare lists so that you know exactly what you need to buy, approximately how much it will cost—and whether you can afford it.

An orderly arrangement of the right kinds of tools makes work on any d.i.y. job easier.

Start right to
be a handyman

The following lists of tools have been carefully selected to help you equip yourself to do minor repair and d.i.y. jobs, and, as your skills develop, add more tools to handle more complicated jobs.

You will be amazed at the number of

jobs you can do with this first collection of simple, but important tools. Remember to buy only top-quality.

Add to your basic tools with the more complete selection shown on the opposite page, and you will be able to master most jobs.

The list of tools on page 7 is recommended as the third step on your way to assembling tools for a good workshop. The investment keeps mounting as you go along, but the increase in your capabilities far outweighs the cost.

As you become more expert, you will want to add even more versatile (and expensive) tools. But by that time, you will be the best judge of which tools best suit your needs.

Your first step is getting these tools: Dovetail saw, pliers, screwdrivers (Phillips and regular), assortment of nails and screws, glue, multi-bladed forming plane, 10-oz. hammer, nail punch, adjustable wrench, scratch awl, machine oil, steel tape measure, shop knife, push drill and bits. Divided tool box (inset), which is simple to make, keeps tools handy.

Next, get these tools: Eight-point cross-cut saw, combination square, sharpening stone, pipe wrench, large screwdriver, 10-inch file, hacksaw, diagonal wire cutters, butane gas blow lamp with soldering tip and flame spreading tip, $\frac{1}{4}$- and $\frac{3}{4}$-inch wood chisels, putty knife, locking pliers, sanding block, $\frac{3}{8}$- or $\frac{1}{2}$-inch electric drill with wood and metal cutting bits, portable woodworker's vice, 24-inch spirit level. A sheet of perforated hardboard (right) on a door or wall provides storage for tools.

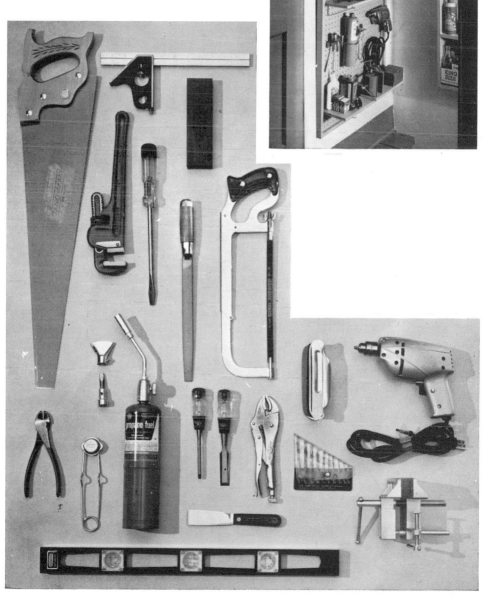

When you are ready for a fully-fledged workshop, give its layout a lot of thought. Three basic needs for any workshop are space, light, and a good work-bench.

If possible pick a place for your workshop where it will have room to grow. A common fault in home workshops is lack of open floor space for large projects. See page 61.

Spend some money and provide plenty of light for your workshop. The importance of adequate light cannot be over-emphasised. If you cannot see your work well enough, you will soon get tired and start making costly mistakes.

Fluorescent fixtures are best for over-all lighting. White paint on the walls and ceilings is the least expensive and most satisfactory way to increase light level. The size and design of your work-bench depends mostly on the space you have. The bench should be high enough so that you do not have to stoop at all to work on it. The height of your hip-bone —about 40 to 42 inches for most men— is about the right bench height.

Third-step tools: Paintbrushes, bulk supplies of paint and sealers, 16-oz. hammer, C-clamps, sabre saw, wiping cloth, steel wool, orbital sander, channel pliers, heavy-duty stapler and staples. Your tool board (inset) now keeps your tools above the work-bench.

Other handy tools and supplies

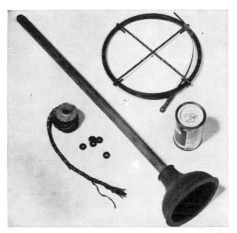

Have a "plumber's friend", plumber's snake, chemical drainpipe cleaner, graphite string, and washers ready for any plumbing emergency. These tools help keep plumbing operating efficiently and may save repairs later. Take care not to crack the basin when unscrewing taps—see page 191.

Bulk supplies: If you have storage space, save time and money by bulk-buying items like paint, thinners, turpentine, linseed oil, cleaning agents, paraffin and emulsion paints. Other items could include putty, sealers for both wood and wallpaper, and various types of fillers.

Electrical spares should include fuses—cartridge and wire—of all ratings, bulbs, switches, bulb-holders, plugs, insulating tape and connectors, junction boxes, cable—both lighting and power. Tools should include insulated pliers and screwdrivers and a testing screwdriver. Read pages 195-202 before tackling any electrical repairs. There are a number of jobs which should be done only by qualified electricians.

Paintbrushes—like any other tool—last longer and give better performance if they are good ones. Pick four-inch brush for outside work, large surfaces; sash "tool" for windows; also enamel, varnish, and stain brushes. Clean paint brushes after every job—they will last much longer. First clean out paint with an appropriate solvent cleaner, then wash in warm soapy water, rinse and dry. Never store brushes standing on their bristles—it is the quickest way to force them out of shape.

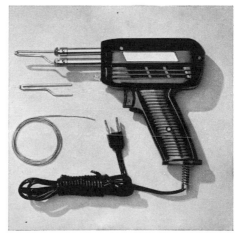

Electric soldering "gun" is another good investment for your workshop. These heat up fast and are especially handy to manipulate. Special tips are made for cutting soft materials such as linoleum or tar paper. See page 146 for instructions on how to solder.

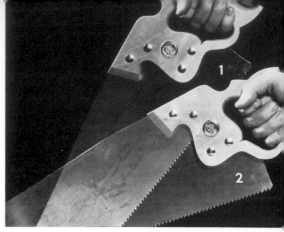

Start saw by using knuckle of thumb to help guide blade. Pull saw towards you, cutting a slot for next downward stroke. Use knuckles for the next few strokes—until the saw is started.

Saw stroke should rock slightly, following a normal arc as arm swings from shoulder. Thus, at end of stroke, saw teeth follow cut along line on board. Weight of saw cuts for you.

How to use a handsaw

A true and square cut on a piece of plywood can be made quickly and accurately if you use this simple trick: Mark a line at the length the wood is to be trimmed. Position a 2 x 4 (or 2 x 2) you know is square along the line, and clamp it to the work. Board now acts as guide to keep saw on the line.

Comparison shows the difference between cross-cut and rip-saws. The cross-cut's teeth (right) are filed to give you a sliding cut across wood fibres while the rip-saw's chisel-like teeth are made to plough with grain of the wood.

Accurate angle cuts into plywood are easy to make if you use a 2 x 4 to guide the saw. Mark the angle to cut on the edge of the plywood and square line across the board. After you have started the saw, clamp a 2 x 4 parallel to cut-off line so that saw just touches edge. Guide will keep saw from wandering.

Nearly every job a handyman tackles requires a handsaw. That makes it important to know how to select, use, and care for saws.

A cross-cut saw, for cutting across the grain, and a ripsaw, for cutting with the grain, are probably the most necessary for all-round use. (The cross-cut works best if you hold it at an angle of about 45 degrees to the wood, and the ripsaw is best at about 60 degrees.)

There are many other kinds of saws that you will want to add to your hand-tool equipment, even if you have a power saw. Some of them are shown on page 12.

Your handsaw, unlike most other tools, generally needs a professional's touch for sharpening.

Use the cross-cut saw to make cuts across grain. Steady the timber you are cutting with the left hand so that the motion of the arm working the saw does not move the board out of position. To avoid sawing into your bench top or whatever you are using to support board, allow about three inches clearance between cut and bench.

Check your work often to make sure it is square

Saw will not bind when ripping long boards (left) if saw cut is kept open with nail or wooden wedge. Move it towards you as you go. A clamp across cut at end of board stops whip.

Square cuts are easy to make (lower left) if you check the saw blade at intervals with a try square. Place blade of square against saw, letting body of it follow along the cut-off line.

If saw wanders off line (below), bring it back to the spot (arrow) where it veered, and start again. This is easier than twisting saw back to the line, then planing edge after the cut is made.

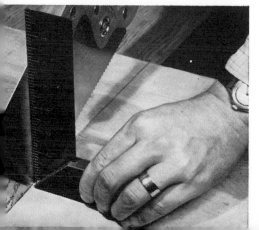

Job at hand determines kind of saw to use

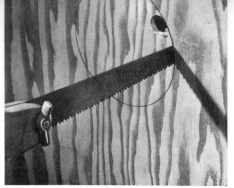

Keyhole saw cuts holes for pipes, electrical outlets, or fixtures in floors, walls, and in ceilings. Tapered blade goes where other saws cannot, and it will cut through tough materials.

Coping saw is curve cutter. Or use it for some inside cuts by drilling starter hole first. Then remove the blade, insert it in hole, and reassemble. Pins (arrow) adjust the blade.

Mitre box is used with tennon saw, designed for accurate cutting with or across grain. Frame of this mitre unit adjusts to almost any angle. Stiff back is ideal for straight cuts.

Cabinet saw—sometimes called dovetail saw —is smaller version of tennon saw with different handle. Use it to cut tennons, grooves, rabbets, and for other fine work.

Thin cuts less than width of saw cut are easy to do if a piece of wood controls saw. Clamp wood to piece you will trim so end extends slightly. When cutting, off-cut acts as guide.

To start cut, nick surface to be cut with a file, then start hacksaw blade in nick. Or use thumb to guide blade until cut is started.

Use both hands to hold the saw. Apply cutting pressure on forward stroke; lift blade off work on return stroke. Hacksaws cut only one way—forwards. Bear down just enough to keep the saw cutting. Do not put too much pressure on forward end. (It blunts teeth, causes blade to skip over the metal.)

How to use a hacksaw

Blades have 14, 18, 24, or 32 teeth per inch. The best blade for general use is an 18 tooth one (top). To cut thin material, use 32-tooth (bottom) for a smooth cut.

For hard cutting, your best tool is the hacksaw. When you use it, a light, steady stroke is best—about 40 to 50 times a minute.

Always insert a new blade in the frame with the teeth pointing away from the handle. Tighten the wing nut until the blade is rigid. Insufficient tension will cause the blade to twist and jam; too much tension will cause the blade to break at the end holes.

If you break a blade, do not insert a new blade in the old cut. It makes a wider cut and will jam. Turn the metal over and start anew from the other side.

For inside cuts, use a pointed hacksaw with replaceable blade. Shaped like a key-hole saw, it works in tight places. Here it cuts tongue in strike plate to catch latch.

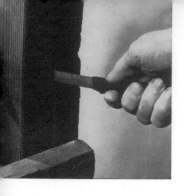

Wrap insulating tape around the end of a blade when you must get into an opening too small for a conventional frame. Saw with slow, even strokes.

Always keep the blade flat on the metal. The more teeth you have going across the metal, the better the saw operates. Avoid holding blade at sharp angle.

To cut a thin sheet of metal, clamp it between two pieces of scrap wood, and cut through all thicknesses. This method makes clean cut without bending metal. Use vice to hold work.

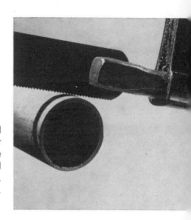

On thin metal, use fine-toothed blades. Keep at least two or three teeth on the metal while cutting it. If you do not, metal will tend to jam between teeth, causing them to strip off blade.

To cut thin metal tubing, insert appropriate sized dowel in it. For any work that is polished and must not be marred, make clamps of soft wallboard and insert between work and vice.

On thick metal, use coarse blades. Even stroke (keep two or three teeth on metal) with fairly heavy pressure gives fast, deep cut. Keep blade tight in frame of the hacksaw to avoid buckling.

Cut wider slots in one sawing operation by adding more blades to saw. End pins are usually long and strong enough to hold several. Teeth should all point the same way.

Reverse the blade to get at a job that is in an awkward position. The blade and the frame have to be assembled round the job, and care must be taken when cutting.

Choosing and using a plane

With a sharp plane, a skilled craftsman can produce a square and true edge to a board. That kind of skill takes practice, but even the unskilled handyman can use a plane to good advantage in shaving a board smooth or trimming a door or drawer.

When you use a plane, take long strokes, striving for a shaving that comes off in a continuous ribbon.

When you smooth the end grain, cut only part of the way across, completing the stroke from the other side. This avoids splitting the corners.

Keep the plane iron sharp; a blunt blade tears wood instead of shaving it.

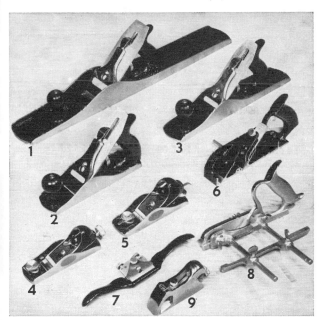

Planes are made for every cutting and smoothing job

More common planes include (1) jointer plane, (2) smoothing, (3) jack, (4) low-angle block, (5) block, (6) rabbet, (7) spokeshave, (8) combination rabbet, and (9) cabinetmaker's. The jack plane is best suited for all-round use by a handyman. Jointer and smoothing planes, as well as jack, are used for coarse or fine work. Low-angle block and regular block are used for planing edge grain and fitting. The spokeshave is designed for smoothing curved surfaces, and the combination rabbet plane will cut ploughs, rabbets, dadoes, and beads. The tiny cabinetmaker's rabbet plane is an excellent tool for mortises, splices, gains, and rabbets.

Know how to dismantle and adjust your plane

Each part of your plane has specific purpose: (1) Adjusting nut for depth of cut; (2) Y adjusting lever attached to nut, (3) lateral lever sets blade square, (4) plane iron and plane iron cap, (5) cam removes the lever cap, (6) lever cap locks on plane iron and cap, (7) lever cap supports cap and irons, (8) frog supports caps, irons, and screw, (9) knob affords handhold for pressure, (10) toe supports knob, (11) mouth accepts plane iron, (12) plane bottom—made for smooth cut, (13) heel supports handle, (14) handle grip for back pressure.

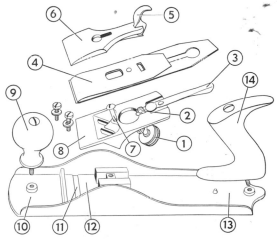

Cut smooth, straight edge by applying correct pressure

Begin stroke by applying most of pressure from hands and arms to knob. Pressure is applied to both knob and handle at middle of stroke, to handle at end. Follow it through.

Hold plane at slight angle to cut you will make. It should shave wood off, not tear or chip it. Strive for ribbon-like shavings by practicing on scrap until plane is set for job.

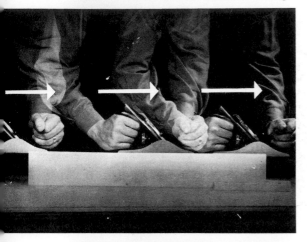

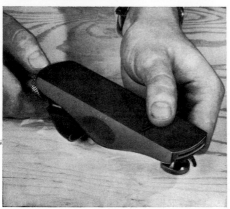

Adjust blade quickly by running thumb lightly along—or sighting down—bottom of plane. For smooth cut, blade should extend hair's width. Set blade with the adjusting nut.

For even shaving, keep blade parallel with plane bottom (shown here out of parallel) by moving lateral adjustment lever. This keeps wood from getting higher on one edge.

To dismantle for sharpening and cleaning, remove plane-iron cap from plane iron by unscrewing screw with lever cap. For re-assembling, see diagram on page 15.

Plane end grain glassy smooth by cutting a slight bevel at corner first (see arrow) to prevent splintering. Or plane half-way from each edge to keep from splitting. Take thin cuts.

Two or three pencil lines on a board will let you see just where edge has been taken down and where bumps remain, when you try to keep an even edge on timber.

Adjustable fence determines width of cut with rabbet plane. It can be used on either side. Double seat for blade lets you work into corners. Tool comes with fitted depth gauge.

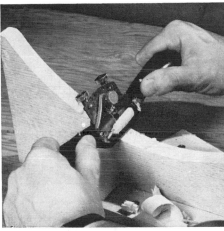

Smooth curved surfaces with a spokeshave, usually pulled instead of pushed like plane. Cut with grain to avoid chipping. Depth of blade is set with screws according to timber.

Combination plane makes dadoes, beads, matching tongue, grooves, rabbets. It is equipped with spurs for end-grain planing, a fence, depth gauge, and lever adjustment.

Jointer plane spans low spots on long, uneven surfaces, smoothing them after higher ridges are trimmed. It is ideal for planing edges to be glued. Use like smoothing plane.

Small rabbet plane is used for trimming rabbetted shoulders, and for splices, mortises, or gains. Can be converted into chisel plane for removing glue or excess wood in corners.

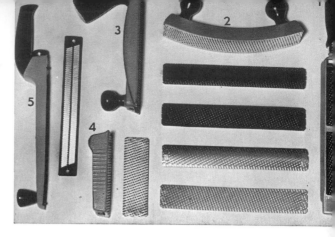

Multi-bladed forming tools are now available in file (1), convex plane (2), and plane (3) shapes. The pocket tool (4) is for one-hand use and for safe, convenient carrying. Tool on the left (5) has a handle that shifts to plane or file shapes.

Blades are made in various grades so that masonry and steel can be cut as well as wood.

Multi-bladed wood forming tool

Multi-bladed tools do a fast, smooth job on wood, will not gouge or splinter—will even plane across grain ends or plywood edges. A plane handle works best on all flat areas; the file type tool is better for free-hand work.

Half round blade, shown here on file handle, trims and forms concave and compound-curved surfaces. It works well on any curved surface where flat tools will not fit. Allow shavings to get away from blade.

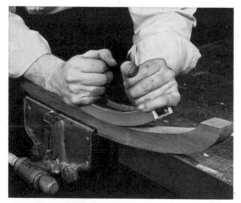

Convex planing tool uses the same flat blade, but bends it to plane recessed areas. It is ideal for cleaning up and smoothing any shaped surface. Could be used instead of spokeshave.

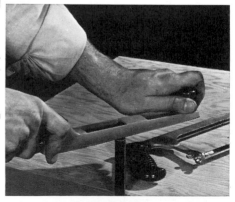

With fine-cut blades, these tools work well on metals up to mild steel. Used as shown, this tool makes fast work of removing the burr on sawn tubing. It works the same way in the smoothing of solder and other metals.

How to use a drawknife, pocket-knife and scraper

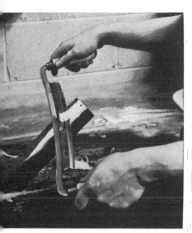 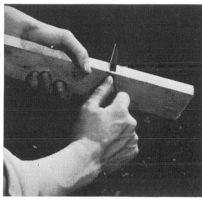 

Drawknife (left) removes wood quickly to rough out a shaped piece. Grasp handles and pull knife to you. Pocket-knife (centre) is handy in workshop. Keep it razor-sharp on oilstone. Cut away from yourself. Scraper (right) is tool to use for scraping off peeling paint or for stripping off sludge softened by a paint remover.

How to use chisels

Your wood chisels are precision tools. Keep them razor sharp. Store them in wall racks or wood-lined drawers where their edges are protected. Never use them to cut anything but wood, and do not prise with them.

Grinding angle for sharpening your chisels is between 20 and 35 degrees, depending on use. For a paring chisel, the best grinding angle is 30 to 35 degrees; for chisels used in hard-wood, the best angle is 20 degrees.

For special woodworking projects and maintenance jobs, this chisel selection comes in handy. (A basic selection of wood chisels is shown on page 20. Across top of picture is a set of swan neck chisels used for fine, exacting work in wood. Specially curved blades make cuts that are difficult with flat blades. The wide metal chisel below is used for cutting bricks and stone. Cold chisel shown at the bottom is used for heavy work on concrete etc.

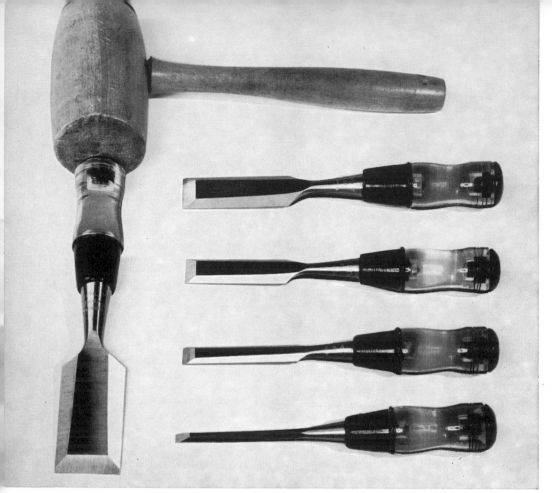

Buy good chisels. A useful set includes these sizes: $\frac{1}{4}$-, $\frac{3}{8}$-, $\frac{1}{2}$-, $\frac{5}{8}$-, $\frac{3}{4}$-inch widths. Never use a hammer on wooden handled chisels. It could both split and roughen the handles, making them uncomfortable to hold.

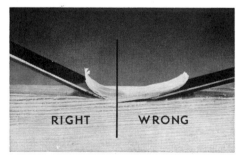

RIGHT WRONG

Any chisel is a knife, its tapered edge slicing and separating wood fibres just like a wedge. Splits will break free (upper left) if the blade travels into downhill grain. Let one hand grip and guide the blade (upper right) while the other hand applies the push on the handle. The cleanest cut comes from a sideways slip as the chisel advances—like the slide of a sharp razor. Recessed cuts (right) where the blade cannot lie flat on the wood with bevel up, are made with the chisel held at an angle, bevel down. Control the cutting action by holding the angle of the chisel constant.

All cross-grain cutting goes best when chisel is held like that pictured, left above. Lift it so corner of edge begins the cut, rock it level as pressure is applied to press through wood.

Mortise cut (above), because cut is shallow, is best done with short-bladed butt chisels. If handle is all wood, strike with mallet.

Deep mortise (left) needs thick-bladed chisels so prising wood away at bottom will not snap steel. Keep flat side towards shoulder of cut; allow for undercut of one-sided bevel.

Keep your wood chisels razor-sharp

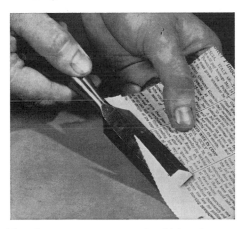

Try the paper test; cut should be clean—not ragged. Another test: Hold blade in good light and look for reflected line of highlight that reveals rounding, blunting of bevel.

Never use chisels as paint scrapers, wedges, screwdrivers, or lid lifters. Wood chisels are made for wood; paint, mud, glue-covered timber blunts edges.

How to use files and rasps

Files and rasps are manufactured in a great variety of shapes and sizes; a good selection is shown below.

A file with a single row of parallel teeth is called single cut; with a second row of teeth criss-crossing the first it is called double cut. Single and double cut files commonly come in four degrees of coarseness: Coarse for rough, fast work; second cut for tough alloys and more finished work; smooth cut for fine finish. For wood, you will want a rasp, which has large teeth for fast cutting.

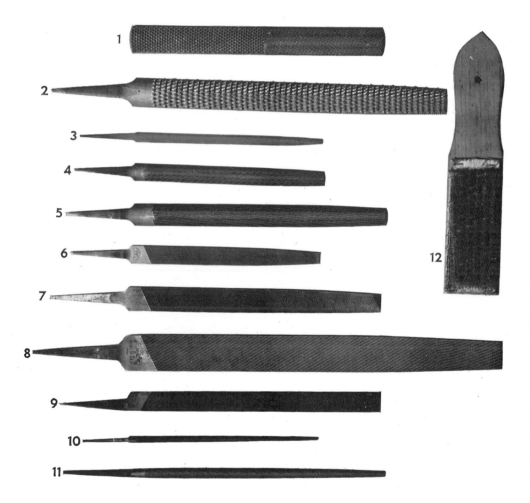

Files and rasps that you will probably use most include those in this selection: (1) 10-inch combination "shoe" rasp; (2) 12-inch half-round wood rasp; (3) 6-inch round; (4) a 6-inch half-round for small surfaces; (5) 10-inch half-round for rough work and concave surfaces; (6) 6-inch smooth-cut mill file for smoothing small pieces of work. A 10-inch smooth-cut mill (7) for smooth finishing; (8) 8- or 10-inch second-cut mill for finishing (mill files are single cut); (9) 10-inch knife for sharp angles; (10) a 6-inch triangular for touching up and sharpening some saws, and so on, (11) 10-inch round for round openings. File brush (12) cleans files.

Files will not chatter—which dulls the teeth—if you keep material to be filed clamped in rigidly and close to the jaws of the vice. To prevent material from being damaged by the jaws of the vice, cushion it with small pieces of wood (if material is wood) or metal. Files are made in different sizes and shapes. The sizes you will use most range from 4 to 12 inches, in shapes of mill, flat, round, half-round and triangular.

Lift file off material on return stroke. This keeps back of teeth from blunting and wearing and damaging sharp cutting edges. However, when you are filing soft metals such as lead, aluminium, copper, some brass alloys, and so on, drag the file across the metal on the return stroke to help clean the teeth. A single-cut file has a single row of parallel teeth. A double-cut file has a second row of tooth criss-crossing the first row of teeth.

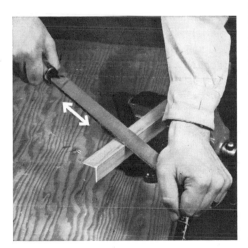

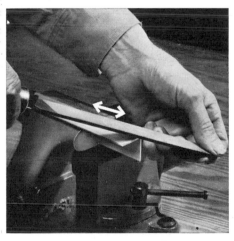

For coarse filing, hold file as shown. Always exert enough pressure on the file to keep it cutting. Too little pressure causes the file to slip and skip over the work; blunts teeth. On all flat surfaces, keep the file parallel. Don't let it rock back and forth or you will tend to round the material as you progress. The range of coarseness and fineness of a file is coarse, second-cut, and smooth. Work you will do determines which file to use.

For smoother cuts and light filing, grip the file this way. Go towards the edge of the material for edge sharpening, then away from it for finishing touches, if a keen edge is not necessary. For draw-filing (finishing touches on long, flat surfaces) push file across material at right angles. A coarse file has a small number of big teeth, while a smooth file has large numbers of fine teeth. Cut of a file is determined by this and spacing of teeth.

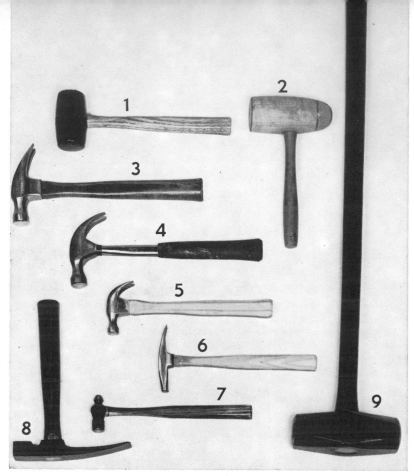

Good assortment of pounding tools includes: (1) and (2) soft-headed hammers which come with various shaped heads for beating out metal, dents in car bodies, etc; (3) and (4) two styles of claw hammer, the latter with an all-metal handle; (5) 13 ounce claw hammer for light work; (6) upholsterer's hammer for driving in tacks; (7) ball-pein for engineering work; (8) mason's hammer; (9) sledge hammer.

How to handle a hammer

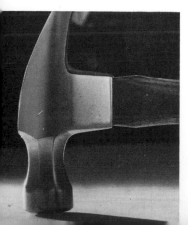

Face of poll of hammer is crowned. This allows you to drive nail flush without leaving tracks. Always buy good quality hammers—ones with heat-treated heads and balanced handles. With care, they can last a lifetime.

Claws of hammer should be well machined to slip easily between nail-heads and timber. Claws should grip head and body of nail firmly. Claw hammers are made in various weights.

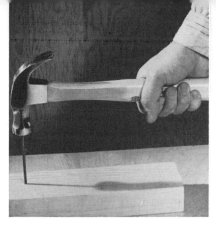

Hold hammer near end of handle for greatest leverage and power when driving nails. Keep face of hammer at right angle to axis of nail. For light work, extend thumb up handle for more control. Hit nail head centrally in all work.

One tap starts nail in timber . . . next blow can be medium stroke. Until nail is started, grip it between thumb and finger, and perpendicular to timber. Ease as head nears surface of timber; finish with light blows to avoid marking surface.

Nails hold better if they are clinched over. Bend nail (that protrudes at least $1\frac{1}{2}$ inches) by striking tip at an angle and force

it down to timber with light taps. Sink point below surface of timber with sharp rap on end of point. Always clench with grain of wood.

Use block for leverage and to prevent marring timber when pulling nails. First pull (without block) should be $\frac{3}{4}$ inch. Insert block against nail and continue.

Use nail punch to countersink nails below surface of timber. Place tip of punch squarely on nailhead and drive it $\frac{1}{16}$ to $\frac{1}{8}$ inch below the surface. Fill the holes.

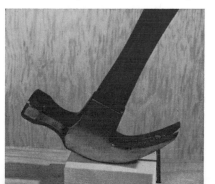
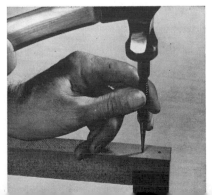

Saw broken handle flush with cheek of head. Punch out rest of handle. Or drill out all wood possible, then split out rest of handle. Do not burn handle out of head; you will destroy temper of the steel.

Measure down handle to where bottom of cheek should fit—just above "shoulder" of handle. Head should be a wedge fit—most "sockets" (eyes) are tapered slightly. You can find hickory handles at hardware and d.i.y. shops. Take along hammer head to check size.

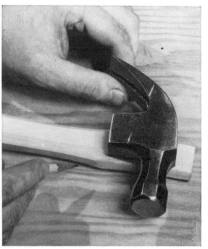

With calipers (or by trial and error), measure and shape handle to fit head snugly. File or grinder cuts handle to size easily; finish with sandpaper. Handle *must* fit tightly.

To expand handle in head, cut slots for wooden wedges. Hacksaw does excellent job. Slots are cut depth of wedges, which should be maple or hickory. Or buy metal wedges at a hardware shop. Lock handle in vice between scrap.

After you tap head on handle as far as it will go and saw off projecting end, drive in the wedges. To drive handle on, strike butt end of it on a solid surface. File top flush. Sand handle lightly and wipe on several coats of linseed oil.

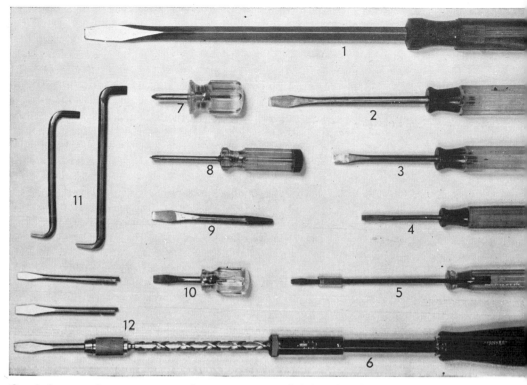

Good, inexpensive assortment of screw-drivers for your workshop includes these: (1) heavy-duty square blade; (2) and (3) medium and small standard blade; (4) small light blade with cabinet tip; (5) a six-inch screw starter. Spiral ratchet (6); (7) stubby Phillips for Phillips-type screws; (8) medium Phillips; (9) bit for hand brace (Phillips also available); (10) short for tight quarters; (11) two sizes offset; (12) bits for spiral ratchet.

How to use screwdrivers

If you have ever had to tighten a loose screw with an improvised tool—like a pocket-knife—you know how important a screwdriver can be.

Screwdrivers are one of the most single-purpose, yet essential, home-maintenance tools you can own.

They do one job: Drive and draw screws. They are not prisers, putty knives, paint paddles, or cold chisels.

One of the handiest of the family is the spiral ratchet (No. 6 in the photograph above). The ratchet can be set so that downward pressure on the handle either drives or draws screws. The ratchet can also be set so it works like a regular screwdriver.

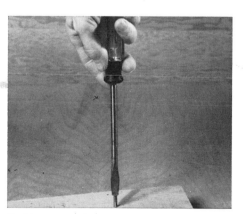

Hold screwdriver handle so it sits firmly in palm of hand. Grip ferrule with thumb, forefinger. To gain power without tip jumping from slot, use longest screwdriver you can.

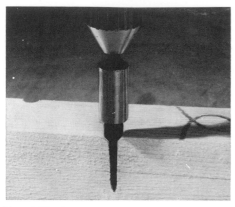

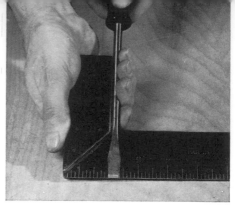

Keep tip square with grinding wheel or file. If it becomes rounded or bevelled, it will tend to rise out of the slot, "stripping" screw so badly that you will not be able to drive or draw it. Keep the screwdriver shank oiled and steel-woolled to stop formation of rust.

Pre-drill pilot holes. Fastest way is with a power outfit. Bit drills hole to right depth, size, countersinks it for screwhead. By hand, bore first hole larger than shank diameter; second one smaller than the threads of screw.

Tip of screwdriver should completely fill slot of screw you are driving or drawing. It should be as wide as screwhead. If tip is too wide, it will mark the wood around screw.

Get more driving power on screw by exerting downward pressure on top of screwdriver with free hand, as shown. If screw is especially hard to drive, withdraw and enlarge pilot hole.

For tough-to-get-at-places, you cannot beat driver equipped with screw holder. Jaws of holder keep driver tip tightly in screw slot until the screw is well started in the hole. You pull back on the driver to release it.

Offset screwdrivers are made for all kinds of close-quarter jobs where regular screwdrivers are too big to go. Blades are at right angles to one another and to shaft at the end so that you can use both of them if needed.

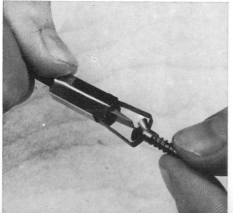

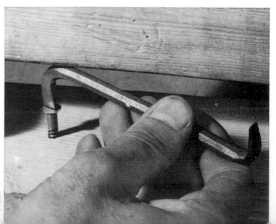

Hole-drilling tools

The family of drills, bits, and braces is a large one, filled with specialists that make any boring job easier.

A brace is the most useful drilling tool for home use. Rapidly approaching it in all-round usefulness is the electric drill, which many users regard as an essential "hand" tool.

When you buy a brace—as with any other tool—get a good one. It should have ratchet and spring-action jaws. Keep the brace well oiled and the auger bits sharp.

One tip to remember in all boring jobs: When you bore through timber stop as soon as the bit's lead screw breaks through on the far side. Then if possible turn the timber over and complete the holes from the back. This prevents the wood from splintering.

Correct grip on brace lets you sight and guide bit at right angle. You get accurate hole, are less likely to break bits.

Oiling points are: Head oiling hole, ends of crank-handle collar, ratchet dogs and collar, chuck shaft, and the chuck shell. Oil frequently.

Basic bits are the auger (centre) for large holes in wood, and twist drills (right) for either wood or metal. Countersink bevels holes for screws.

Special drills speed up particular jobs

Using a hand drill is a fast and easy way to bore or drill small holes in wood or metal. Start holes in wood with a bradawl first to keep drill from slipping. Centre-punch metal. Exert even pressure on drill handle and turn the crank slowly.

Expansive bit cuts 1- to 3-inch holes by easy adjustment of extension cutters. Screw must be tight to keep cutters from slipping, when bit is forced into stock. Interchangeable short and long cutters give a big range of hole sizes.

Screw mates are shaped like screws and have sharp cutting edges that bore holes the right diameter and depth and countersink in one operation. They are made to match standard screws. Shank locks in power drill or hand brace.

Safety First

Remember that all tools should be kept out of the reach of children. Even a screw-driver could cause permanent injury.

Variety of boring tools increases handyman's scope

In addition to the boring devices shown on these pages, there are metal guides with which you can drill holes for dowels perfectly straight and to the correct depth —there is no question of over drilling, and there is perfect hole alignment on the second piece of timber—no intricate measuring is necessary.

The other useful boring tool, often forgotten in these days of the power drill, is the gimlet. It is available in various sizes and comes into its own in places where the power drill or brace and bit cannot be used. Keep the gimlet sharp— a blunt tool requires a lot of pressure and tends to split the wood.

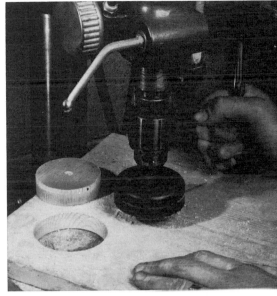

Hole saw cuts holes larger than regular bits, comes in assorted sizes. Pilot drill starts it in wood or metal that is not too thick. Teeth leave clean sides in stock, eliminate splintered and chipped surfaces. Force in material slowly

Holes in masonry are easy with carbon-tipped drill or with punch. Carbon-tipped bit in power unit has spiral flutes that remove powdered dust. To keep dust from clogging, twist punch as you hammer.

Push drill is made to order for drilling pilot holes for screws, brads, nails, and many more small jobs. Spiral drive operates smoothly in all woods—returns the handle after each stroke. Handle contains variety of drill sizes.

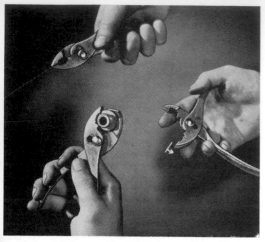

Positions. Fine serrations at tip of jaws grip small objects (top). Coarser teeth at middle are for larger jobs (left). To change to a wider bite, open the jaws wide so the pivot bolt will slide into the other slot.

Adjustable Grips

Of all the holding tools, you will probably use your grips the most. Uses range from snipping off wire and taking a kink out of a bent nail to serving as a wrench on small nuts.

A good pair of grips costs comparatively little, so avoid buying cheap ones. There is no greater irritation than trying to work with grips that have poorly machined jaws or a pivot bolt that slips unexpectedly.

Serrations in the grips should be kept clean. Rake out with a wire brush or three-cornered file.

Tighten bolt. A loose pivot nut and bolt will impair the wire-cutting and gripping action. Tighten bolt and nut for free play without any wobbling. Lock the nut tight by burring threads with punch. There are several different types of grips, so this tightening process will not apply to them all.

To speed work, handle your grips this way. When you hold the grips, keep the little finger inside one of the handles. This lets you open the jaws easily without using the other hand.

More comfortable grip is furnished by length of rubber tubing slipped over handles. Spring action of tubing will cause grips to open by themselves, enabling you to leave one hand free.

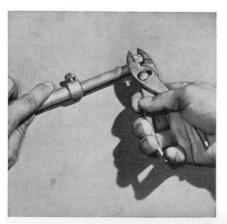

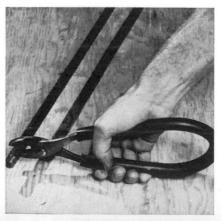

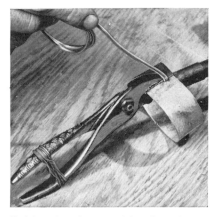

Rubber bands around handles of grips give the tool a vice-like hold on work which must be held in position for soldering, drilling, or similar small jobs.

Grips help vice hold pipe or similar object when you clamp both pipe and grips in vice. Additional "grip" lets you apply necessary leverage without making it slip.

Pull tiny brads, escutcheon pins, tacks, and so on with long-nose grips instead of hammer claws, to avoid damaging wood. Nail lifts out as you roll grips.

Special tools speed certain jobs. Long-nosed pliers (left) help in electrical work; pincers (centre) pull nails, cut wire; tin snips (right) slice through sheet metal.

Drive brads with grips on small jobs that might be damaged by hammer. Here brads are driven into a picture frame. Paper prevents marking frame.

Adhesive bandages cushion serrated jaws of grips, so that you can use them on all delicate work without marking the job. Put on as shown, or wrap in layers.

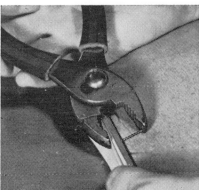

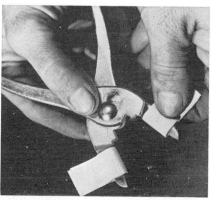

If grip joint binds, open handles to binding point and oil. Position pliers on a block and tap gently around joint with a small or medium-sized ball-pein hammer. Do not strike edges of pin or you will bind it more.

Slip-joint grips that need frequent tightening can be helped by this procedure. Tighten the nut so grips open and close smoothly. Then burr the threads in front of the nut with a hammer and centre punch.

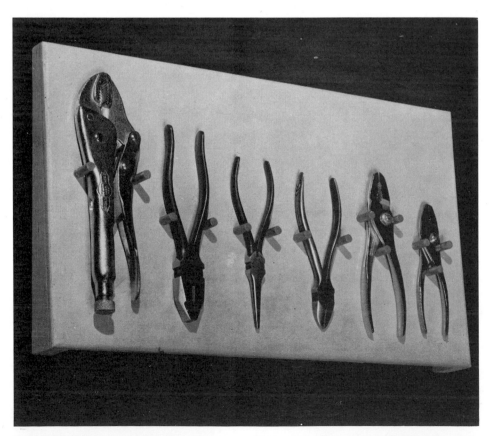

Hang your grips in a convenient place on a board like this. They are much easier to locate and grasp once you have found them.

Edges and points are protected from accidental damage that sometimes occurs when tools are cluttered together in drawers or boxes.

How to use wrenches and spanners

Good wrenches are important tools. You will want to buy the best for two reasons: (1) Good ones last longer, and (2) Cheap wrenches slip easily, causing grazed knuckles.

When you're using a wrench, you should always pull, not push. If you push and the nut breaks loose unexpectedly you are almost certain to hit your knuckles against something.

Keep wrenches clean with paraffin; greasy tools slip. And don't hammer on a wrench or spanner handle or slip a length of pipe over it for more leverage —something will break.

Here is a selection of spanners and wrenches with tips on how they should be used.

Adjustable wrench should be first you buy. With one big and one small, you will be ready to do most simple nut-and-bolt repair jobs. Keep its mechanism clean.

Pipe wrenches are the second most useful general maintenance type. You need two—one to hold with, one to turn with. The 10 inch and 14 inch deal with most domestic plumbing.

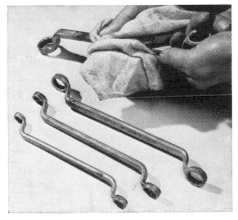

Off-set ring spanners lend themselves best to hex-head bolts and nuts, with 12 "points" which let you change position on nut with only a small handle movement. Keep free of grease.

Open-end spanners are inexpensive. Do not buy the cheapest set; get good steel. Nut, bolt, and wrench standards make open ends a snug fit in proper size, and they cannot slip.

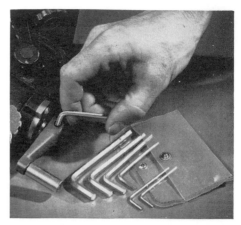

Socket spanner sets range in price from a pound or so to about anything you want to pay. Shown (top to bottom): T-, flexible-head, speed, ratchet handles, sockets.

Hex wrenches are those little, L-shaped models that fit the hex sockets of set-screws on equipment pulleys and machinery assemblies. The wrenches come in assorted sizes.

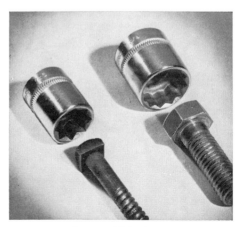

Adjustable wrench must fit nut tightly so it will not slip. Place opening on nut, then make the loose jaw tight before turning on nut. You will avoid slipping and skinned knuckles.

Square or hex—which do you use more frequently? Socket on left (more readily available of the two) is "8-point" for use with square nuts; "12-point", right, for hex nuts.

Tools for measuring and marking

Precise measurements, square cuts, level and plumb installations—these make the difference between work you can be proud of and work that is ill-fitting and unsightly.

Observe the simple rule, "Measure twice; cut once," to save time and avoid waste of materials.

There are many special tools that help you measure and mark accurately. Most essential, however, is a sharp pencil or point that puts a line exactly where you want it.

The right tools and methods can short-cut your work. Some common tools are pictured in this chapter, with advice on how to use them.

One good measuring "tool" not to be overlooked is your own hand. If you know the measurement between first and second joint lines (underside) of your forefingers, breadth across knuckles or palm on a flat surface with thumb extended, as well as length of your arm from shoulder to fingertip, you can do a lot of rough measuring without the usual tools.

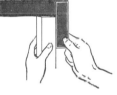

A framing square is large enough to be highly accurate in squaring timber and in guiding square lines (as in the picture). A versatile measuring tool, the framing square generally has several scales printed on its face which assist a builder in computing angle cuts for such projects as framing a house. A small square (shown in drawing) is handy for squaring the ends of battens.

Mark for accuracy with two fine pencil lines or scratches. Make them by holding a sharp pencil (or knife or scratch-awl point) at exact position desired.

Flexible steel rules give accurate measurements for both inside and outside curves, yet are rigid enough to extend 8 to 10 feet vertically. Zigzag folding rules are also handy.

  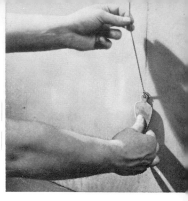

Marking gauge is the most accurate tool for scribing lines parallel to grain. Use a rule to set the marking spur, a good check on the printed markings on the gauge. Keep gauge pressed tight against board all the time.

Plumb bob establishes a true, vertical line to guide framing, set poles, and do other similar jobs. Suspend bob on a string, and wait for the point to come to rest. Here a plumb bob is used with a frameing square to make sure two joined pieces of timber are square and true.

Chalk line is used to mark a straight line on any flat surface, horizontal or vertical. Pull a cake of marking chalk along a light, twisted cord, and tie cord to nail. Pull taut along surface, snap to mark.

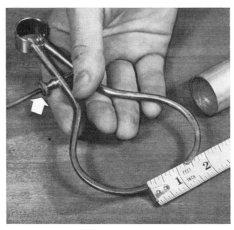

Outside calipers find diameters easily. Adjust them to fit snugly, but not tightly, at widest part of round. Set or read by placing one point at ruler end, other on fine markings.

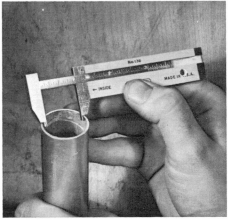

Caliper rules—designed for inside and outside measurements of cylinders—have graduated scales for accuracy. Adjust metal slide by pulling out, and positioning it on cylinder.

Dividers mark circles or small arcs or you can also use them for stepping off a series of measurements along scribed line. Compass, with pencil on one leg, is used the same way.

Bevel gauge will duplicate angles, or you can adjust it to the angle you want with protractor of framing square. Blade can be set from 0 to 180 degrees. Thumbscrew locks blade.

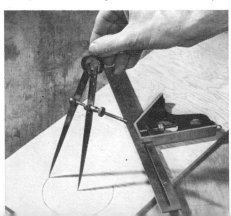 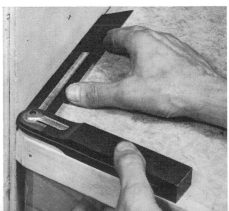

This knot lets you hold tension with one hand and tie end of taut line at same time with other. Form loops with free hand, pull knot tight without releasing the line.

Measure by balance. Then without a rule you can saw a board almost exactly into two equal lengths. Rest board on your hammer handle, saw where it balances.

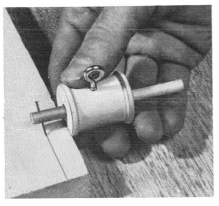

Marking gauge is easy to make from a spool, dowel, brad, and a screw eye. Screw eye is turned into bored hole, locks gauge at selected width to keep line true.

Visual aids can be used to a considerable extent when working outside the workshop, and therefore without its aids. For instance, fence posts can be set upright in an almost perfect vertical position by lining them up visually with a known vertical line—like the corner of a building.

This method can be used quite successfully to erect small sheds and greenhouses.

A word of warning about horizontal fixings—do not line up with the ridge of a roof because it may have sagged a little over the years.

Large arcs and circles that are too big to make on compass or dividers are most accurately marked with the use of trammel points (see sketch). These two steel points slide along a wooden bar and clamp in position with setscrews. Lacking trammel points you can do the job with a pair of nails driven through a wooden bar as shown in picture.

Profiles made easy

The Temco Template former is an extremely versatile tool and can be used by the skilled or unskilled do-it-yourselfer with the same accuracy.

It reproduces simultaneously male and female profiles of any projection or form; saves time and materials; and gives a job of neat and professional finish.

To use, simply .place the former against the object and gently push into the outlines. A reproduction of the outline is formed which can be transferred as required.

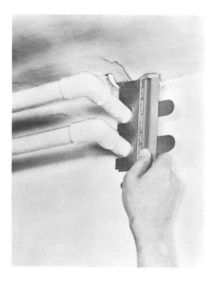

Laying all types of flooring. It is possible to make a pattern of complicated door beadings very quickly, saving hours of tedious measuring and giving a neater finish. Make a pattern (as shown above) and then place in the correct position on the floor covering and cut out.

When wallpapering, the former will help in getting round awkward pipes quickly and neatly (above and below). Transfer the profile direct on to the wallpaper, cut out, and hang paper.

Covering wide areas is no problem. Simply join two or more formers together to obtain a profile of a large area. The formers are held together with a small connecting plate and can be used at 90 degrees.

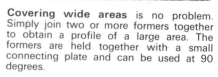

Levelling equipment

For many jobs, your tool kit is not complete until you have one or more of these inexpensive aids. The carpenter's level is used for a wide range of jobs, from horizontal and vertical levelling to simple contour sighting. Look over your hardware shop's stock of levelling tools to find the right ones for your needs.

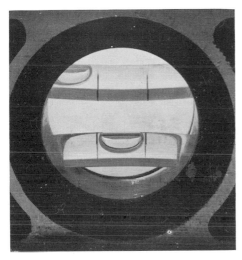

When bubble in spirit level looks like this, work (horizontal or vertical) is level. Standard carpenter's level has three double vials.

It is as simple as it looks: put level on work, and move work until bubble settles to level. Read only vial with the curved side upward.

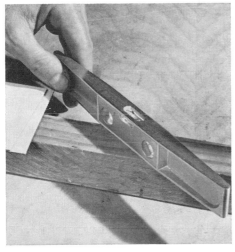

To test for accuracy, set level on flat surface and adjust one end until bubble is dead centre. Then reverse ends. If bubble is off centre, your level needs replacing or adjusting if it has been designed for vial replacement.

Abrasives

Selecting the right abrasive for the job and learning how to use it can save you money and can save you countless hours of tedious sanding and rubbing to get wood, metal and other materials ready for final finishing.

Here is a round-up of the more common abrasive materials you can buy for woodworking and for finishing projects —along with several tricks you can use to cut in half the time spent on the tedious job of sanding.

Coated abrasives: (1) crocus cloth (red) for metal; (2) silicon carbide (dark grey) for soft metal, glass; (3) garnet (reddish), general woodworking; (4) emery (black), metal; (5) aluminium oxide (brownish), wood, metal; (6) flint (yellowish white), paint, soft wood.

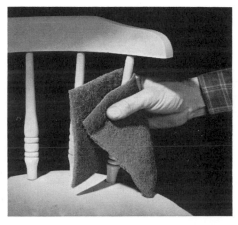

This new abrasive has the look of coarse felt. It is a $\frac{1}{4}$-inch thick pad of nylon fibres, coated with fine abrasive particles. For wood finishing this washable pad is used for rubbing sealer coats, scuffing between varnish coats, and applying satin finishes.

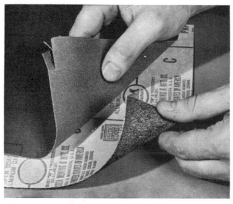

Backing materials are classified as follows: A is light-weight; B, C and D middle-weight; E for the coarse grits, especially for use on mechanical sanders. Cloth backings are J—a light and flexible backing—and X—a stronger backing which resists stretching.

Coatings include closed coat (left) which cuts fast because of more abrasive particles per square inch than open coat. Latter cuts slower, but will not clog as quickly. If abrasives do clog, clean with brush (or file card for a difficult case) to renew cutting action.

Try these sanding techniques for better results

Sand with grain of wood. You will tear fibres of wood if you go across the grain and will never completely erase the marks made. Start with coarse or medium paper and finish with a fine one. It is best never to skip more than one grit size in sanding process.

Round corners and edges of timber slightly to make finish stick better. Cork sanding block improves contact between abrasive and timber. Tiny teeth in each end of block hold abrasive in place to prevent it tearing.

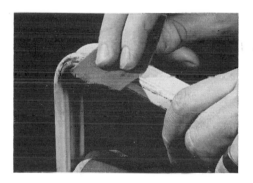

"Feather" edges of paint film on metal and wooden surfaces that are to be spot-primed. Re-paint spots with as many coats as needed to match surrounding painted area. Aluminium oxide paper is good for removing rust.

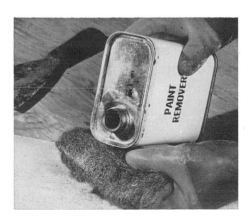

Softened finishes—especially in grooves and on corners of furniture pieces—are easy to remove with steel wool after you soak the wool in paint remover. Use steel wool on the softer woods where a scraper's blade may mar or damage surface while removing finish.

For a hand-rubbed finish, use powdered pumice. Apply the powdered abrasive with felt pad dampened with linseed oil. Work with the grain of the wood and check often to be sure you do not cut finish. Clean off work with a clean dry rag or brush.

Code

PAPER BACKING—Supplied in 4 Weights	
A	Very light and pliable
C	Medium heavy and flexible
D	Stronger than ''C''; moderately flexible
E	Tough durable paper for mechanised applications

CLOTH BACKING—Supplied in 2 Weights	
J	Lightweight pliable cloth for use where extreme flexibility is needed
X	Heavier, stronger and more stretch resistant

TYPES OF COATING	
CL	CLOSED COAT. Denotes complete coverage of the backing surface with grain. Used where a high rate of stock removal and a heavy working pressure are required.
OP	OPEN COAT. Indicates a 50 to 70% grain coverage. Very effective when sanding materials which tend to load the abrasive.

Grade markings refer to the size of the grain of the compound used, and it differs with each variety of material used. In addition, different manufacturers have different markings. The table opposite will help you to select the right paper for the right job.

Next to the diamond in hardness, silicon-carbide abrasive is an electric-furnace-formed, blackish cinder of sand and coke. Below this on the abrasive scale is aluminium oxide, another product of electric-furnace fusing.

Garnet is slightly softer than aluminium oxide, while emery comes next down the scale of hardness. Flint is a sharp-grained form of quartz rock: Crocus is a dust-fine iron oxide.

Silicon carbide on a water-proof backing is used wet for rubbing down metal surfaces.

MATERIAL	GRIT RANGE	BACKING	ABRASIVE	COATING	BELTS	DISCS	ROLLS	SHEETS	APPLICATIONS
FLOOR SANDING PAPER	24—36	E	SIC	OP	●		●		Very open coat material for floor sanding.
ABRASIVE PAPER	24—400	E	SIC	CL	●	●	●	●	For leather, rubber, plastic, etc.
ABRASIVE PAPER	60—180	E	SIC	OP	●	●	●	●	
ABRASIVE PAPER	180—320	C	SIC	OP	●	●	●	●	A flexible product used mainly for polyester sanding.
"RED-I-CUT" WATERPROOF PAPER	60—400	C	SIC	CL		●	●	●	
"RED-I-CUT" WATERPROOF PAPER	220—500	A	SIC	CL		●	●	●	Wet and dry rubbing down of under-coats, colour coats, lacquers and
WATERPROOF PAPER TYPE 2	60—400	C	SIC	CL		●	●	●	varnishes. For extreme flexibility, use "Red-i-Cut" Waterproof Paper.
"LUBRICOAT" FINISHING PAPER	150—320	A	SIC	OP		●	●	●	Specially recommended for dry sanding materials which tend to load.
"LUBRICOAT" ABRASIVE PAPER	60—	E	SIC	OP		●	●	●	
FINISHING PAPER	150—320	A	SIC	OP		●	●	●	Dry sanding of undercoats, fillers, etc.
EMERY CLOTH	3—00		EMERY	CL					General workshop use.
SANDER DISC (GLUE)	16R—120	Fibre	ALO	CL		● (Flat)			For portable sanding machines.
SANDER DISC (GLUE)	16R—36	Fibre	SIC	CL		● (Flat and Depressed)			Use ALO for steel; SIC for low tensile
RESIN SANDER DISC	16R—120	Fibre	ALO	CL		● (Flat and Depressed)			materials such as stone, glass, plastics,
RESIN SANDER DISC	10R—120	Fibre	SIC	CL		● (Flat and Depressed)			etc.
BELT PAPER TYPE 2	30—220	E	ALO	CL	●	●	●	●	
BELT PAPER	30—320	E	ALO	CL	●	●	●	●	
BELT PAPER	30—120	E	ALO	OP	●	●	●	●	WOODWORKING
BELT CLOTH	24—100	X	ALO	CL	●	●	●	●	Sanding and finishing hard woods
BELT CLOTH	60—120	J	ALO	CL	●	●	●	●	on high-speed belt and drum sanding
BELT CLOTH	60—120	J	ALO	OP	●	●	●	●	machines
MOULDING CLOTH	120	J	ALO	OP	●	●	●	●	
BELT PAPER	24—150	E	GAR	CL	●	●	●	●	Sanding and finishing soft-woods
BELT PAPER	40—120	E	GAR	OP	●	●	●	●	on low-speed machines.
BELT CLOTH	30—120	X	GAR	CL	●	●	●	●	Used also for end grain sanding.
FINISHING PAPER	100—240	A	GAR	OP				●	Dry sanding by hand or with reciprocat-
CABINET PAPER	36—80	D	GAR	OP				●	ing and oscillating machines.
CABINET PAPER	100—150	C	GAR	OP				●	
ABRASIVE CLOTH	24—100	X	SIC	CL	●	●	●	●	METALWORKING
ABRASIVE CLOTH	120—320	J	SIC	CL	●	●	●	●	For work on metals of low tensile
RESIN ABRASIVE CLOTH TYPE 3	50—180	X	SIC	M	●	●	●	●	strength. Use Resin Abrasive Cloth, Type 6 for the more punishing opera-
RESIN ABRASIVE CLOTH TYPE 6	24—120	X	SIC	M	●	●	●	●	tions. In bond strength, the abrasive cloth Type 3 lies between Type 6 material and Abrasive Cloth.
INDUSTRIAL CLOTH	24—320	X	ALO	CL	●	●	●	●	Grinding and polishing all steels. Use
METAL CLOTH	24—320	J	ALO	CL	●	●	●	●	Resin Industrial Cloth for the more
RESIN INDUS. CLOTH	24—320	X	ALO	CL	●	●	●	●	punishing applications; Industrial Cloth and Metal Cloth for less severe work.
WATERPROOF CLOTH	36—500	X	SIC	CL	●	●	●	●	Wet grinding metal, glass and plastics.
WATERPROOF CLOTH	36—240	X	ALO	CL	●	●	●	●	

Selection and use of scrapers

Given a razor-sharp edge, scrapers are unequalled for shaving fine wood to glassy smoothness before you sand for finishing or refinishing.

Scrapers are the tools to use, also, on veneer surfaces (instead of using a plane), for removing old paint and varnish and wall-paper. And scrapers are ideal for cutting away humps and ridges on most uneven or mis-matched surfaces. They are even useful for applying patching materials in repairing small holes in wood or plaster.

Scrapers are manufactured in a wide variety of shapes and sizes, depending on the job they are intended to perform.

In general, scrapers utilize a wide, straight blade, ground or filed with a slight bevel on the cutting edge. The handles vary according to the job to be done and to differing degrees of comfort and convenience during use. You are sure to fine an assortment that will be invaluable for routine maintenance.

These general-purpose scrapers will handle most jobs

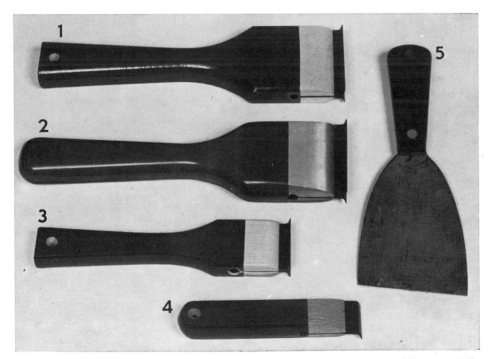

Above are five different types of scrapers. Nos. (1) and (2) have long handles to give the extra leverage needed on heavy jobs, while (3) and (4) are for lighter jobs. (4) is especially useful in tight quarters. (5) is for scraping walls, also for filling small holes and cracks.

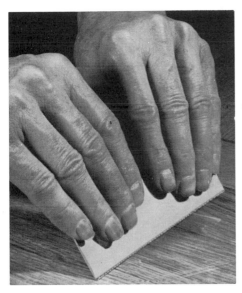

Hand scrapers are small rectangles of steel that produce fine shavings. (not dust) when they are pulled across a wood surface at the proper angle. Use both hands, thumbs and/or fingers when applying pressure. Hold blade at 75 degrees to direction of movement.

Cabinet scraper is used for final smoothing before sanding. This scraper is good on surfaces with irregular grain where a smoothing plane cannot go. When you can, scrape with grain, holding scraper at slight angle. Blade is dull when it makes dust instead of shavings.

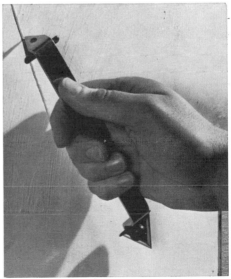

Use both hands, if possible, when you operate the double-blade scraper. Scrape to grain of wood at an angle, or with the grain whenever it is possible. On paint, or varnish, bear just hard enough to remove it. The surface should be smooth when you have finished.

Crack scraper has self-sharpening, replaceable cutters for shaving V-shaped grooves in plaster for permanent repair jobs. Double-edged scrapers like this can be used for removing putty in window frames. Use with a pulling action rather than a pushing one.

Use these sharpening tips for good cutting edges

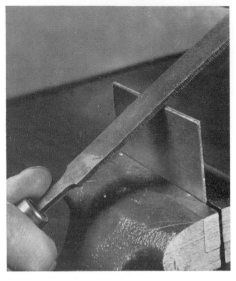

1. Remove hook edge on flat side of a scraper with a file. For hand scrapers, dress the square edge by draw-filing it (running the file lengthwise, but flat, across the edge of the scraper). It is best to use a slow, uniform stroke. When you are finished with this, the edge should be flat and square. Keep blade fairly low in the jaws of the vice.

2. Grind or file the edge of a scraper blade to an angle of approximately 45 degrees. Keep the edge straight, but round the corners just slightly. Strokes should be cross-wise and towards the edge of the blade as shown. File away until all burrs and nicks disappear. To sharpen double-edged scraper, file against bevel, keeping the original angle.

4. Burnish· flat edge of a scraper blade to draw the edge. Hold burnisher slightly more than 45-degree angle on succeeding strokes until the last one is about 75 degrees. This produces a hook edge (2, left). Hand scrapers: Burnish the sides. Then turn drawn U-shaped edges by stroking burnisher across edge. Do first stroke at 90 degrees and continue at 75 degrees for burr edge (1).

3. Whet the bevel side of scraper blade on an oilstone. Then turn the blade over on its face side and whet to remove the wire edge. When finished, the blade should be sharp. When sharpening hand scrapers, whet the edge until file marks disappear and the surface is smooth. Hold the blade perpendicular to oilstone, push back and forth.

Accessory units make this a versatile tool. Pencil burner unit (left) gives a fine pencil-point flame. Soldering irons can be heated with this lamp. The flame spreader tip (right) provides a widened flame area for burning off paint and for heating large areas.

Push-button lamp has pilot light that burns until bottom button (below thumb) is depressed. While button is down, torch sends out a blast of flame. Releasing reduces flame to pilot light.

Butane Gas blow lamp

When you want concentrated heat for some building or repair job, there are few better ways of getting it than by using a handy butane lamp.

Butane lamps have grown rapidly in popularity over the past few years. The fuel comes in disposable metal cylinders and is under pressure so that no hand pumping is necessary. You just hold a lighted match under the end of the tip and slowly release enough gas to light it. On no account should the valve be unscrewed until the gas cylinder is empty—always keep a spare by you. No pre-heating is necessary to start the torch as is necessary with paraffin blow lamps.

For emergency lighting in both home and workshop, the "Clansman" butane gas lantern can be stood or hung and has a light output of 150 candle power with seven to eight hours burning time from one gas cylinder. The same cylinder also fits a butane gas blow lamp from the same range.

Burner unit of torch unthreads from empty fuel cylinder for refueling. Seat unit only hand-tight on to new cylinder.

Use of sharpening stones

It is much easier to work with tools if they are kept sharp. Only rough, inaccurate work can be expected from a blunt tool; it requires more power to use and may actually be dangerous.

Because a blunt edge reflects light, you can easily see if a tool is sharp. Hold it up to the light, and if the cutting edge shows traces of a white line, it needs sharpening.

In general, there are two steps in sharpening most tools with abrasives: shaping the first bevel on a grinding wheel, if required; and honing the second, or cutting bevel, on an oilstone. In most cases, grinding and honing are done against the edge. The first bevel could be ground on a coarse stone, but a wheel gives a concave bevel, familiarly known as "hollow ground", which lasts longer and cuts better.

The wet sandstone wheel has the advantage of not overheating work, but it has been largely replaced by faster-cutting artificial stones.

An aluminium oxide wheel of medium grit, powered by hand or motor, suits all-round use. Dip tool frequently in water, or the edge being ground may overheat and lose its temper, indicated by blueness. A carefully ground first bevel can be re-sharpened many times on an oilstone before it needs re-grinding.

Artificial oilstones are made of silicon carbide or of aluminium oxide. Both are available with coarse surface on one side, and a fine surface on the other.

A combination coarse-fine aluminium oxide stone is best for all-round use. Like all oilstones, it is used with a light oil. When honing, try to wear stone evenly. Keep surface clean and wipe with a paraffin rag before use.

Keep tool edges sharp, and you will rarely have a major sharpening job.

New oilstones should be saturated with a light oil before use (left), and kept oiled and dust-free thereafter. Silicon carbine powder (about 80 grit), mixed with a little water on a sheet of glass, is used to grind down an oilstone that has been worn uneven by use (right). Make or buy a case for your stone to protect it from dirt and damage. When you are using the stone, use its entire surface to avoid wearing it low in places. Keep uniform pressure on tool being sharpened; use plenty of oil.

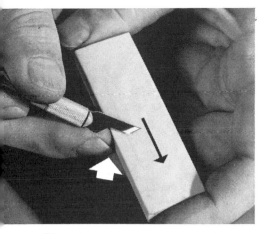

Tiny edges are best honed on fine-textured little stone. Let finger ride on edge of stone to help control stroke and angle. Turn blade, rotate wrist for return stroke.

No grinder? Guide bevel with clamp (or tool you can buy) on coarse side of stone, riding lightly. This grind is flat—but produces sharp edge when you turn stone, finish on fine side.

Angle on stone is automatic if you rock blade slightly, until both heel and toe of concavity are in contact. Then hone away from yourself with a full-arm motion.

Single stroke on back of tool, with blade perfectly flat on stone, is usually enough to remove the honing "burr" and put final touch on edge. Heel-toe honing of a concave grind shows here.

Adjustable rest is easy to improvise. Long angle, cut from hardwood, gives tool broad area to rest on, helps you grind it accurately. Match the original bevel.

Hollow-ground edge that wheel gives to your tools is easiest to hone, can be made razor sharp many times before re-grinding. Move edge laterally across blade in light passes.

Sharpening jobs

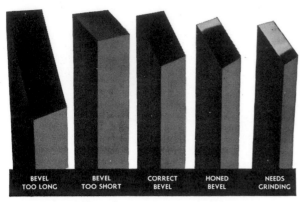

BEVEL TOO LONG   BEVEL TOO SHORT   CORRECT BEVEL   HONED BEVEL   NEEDS GRINDING

Correct bevel is important. Long bevel nicks easily, short bevel will not enter wood.

Cutting tools are not much good unless they are sharp, and each of them has its own sharpening techniques. A representative group of tools and sharpening methods appears here.

As a general rule, frequent honing of an edge will postpone the need for a grinding job. But when the time comes to grind a tool, do not press the work so fast that you burn the edge.

In addition to grinding wheels and oilstones, you will need files to do some of the sharpening jobs.

Whet plane iron on oilstone to get sharp cutting edge. Hold the blade at 25- to 30-degree angle, with the back edge slightly raised. Bolt fastened to blade holds angle.

Very small tools are hard to hold up to a grinding wheel. Make a simple jig with slot in end of piece of hardwood, and thumb screw to hold blade. Use jig as usual on rest.

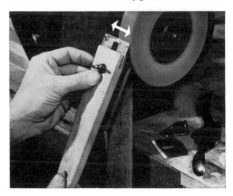

Wood chisels, plane irons are sharpened similarly. Check edge for squareness with a try square. Square the edge, and remove nicks by touching it to the grinding wheel.

For grinding hold the blade at 25-degree angle. Bevel should be little longer than twice the thickness of the blade. Move the blade to the side, grinding until a burr appears.

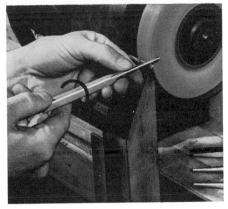

Flatten punch face by twisting it against a wheel, then re-shape end lightly against the side. Turn centre, prick punches against wheel at their original angle, restore point.

Cold chisels blunt fast, once true edge is gone. Touch them up often. Twist butt of chisel against wheel to remove burr. Bevel reduces "brooming" when you pound it.

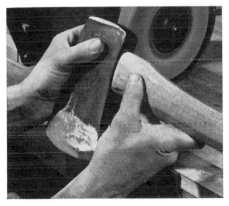

Single-bit axe should have battered head end ground smooth. Grind edge well back on flat, so it will not become too thick. Best axe edge is rounded, so it will not stick.

Hardened edges, such as those on the cutting pliers, resist filing. Use handstone on them with tool in vice for control of sharpening angle. Keep both the edges parallel.

Sharpen points of awls, punches, etc., on stone's edge. Side of case provides for angle to guide strokes. In this way you avoid wearing uneven ridges into a stone.

Gouges can be re-ground on a grindstone in the same way as an ordinary chisel. Take care not to grind too much on the centre, so making the bevel on the outside edges shorter than in the middle. While grinding, the blade must be revolved. Special slip stones are manufactured for use on the inside bevel gouge. Great care should be taken when removing the "wire edge" from a gouge.

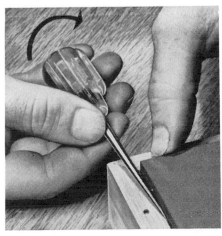

A tool holder you can buy for a grinder sharpens drills to original perfection. On this model, make adjustment for size of drill, then swing holder across the wheel.

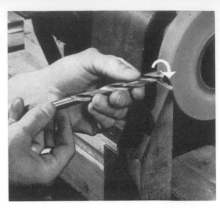

Twist drill bits, hand held for sharpening, should be moved slowly, with twisting motion, across face or side of wheel. Heel of cutting face must be lower than lip.

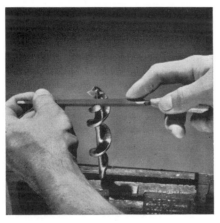

To sharpen auger bit, clamp in vice, use fine file. Sharpen lips like a chisel, at 20-degree angle. Do not touch outside curve of lips except to smooth off wire edges.

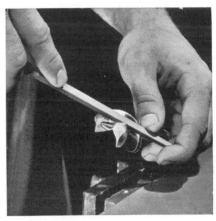

Cutting edges on a bit are for depth just like two chisels at the end of the twists. File as pictured, on upward side of edge, pressing only on forward stroke.

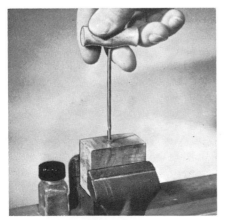

To sharpen gimlet, bore ¾-inch deep hole in hardwood. Fill with flour abrasive, oil. Re-insert gimlet, bore deeper. To finish, repeat in softwood without oil.

Bit file you can buy is made just for sharpening auger bits. One end has uncut edges, and the other, uncut sides. File as shown. Use file also to touch up the lead screw.

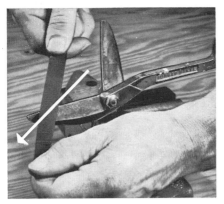

Flat cut of file is ideal for edges that are bevelled—not sharp. Stroke across the edge away from you. Use full length of file to stroke diagonally along entire edge.

Screwdriver tip must be square and flat. File it when it becomes rounded. Carry stroke up side so taper does not increase (which causes the tip to slip).

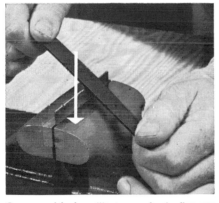

Scraper blade will give perfectly flat cut when filed at slight bevel across the edge. Lock the edge of scraper being filed next to vice jaws to prevent damaging vibration. Each stroke should cover full blade.

Grass clippers take the same shear-cut bevel as tin snips or scissors. Stroke smoothly from heel of edge to tip, along the full length of the file. Never file the flat surfaces between the blades.

Safety First

Remember that all tools should be kept out of the reach of children. Even a screw-driver could cause permanent injury.

Pliers grip better when the teeth and knurled ends on the jaws are kept clean and sharp. Use a small, three-cornered file to touch them up after they have become blunted. File individual teeth to a point for best gripping. File wire-cutters horizontally.

Keep knives and scissors sharp

You will get more satisfactory use of your knives and scissors if you keep their cutting edges sharp.

New, sharp household knives are best kept in condition with a sharpening steel until the fine edge wears off, and then they must be re-ground.

The edges of most hollow-ground knives can be restored with an oilstone. Home abrasive sharpeners also do a good job. Do not try to sharpen knives that have saw-tooth or serrated edges.

Some sharpeners have sets of hardened steel discs instead of abrasive stones. They give a quick edge to the cheaper grades of knives, but are not advocated for the finer grades, especially those that are hollow ground.

The best sharpener for a pocket-knife is a simple oilstone. Grind only when the knife is very blunt. Scissors should be ground at right angles to the blade, then honed on oilstone.

1 *Stroke down one side . . .*

Sharpen your carving knife with a sharpening steel. First, swing knife down length of steel with light stroke. (Arrow shows swing to cover entire blade length).

2 *Then up the other . . .*

Second stroke. Make the second stroke ecactly as you did first, except make it on the opposite side of sharpening steel. Continue stroking alternate sides until sharp.

Hone knife edge is wedge-shaped for easy cutting and long use. Stroke one way, then rotate knife for backstroke. Avoid grinding if possible. Thin blades overheat.

Grinding pocket-knife. Moving blade from side to side, hold it so metal is removed well back from cutting edge. Tilt blade slowly until grinding reaches edge.

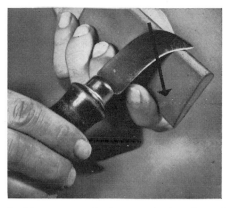

Inside curves—linoleum and other shaped knives need a slip stone. Select curve of round end slip stone that fits the knife you are honing. Careful slip work retains shape.

Stainless steel cutlery can be sharpened without scratching with a fine-grit silicon carbide stone of this shape. Whet the blade with circular motions on each side.

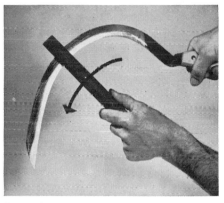

Sweeping curve from heel to tip is proper movement for sharpening a sickle. Use slim scythestone to avoid cutting yourself. Switch ends, sides of the stones to distribute wear.

An electric sharpener gives a quick sharp edge to both knives and scissors. It is a miniature grinder—and, because it is easy to do, there is a tendency to overdo the sharpening, thus shortening the life of the knife. Let the grinding wheel do the work—very little pressure is needed.

Oilstone will keep scissors sharp. Here the free half of scissors helps guide angle required to maintain proper bevel on blade. Stroke forward on fine side of stone.

How to build a work-bench

Here is a simple work-bench that is sturdy enough for any work shop.

Even if you are inexperienced, you can build it by following these instructions. The basic design is easy to alter, too, to suit your needs. For example, you can use block board on top, round the corners of the 2 × 4

legs, or replace the wire braces with closed plywood ends.

If you are much taller than 5 feet 11 inches, the bench should be higher. Measure from head of your hip-bone to floor, subtract $1\frac{3}{4}$ inches to allow for thickness of the bench top, then change length of leg pieces to match.

Finished bench is simple and sturdy. The only tools you need to build it are saw, screwdriver, hammer, carpenter's square, wrench, brace, and bits. A sheet of 3-plywood or hardboard on the bench top forms a smooth working surface that can be replaced easily when it becomes worn.

Upper frame is best assembled on a solid, level surface. See the materials list on page 60 for the number of pieces and their dimensions. Screws needed are listed. Lay out upper frame parts first; drill holes through the side-pieces to meet cross-pieces; then drive screws. Use three $2\frac{1}{2}$-inch screws at each joint. Drive flush or countersink screw heads. Now you are ready to fasten the legs to the upper frame.

A large C-clamp will hold the legs in position while you are drilling the bolt holes. Use a $\frac{3}{8}$-inch bit and stagger the holes, leaving room for the 6-inch side bolt between the two 4-inch bolts. Tighten the bolts until the washers seat themselves in the wood. The clamping action of the three bolts from two directions ties the whole upper frame solidly to the legs. After you have finished all construction of the bench, you may want to anchor the legs to the floor for a really sturdy bench. Do this by fastening four 3-inch lengths of $1\frac{1}{2}$- by $1\frac{1}{2}$- by $\frac{1}{8}$-inch angle iron to the bottom ends of the legs so that a flat surface is flush with ends of legs and flat on the floor. Drill holes in floor for sturdy masonry fasteners and bolt the bench down. If the floor is wooden, screw angle iron braces to it.

Two lower frame pieces are located by measuring up 8 inches from the bottom of each leg. Then drill the holes for eight remaining 4-inch bolts, tap them into place, and tighten them. The plywood panels will help to strengthen the frame. The $\frac{3}{4}$-inch plywood shelf panel goes in next. Holes for screws can be drilled before panel is set in place. Space 11 holes evenly along front and back edges. Leave a $\frac{1}{4}$-inch space at back of shelf panel for back panel. Install screws in back edge first.

Slip back panel down behind edge of shelf panel so it rests on the back lower frame. From behind drive nine $\frac{5}{8}$-inch screws in lower edge of the back panel and edge of shelf panel. Then align ends of back panel with leg edges (squaring up the frame), drive five more $\frac{5}{8}$-inch screws through the plywood into each back leg. For side bracing, use wire braces. Take nuts and washers from diagonally opposite bolts, measure correct distances on braces, then bend rods into loops at those points, and hook over bolts. Replace washers and nut. Then, holding carpenter's square, tighten the wire braces with screwdriver until frame is pulled square. After bench is in use, check for tightness and line occasionally. Alternative bracing method is to fasten a panel of plywood to the edges of the legs.

Fasten top planks to cross-pieces with 2½-inch screws—drive two into each cross-piece. Begin with back plank first. Planks overlap frame 10 inches at each end. Push other planks against first, screw in place. Drive screws flush with surface of planks, or even countersink them. Plywood top goes on next. Blockboard could be used instead of planks.

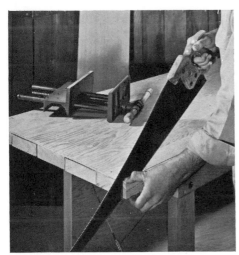

Fasten top panel of plywood to planks with ⅝-inch screws spaced evenly along all edges. Sink screws well into top. Install the plywood backboard with nine 1½-inch screws. The lower edge should line with lower edge of rear plank. Finally, install a good quality vice and other accessories you may require.

List of materials for work-bench

Upper frame

2 pieces 2 × 4, 52 inches long
4 pieces 2 × 4, 23 inches long
24 flathead screws, 2½ inches, No. 12

Legs

4 pieces 2 × 4, 34½ inches long
4 carriage bolts, ⅜ × 6 inches, with nuts and washers
8 carriage bolts, ⅜ × 4 inches, with nuts and washers

Lower frame

2 pieces 2 × 4, 48¾ inches long
8 carriage bolts, ⅜ × 4 inches, with nuts and washers

Shelf panel

1 piece ⅝-inch plywood, 41½ × 19½ inches. (Alternative size, if braces are omitted and plywood ends used instead: 48¾ × 19½ inches)
22 flathead screws, 1¼ inches, No. 10

Back panel

1 piece ¼-inch plywood, 48¾ × 19½ inches
19 flathead screws, ⅝ inch, No. 6

End braces

4 braces, 36 inches long (Alternatively, omitting braces: 2 pieces ¼-inch plywood, 23 × 23 inches; 34 flathead screws, ⅝-inch, No. 6)

Top planks

5 pieces 2 × 6, 72 inches long
40 flathead screws, 2½ inches, No. 12

Top panel

1 piece ¼-inch plywood, 28 × 72 inches
1 dozen flathead screws, ⅝ inch, No. 6

Backboard

1 piece 1 × 12, 72 inches long
9 flathead screws, 1½ inches, No. 10

Vice

Any standard woodworking vice.

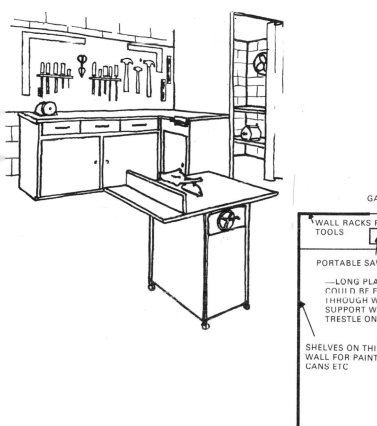

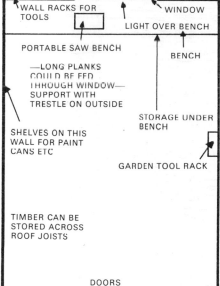

GARAGE WORKSHOP

WALL RACKS FOR TOOLS

WINDOW

LIGHT OVER BENCH

PORTABLE SAW BENCH

BENCH

—LONG PLANKS COULD BE FED THROUGH WINDOW— SUPPORT WITH TRESTLE ON OUTSIDE

STORAGE UNDER BENCH

SHELVES ON THIS WALL FOR PAINT CANS ETC

GARDEN TOOL RACK

TIMBER CAN BE STORED ACROSS ROOF JOISTS

DOORS

Workshop planning ideas

How you finally plan your workshop depends to a large extent on the space available and the sort of work you intend to do.

If you wish to store and use sheet materials such as ply, hardboard, chipboard, blockboard, etc., then there must be adequate space in which to work with them. It follows that you will cut by machine so, with this in mind, the question of space allocation is very important.

The bench should be the same height as the saw bench so that extra long work can be supported. In order to have maximum floor space, the saw bench should be portable so that it can be moved aside; and work benches, tool storage racks and cupboards, and large pieces of equipment (bandsaw, lathe, etc.) should be placed in convenient positions round the walls.

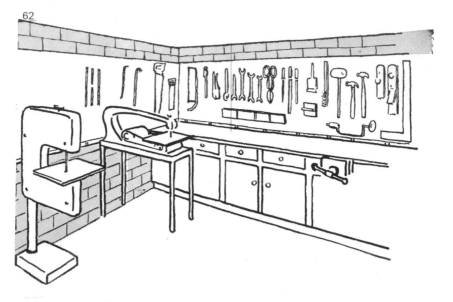

AN ENGINEER'S WORKSHOP

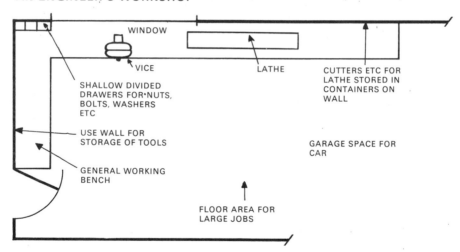

In both small and large workshops, it is good practice to store hand tools on the walls. Special racks can be made. Or pegboard can be mounted on battens and then fixed to the walls. Used with the special fittings available, pegboard provides endless storage for all types of tools.

If you have very limited space, perhaps at the window wall end of the garage, then you might consider placing the work bench under the window. Then place your portable bench saw in such a position that long planks can be ripped by feeding them into the saw and then out through the window, supporting the end of each plank on a light-weight trestle.

In workshops large or small, the siting of the vice is always a problem. But, particularly in the small workshop, its placing is most important. Give a lot of thought to this problem and take into account the jobs for which you are most likely to need a vice. You should also consider the various types of vice because the design chosen could be the deciding factor in siting its position in the workshop.

The overall lighting of the workshop should be given considerable thought. On pages 201-2 there are some ideas to follow.

Which power tools for you?

A portable tool is your best buy if your main interest is remodelling, building, or home maintenance, as it can be transported and used anywhere there is electrical power within reasonable reach.

This type of equipment is very sturdy but there is a capacity limit. If you require to go above this limit for long periods, then you should consider buying the heavier industrial power tools, three of which are shown below. The various attachments to the $\frac{5}{16}''$ and $\frac{3}{8}''$ power drills are described fully on pages

These four basic portable tools put power in your hands

Electric drill is the unquestioned king of all power tools. This compact tool should be your first buy. Besides drilling holes in all imaginable types of materials, attachments are available for all kinds of uses from sanding and polishing to brushing and turning.

For heavy duty cutting, the circular saw is the tool to choose. But it is only a worth-while investment if you plan to do all your own cutting from sheets of ply and hardboard and from baulk timber. If you do however, it will pay for itself many times over.

The sabre saw, with its relatively low price and ability to make both straight and curved cuts, has become a popular standard tool. It cuts one-inch material easily and can handle 2 × 4. A variety of blades equips it to handle wood or metal.

An orbital sander is ideal if you are doing much sanding. The reciprocal sanders are useful as well. These power tools are a good buy because they have the capacity for heavy-duty or smooth finish work depending on type of abrasive paper.

Electric drill—one-tool shop

By far the most popular—and probablt the most useful—power tool you can buy is the electric drill. While the tool is called a drill, it can, with its many attachments, perform dozens of handyman jobs.

Among the tasks the versatile $\frac{5}{16}$-inch drill can handle are: drilling holes in wood or metal; sawing wood or metal; grinding; honing; buffing; sanding and wire brushing; driving screws; polishing, and stirring and spraying paint.

You can buy another attachment that will trim a hedge, and with carbon-tipped drills, you can make holes in concrete and masonry.

Drill kits can include a stand that holds the drill in a horizontal position. In this position, it can be a grinder, polisher, and so on.

Available, too, is a vertical stand that allows the drill to be used as a drill press.

In addition to all these uses, the drill can be used as a motor for a number of larger, stationary tools built to operate on its power. Among these are a lathe and jig saw.

As with all electric motors, the power unit in your drill is more likely to be damaged by dust than by use. Keep the drill stored in a bench drawer—safe from dust.

The $\frac{3}{8}$-inch or $\frac{1}{2}$-inch drill is pistol-shaped. Cheaper $\frac{5}{16}$-inch drills are single speed, and therefore require the speed reducer attachment for some jobs. Dearer types have a 2-speed or a variable speed control. Clean and lubricate according to the manufacturer's instructions, store in a dry, dust-free place.

If your drill is not of the variable speed type, then you should consider getting a speed reducer, especially for jobs such as drilling masonry, metal, brickwork, and for driving screws. The reducer cuts the drill's speed to one third. Always use good quality bits, and use a vice or clamps to hold work steady.

The buff on the arbor makes a metal polisher of your rig. Used with jeweller's rouge, it will put a mirror finish on any metal surface from steel to aluminium, including copper-bottomed cooking pans.

As a bench motor, the drill will do numerous jobs with ease. It will make a first class unit for bench sawing or sanding. You can buff metal, use it as a grinder—to sharpen knives, scissors, etc. By using the various brushes (wire and bristle), you can save hours of work on tedious cleaning jobs.

On the Bench . . .

As a disc sander: use a rubber disc to back up sanding sheet. It will smooth joints, level plastic wood, do other sanding jobs.

Knife wheel fits in regular chuck. It has V-groove at the best angle for sharpening knives, plus a metal guide designed to give a bevel when grinding scissors.

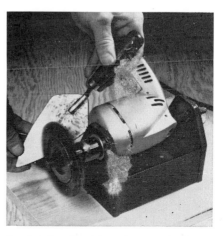

A wire brush makes short work of rust, stubborn dirt. Use a brush to smooth the surfaces when working with metals. Bristles come soft, medium and hard.

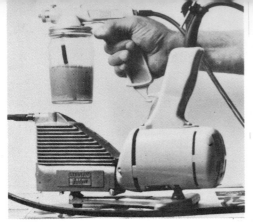

The compressor and paint sprayer gives a really professional finish with paints, cellulose, stains and varnishes. The spray gun is trigger controlled with adjustable nozzle for different fluids. Compressor will also inflate car tyres. Ideal for power spraying lime washes and insecticides.

The circular saw attachment can also be used with the saw table (below).

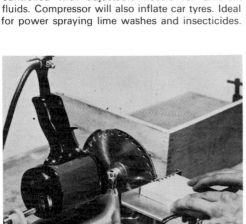

The strong multi-purpose saw table (21" x 14" x 11½" high) converts the circular saw or jig saw to bench operation, leaving hands free to guide the work. It has a calibrated gauge.

The comb jointer cuts accurate joints for drawers, boxes, cabinets—automatically. For use on timber, plywood or laminates up to 1" thick.

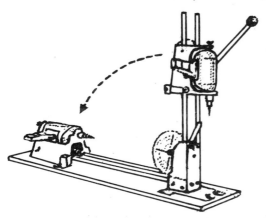

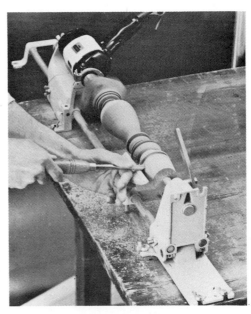

With the lathe/drill stand attachment, you have all that is needed for accurate wood or metal turning and bench drilling. (See above and right.)

... and Outside

Hedge clipper has a gear box converting rotary motion of drill into a piston-like movement. Adjustable for right and left hand working.

The drill is turned into a grass cutter with this attachment. It is light weight and easy to manoeuvre on steep banks. Has a depth of cut adjustable between $\frac{1}{2}$" and $1\frac{1}{4}$" with 12"-width of cut.

Carbon-tipped drills cut concrete or other masonry. Keep constant pressure on drill for steady cutting so you will not blunt drill.

Outside jobs, such as repairing fences or drilling holes in brickwork, are quickly and easily carried out with the power drill. On round timber, use a centre punch to give the bit easy, correct slant.

As portable grinder, drill goes with you to stationary jobs away from the work shop. Works well, too, with lamb's wool cap to polish family car.

Sanding discs

This abrasive disc sands, shapes and cuts, and can be used on wood, stone, hardboard, acoustic tiles, fibreglass, plastics, asbestos, marble, brickwork, metal and painted surfaces.

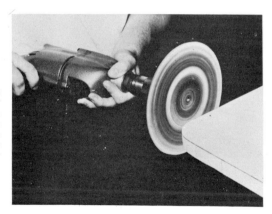

For sanding and shaping, the disc is simply attached to a 5″ or 6″ diameter rubber backing pad and then attached to the power tool. When using, apply minimum of pressure, letting the abrasive disc do its work without undue pressure. The disc resists clogging and is double-sided for long life.

For cutting, the disc should be firmly mounted on a saw arbor. It makes short work of cutting such materials as wood, stone, copper, asbestos sheeting, etc. **When being used as a cutting tool, it is wise to wear goggles to protect eyes from throw-out of material.**

Hand files

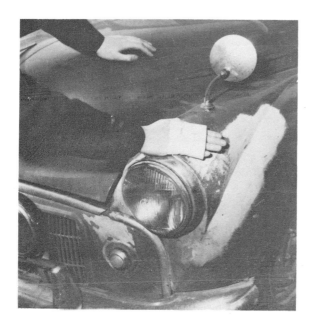

This "hand" file is an ideal method of smoothing, shaping, trimming, profiling, and rubbing down rough surfaces. It will get into awkward places which are out of reach of the abrasive disc or file. It lasts approximately fifty times longer than ordinary sandpaper. If clogging occurs, tap it and debris will fall clear.

Portable power tools

Portable power tools bring great versatility to your workshop. They perform jobs like those done by many pieces of stationary power equipment, but have the advantage of being easily transported to the project—wherever it is located.

This section shows five of the common portable power tools. They are the router, sander, handsaw, chain saw, and sabre saw.

Many of the portable tools have special stands which change them into stationary tools. Others have built-in or attached guides that assure accurate operation.

These items are costly so, before you buy, consider carefully how much work it will really save you.

When hand-shaping, you ride the "bed" of the router along the surface of your work, while the stub end on the spindle regulates the depth of the cut. A smooth, steady movement of the router will produce cuts so smooth that sand-papering can hardly improve their finish.

Use the router in its "name" sense to do decorative work, to set hinges, or, perhaps, to groove a carving board, or decorate a serving tray.

The orbital sander is so called because the pad moves in a tiny circle. The vibrator sander has a pad moving in a straight line with a reciprocating stroke. Can be used on wood, metal or plastic.

Belt sander with coarse paper cuts away wood like a plane, takes you right down to next-to-final sanding with fine grades of sandpaper. Use with grain. Will also remove paint and varnish.

Portable electric saw is used for many jobs

Large jobs are soon finished when a portable electric saw cuts them for you. As in the example here, all you have to do is steer the saw while the motor does the work of cutting the 4 × 8-foot sheet of plywood. Make sure sheets of this size are adequately supported before starting to cut.

This table saw results from mounting a portable electric saw or drill in position under the table top. Saw is fastened with machine screws and can be raised or lowered for depth of cut. The tables come with a ripping fence and a mitre gauge.

Follow line (arrow) with a portable electric saw the same as with a hand saw. Most models have easy-to-see point which runs along the line. Saw seems heavy at first, but since its weight rests on the timber, you soon learn to handle it with confidence.

Abrasive wheels on portable electric saw let you score brick or block for accurate breaking—cut sheet metal—plastics—and a wide variety of similar materials. The saw manufacturers provide wheels adapted to specific types of materials to cut. By using proper wheels, you save time.

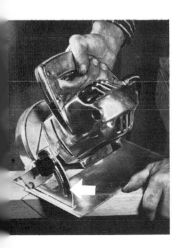

Bevel cuts with the portable saw, shown here making a compound mitre, are done by adjusting the shoe to the required angle and locking it on the calibrated arc (arrow). This tilts the saw. It still rides on the shoe, and the cutting motion of the tool is the same as in straight cross-cutting jobs.

Chain saw is variation of portable electric saw which has its teeth spaced along an endless chain similar to the one used to drive a bicycle. As it is driven around its steel frame, the chain blade makes firewood quickly from logs, posts and tree limbs. Some saws are powered by small petrol motors.

Sabre Saws   Circular Saws

Wood Cutting Blades

Set teeth. For rough curve, scroll, pocket work. 3″ long. 7 teeth to the inch.

Set teeth. For rough curve, scroll, pocket work. 3″ long. 10 teeth to the inch.

Hollow ground teeth. For medium curves and pocket work. 3″ long. 8 teeth to the inch.

Hollow ground teeth. For medium curve work. 4″ long. 10 teeth to the inch.

Hollow ground teeth. For medium curve work. 4″ long. 6 teeth to the inch.

Hollow ground teeth. For straight cuts. 4″ long. 10 teeth to the inch.

Metal Cutting Blades

Set teeth. For medium straight cuts in metal. 2⅞″ long. 14 teeth to the inch.

Set teeth. For medium straight cuts in metal. 2⅞″ long. 32 teeth to the inch.

Plastic Cutting Blades

Hollow ground teeth. For finish straight cuts in plastic. 4″ long. 6 teeth to the inch.

Hollow ground teeth. For finish curve and pocket work in plastic. 3″ long. 6 teeth to the inch.

Knife Cutting Blade

Knife cuts blade for curve and pocket work. 2⅛″ long.

Flush Cutting Blade

Set teeth. Flush cutting blade used for straight cuts. 4″ long. 7 teeth to the inch.

Right Angle Blade

Set teeth. Right angle blade used for curve and pocketwork. 3″ long. 10 teeth to the inch.

Portable Saw Blades

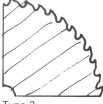

Type 1
Course tooth
Combination
Rip & Cross
Cut Blade

Type 2
Fine Tooth
Combination Rip
& Cross Cut Blade

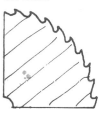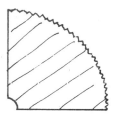

Type 3
Rip Blade

Type 4
Cross Cut Blade

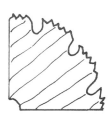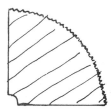

Type 5
Combination
Mitre Blade

Type 6
Plywood
Cutting Blade

Carbide Tipped Saw Blades

Sabre saw cuts more than curves

Sabre saw has gears which convert motor's spin to stroke action, driving a small, thin blade. It cuts curves, including inside cuts, faster, smoother than the hand coping saw usually used.

Cutting 2 x 4s is slow, but it is faster than doing it with a handsaw—and much easier. Make a guide fence to ensure a square cut. Guide is two short pieces of wood nailed at right angles to form a handy "T" square.

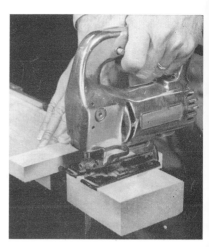

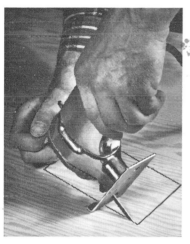

The blade is stiff enough to cut its own smooth, clean opening for "pocket sawing" and keyhole work. Ride saw on tip of shoe, lower blade slowly until it touches work, cuts all the way through.

Some models have auxiliary rip fence that also acts as a circle cutting guide as shown. If yours does not, you can fasten a piece of hardboard to saw base and drill holes at the proper radius of the circle you intend to saw around.

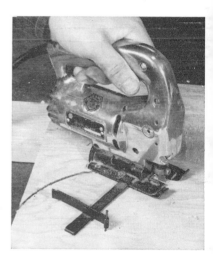

Blade for cutting metal makes short work of iron or copper pipe, sheet metal too thick to cut with tin snips, and many other metal cutting jobs. These blades are rather brittle, avoid twisting as you cut.

You can cut a perfectly straight line in plywood if you use a board fence to guide your saw. Extend the board beyond edge of plywood so that the foot of the saw will be guided as you begin making cut.

How to use a circular saw

Usually the first large power tool that a serious amateur craftsman buys is the circular saw. It has a fast-moving circular blade with teeth around the edge, and no other machine surpasses it in cutting a straight line.

It can make a variety of other cuts, too—mitres, compound mitres, grooves, bevels, spirals, coves, and mouldings. Equipped with the right blades or abrasive wheels, it can be used to work metals, plastics, bone, or stone. You can also turn it into a disc sander or a grindstone.

Most circular saws designed for home workshops have blades 8 to 10 inches in diameter; the larger size is the more versatile.

In home-size circular saws, the circular blade has a $\frac{1}{2}$″ or $\frac{5}{8}$″ hole in the centre, and is attached to an arbor that whirls it. Depth of the cut is sometimes determined by raising or lowering the saw table, but usually by raising and lowering the saw blade.

Nearly all circular saws nowadays have tilting arbors—that is, the blade rather than the table is tilted to produce slanted or bevelled cuts. The tilt can be regulated precisely, and the blade locked firm at any position up to 45 degrees.

Primarily for ripping long boards, the fence is a long, rigid guide parallel to the blade. Cross-cutting and mitring are done with the aid of the sliding mitre gauge.

The equipment described in the following pages is expensive, and each piece needs a fair amount of space in which to be operated. And, if the equipment is to pay its way, it needs to be regularly employed. In view of this, it is worth taking a long look at the power drill with its variety of attachments.

For jigs that will give you additional help in sawing, see page 89.

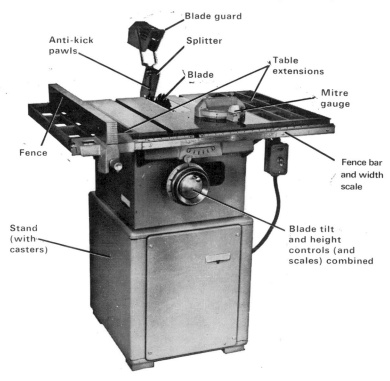

Blade guard

Anti-kick pawls

Splitter

Blade

Table extensions

Mitre gauge

Fence

Fence bar and width scale

Stand (with casters)

Blade tilt and height controls (and scales) combined

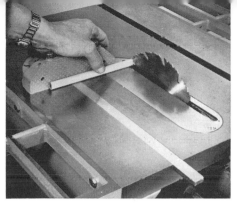

For accurate cutting, table and blade must be parallel. Check: Stick held tightly against mitre gauge should hit corresponding points of blade, front and rear. If not, loosen table-mount or arbor bolts, adjust and retighten.

Easy check for squareness of mitre gauge: Simply sight gauge face against front of table. Light shining up from floor will help you detect inaccuracy. Set zero pointer and stops precisely when gauge is locked true.

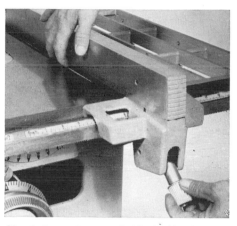

Check fence for parallel by locking it along a mitre-gauge groove, feeling with fingers to detect any deviation from front to back of table. To make corrections, loosen screws or bolts under front casting, reset and tighten.

Blade should be perpendicular to table when tilt gauge (lower left) indicates it. Set blade with square, then set the gauge or the pointer, and finally, set stop nuts or locks. Re-check occasionally as you use the saw.

Tilting blade while cutting a mitre forms a compound mitre. Mitreing requires firm grip, or clamps to prevent side creep. Or face the mitre gauge with sand-paper to prevent slipping.

Accessory sanding disc (make one of plywood, garnet paper) does good job of edge sanding. Here guide is off-parallel; work starts through rear (wide) side so sanding contact is downward.

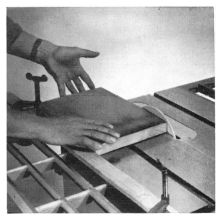

How to use a radial-arm saw

The radial-arm saw is an old-time industrial stand-by that has been scaled down in size for handyman use.

It is different from the standard table saw in these respects:

The saw blade, mounted on a moveable head, slides in tracks or along a shaft. You move the blade along this radial arm in all across-the-timber operations. For along-the-timber cuts, rotate saw head 90 degrees, lock in position, and run through.

The blade is above your work, surrounded by protective guards. Marks on top of timber are visible as you cut with saw or attachments.

The head rotates 360 degrees on a vertical axis, and from vertical to flat on a horizontal axis—or in any combination of both adjustments. Meanwhile radial arm swings through 360 degrees—again in combination with either or both blade adjustments. The number of mitres, compound mitres, angles which can be cut is limitless.

The arm is raised or lowered by a crank to adjust for depth of cut.

Since timber is positioned laterally across table whether you rip or cross-cut, radial-arm saw can be placed against wall to save workshop space.

Radial-arm saws are either direct drive or driven through shaft and gear. Since the spindle is above and easy to get at, it represents a mounted motor, to which a variety of spinning-cutting-drilling tools can be attached.

With shaper, rabbetter, sander, planer, jointer, or other tools on the spindle, all of its flexibility remains. You can set the head or arm or both at any angle for cutting or drilling.

The timber stands still when you cross-cut with a radial-arm saw. Long, heavy planks, with the ends supported, are as easy to cut as tiny mouldings, because you move the saw along the smooth-running radial arm—rather than moving the board. For ripping, you rotate saw head 90 degrees, where it locks with an automatic stop, then push timber through. Set width of rip on scale mounted on radial arm, lock head in position.

For mitre cut, swing the radial arm to the left or right, and draw the saw through, as in cross-cutting. The timber is not moved for cut. The arm locks automatically at the most used angles.

For cutting grooves, saw handles just as in cross-cutting, except that cross-cut blade is exchanged for a blade that is designed for the job. Blade changing is simple, since the spindle is easy to get at.

Compound mitres utilise two-way flexibility of the saw. Turn arm to required setting for one angle. Swing saw head to other angle, pull saw through, while holding board snug against stop.

Rip adjustments on radial-arm saw are made by setting head according to inch scale on arm, then locking it. For wide rips, e.g. ply or hardboard panels, the fence is moved to a rear position.

Flexibility of saw is illustrated in this dishing operation, which will end up as an ashtray of hardwood. Spinning blade is swung in series of passes as block is turned. and held against stop.

Blade sets quickly at any angle. Loosen lever, position blade, tighten. With entire blade above table, it is easy to adjust for settings "scribed" from existing work with sliding T bevel.

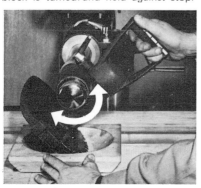

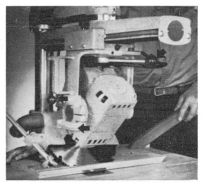

Using a drill press

The drill press is another expensive piece of machinery. It is, however, a versatile tool because, in addition to drilling, it will do jobs from grinding to routing and carving to dovetailing, and it will also stir paint.

Heart of the drill press is the spindle, a shaft driven from the top by a pulley. At the bottom end of the spindle is the chuck, a clamping device to hold drills.

A steel sleeve, called the quill, supports the spindle. A hand lever, meshing with teeth on the quill, raises and lowers quill and spindle to press the drill into the work. You can lock the press for routing, and so on.

Size of the drill press is designated by twice the distance from the spindle centre to the edge of the upright column. Most will drill up to $\frac{1}{2}$ inch holes in metal and 2 inch holes in wood.

To change speed, the belt and pulley guard is lifted and the belt is pushed from one stepped pulley to another, depending on speed required. When operating, turn the pulley wheel with one hand, moving the belt across with the other.

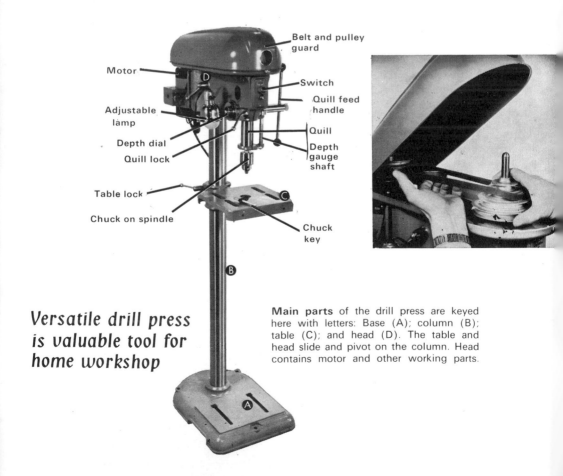

Belt and pulley guard

Motor

Switch

Quill feed handle

Adjustable lamp

Quill

Depth dial

Depth gauge shaft

Quill lock

Table lock

Chuck on spindle

Chuck key

Versatile drill press is valuable tool for home workshop

Main parts of the drill press are keyed here with letters: Base (A); column (B); table (C); and head (D). The table and head slide and pivot on the column. Head contains motor and other working parts.

Using a band saw

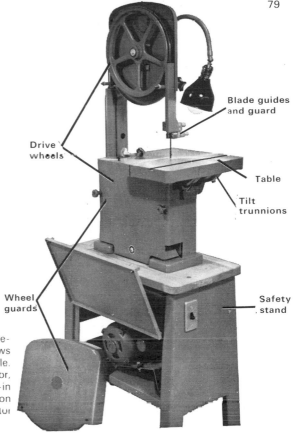

Drive wheels

Blade guides and guard

Table

Tilt trunnions

Wheel guards

Safety stand

Top wheel guard has been removed to show how blade follows around and down through table. Enclosed stand houses motor, pulleys, belt, and has built-in switch. Same saw can stand on bench with a side-mounted motor and belt guard.

For cutting graceful and intricate curves in a thick piece of wood, no home-workshop power tool can surpass the band saw. But once again, it is an expensive tool to have unless it is in regular use.

The band saw will cut much heavier material than the scroll saws, and do it faster and smoother. It will make straight cuts as well as curved.

The wheels of the band saw propel the blade belt-on-pulley fashion, so that its downward-pointed teeth travel continuously downward through a hole in the saw table. Cutting action is smooth and free of vibration. Blades are easy to change; they vary in width and coarseness of teeth.

All moving parts are enclosed in housings and guards, leaving only as much of blade exposed as needed for thickness of material being cut.

Turn knob (A) until blade is taut but springs a bit between fingers As saw runs, adjust wheel tilt (B) to centre blade on wheel tyres. Knob (C) locks upper blade guides.

Set clearance of guide blocks (A), (B) by squeezing them against blade with scrap of paper on each side. Blade clears idlers (C)—which hold it against rear motion—by 1/64 inch.

To square table with blade, check with a square, as shown, with tilt-lock knob (A) loosened. After trueing table, tighten tilt knob and reset pointer (B) to zero. The table will not stay accurately tiltable unless the mounting bolts (C) are tight.

To fold blade, grip mid-point of each side between thumb, fingers—palms up, thumbs out. Roll hands inward and together at the same time. Cross hands to bring 3 small loops together.

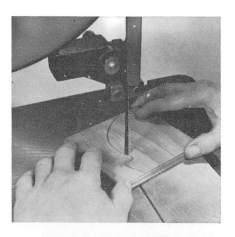

With same blade used for cutting wood, cut non-ferrous metals—such as aluminium, copper or soft brass. Back thin sheet metals with wood; thick sheets cut smoothly unbacked. Table slot is for removal, insertion of blades.

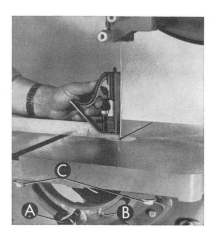

You cannot turn sharply with band-saw blade; it has to enter, back out, try again from another angle. First cut here was down left side. Second came down on right, backed, curved to end of first. Fourth will meet bottom of second; nibbling will square bottom.

Do not try to turn corner sharper than blade you are using can swing. A $\frac{1}{8}$″ blade will turn $\frac{1}{4}$″ radius; $\frac{1}{4}$″ blade will turn $\frac{3}{4}$″ radius; $\frac{3}{8}$″ will turn 1; $\frac{1}{2}$″ needs a wide $1\frac{1}{4}$″ curve. Use $\frac{3}{8}$″ or $\frac{1}{2}$″ blades for straight sawing in heavy material.

Using a jointer

With a power jointer, anyone can plane the edge of a board perfectly square and straight.

Aside from this primary function, the jointer will cut rabbets, chamfers, bevels, tapers, and tenons. Or it can plane the surface of a board as well as the edge, and thus is often called a jointer-planer.

Its only working part is a steel cylinder, slotted to carry three straight knives which are bevelled, like hand-plane blades, to a keen edge.

Unless the rear table is stationary, it is set and locked the same level as the blades just ahead of it for ordinary edge planing. The front table is cranked into position as much lower than the blades as the thickness of wood to be planed from the board.

For safety, every jointer has a flat guard which covers the blades except for the part engaging the wood.

This is also an expensive tool and therefore not worthwhile unless it is in regular use.

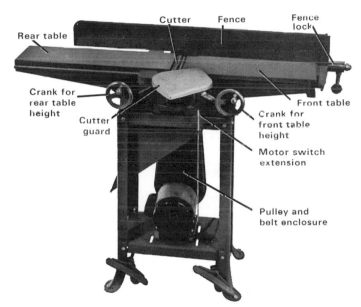

Cutter Fence Fence lock

Rear table

Crank for rear table height

Cutter guard

Front table

Crank for front table height

Motor switch extension

Pulley and belt enclosure

Main parts of the jointer: Front and rear tables are surfaces across which a board slides as it passes over the cutter between. The fence adjusts and locks in place. The front table is raised and lowered by a crank. Sometimes the rear table also is adjustable. The cutter guard is open here to show the cutterhead. The motor, mounted below on stand, has a handy switch extension. Pulleys and belt leading from motor to jointer are fully enclosed. Chute below cutter directs shavings into container.

As board edge slides from rear (infeed) table, knives plane away amount of wood determined by lowering of infeed table (two arrows, lower left). Infeed and outfeed tables are parallel, so cut will be constant depth if knives are adjusted and board is held firm on tables. Cut will be square if fence is set accurately and board is held flat against it. Cutter guard (off for picture) should *always* be in place.

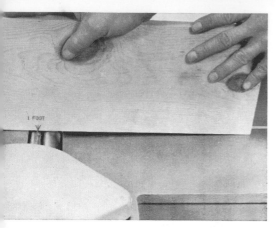

Jointer will cut perfect tapers accurately. Since tapers are measured "so much per foot", mark off one foot at rear of board. Set infeed table to take bite exactly the depth of desired taper per foot. Lower board on to both tables, as shown, with knives just touching at mark. Start jointer, and make a pass. Subsequent passes with the board resting on the tapered cut will finish the entire length of the board.

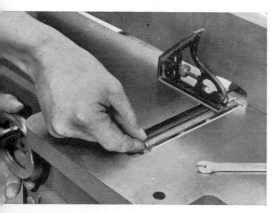

For accurate cuts, knives must be at the exact height of the rear (outfeed) table. If the rear table is not adjustable, raise or lower the knives in the cutter head until they are exactly right. Adjustment can be made with rear table if it is movable. Lay a perfect straight-edge on table, then listen carefully as you use one hand to rock each knife back and forth under the straight-edge. When the click of contact dwindles to silence, knives are at the proper height.

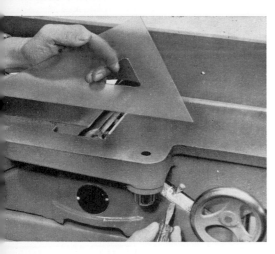

When the knives and rear table are in perfect alignment, adjust the front table so that its depth scale reads accurately. A long (and absolutely straight) edge should be laid across both tables, and the front table raised or lowered until the straight-edge is resting flat across both surfaces. Then change the depth-scale pointer to read "zero". When you run material across jointer, be certain that there are no nails in it. Nails will chip knives, and chipped knives will produce grooves.

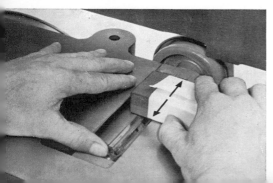

Between sharpenings, jointer knives can be honed into keenness this way: Wrap the hone in paper so it will not scratch the table, but leave one end free to dress the knives. Crank the front table down until the hone lies flat on bevel of a knife. Use the tip of your thumb to hold each knife up against the surface of the stone as the hone is passed back and forth. Use of paraffin or a very light oil will help the hone produce a keener edge on the knives.

How to use a grinder

It makes no difference whether the tools you work with are hand tools or power—they still have cutting edges that must be sharpened now and then. So a power grinder is a useful item for anybody's workshop.

A grinder that spins only one stone is the minimum essential. Or you can buy a spindle head to hold a stone at one end, and maybe a wire wheel or a cloth buffer at the other. You can go on up to a precision grinder worthy of a toolmaker's attention, and pay accordingly. Or you can go the middle way in price and precision, and have a perfectly satisfactory tool.

For most handymen, there is no combination quite so versatile as one offering a grindstone, a buffer, and a power-driven hone all in one machine. Anybody can produce keen edges with that combination.

For safety's sake, do not overlook the most important feature of a grinder —guards around wheels and belts. And wear goggles when you grind.

Important feature is firm, adjustable rest to support heavy, fast-fed grinding. Otherwise, stone may jerk work from grasp. Unsteady hand-held-grinding soon wears the stone out of round. Move the work back and forth across the stone to keep face of stone straight.

Side of stone (if kept ungouged by careful movement of work) is a good flat place for many precision jobs. Unlike rough jobs, drill can be done without tool rest. In such instances, keep steady hand, feed work lightly to produce smooth edge, prevent overheating.

Diamond wheel dresser cuts and trues up hardest grindstone wheel. Dresser must be clamped firm in device to regulate feed, kept steady by the rest as it passes lightly back and forth across stone. Cheaper one (slower, less true than diamond) is made of hard steel.

Rotary hone brings edged tools to near-razor keenness. This hone turns over for either medium-coarse or fine grit. A "wet" hone, it requires light oily dripping as tool is honed. Adjustable rest keeps tool at exact angle as it is moved for even wear across stone.

How to use a multi-purpose machine

If you are looking for the limit in power-tool versatility, get yourself one of the multi-purpose machines. There is quite a variety of them these days—from a tiny hobby workshop model to the high-power machine that can fashion anything short of a timbered bridge.

The advantages of such multi-plicity are many. Such a machine uses only one motor for all its functions. Most designs in this category are built to be easily movable or portable, and they can go to the job—often saving considerable time. They conserve space, a valuable asset if your workshop space is limited.

Basically, a multi-purpose power machine is a circular saw, a drill press, a disc sander, and either a lathe or a jointer. It may get its multiplicity of function by being a coupling-up of these separate tools. Or it may be a singular design with parts that adjust and inter-relate to let it become first one tool and then another.

It may have only these four basic functions. Or, with one make at least, accessories may be added to turn the machine into almost every conceivable kind of woodworking power tool.

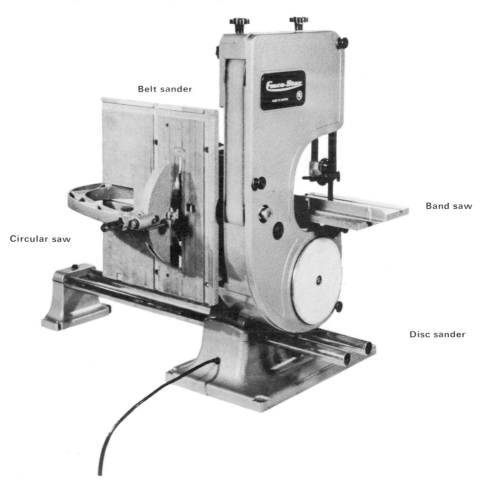

Belt sander

Circular saw

Band saw

Disc sander

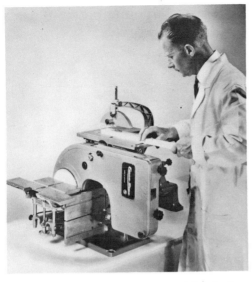

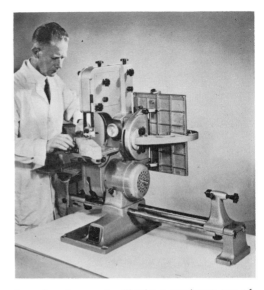

As a circular saw, it can be used for ripping, cutting and mitreing timber up to 2″ thick. The guard shield can be removed for cutting large panels and boards, the workpiece being placed across the table and support. The circular saw table can be raised and lowered and angled through 45 degrees. Slots and grooves can be cut up to a maximum of $\frac{1}{2}$″ wide by fitting wobble saw discs.

As a band saw, it will take a maximum cut of $4\frac{3}{4}$″ and by fitting any one of a selection of blades it can be used for ripping, cross and contour cutting. Table can be tilted through 45 degrees and a knife blade may be fitted for cutting materials such as paper, felt, leather and plastics.

Wood turning with the necessary attachments is another side line of this versatile machine. Picture (left) shows the finishing touches being carried out on a wooden bowl, while (right) a table leg is newly finished. Note how the chisels are being held for these two operations.

As a disc sander, it will round off or face timber ends at any angle.

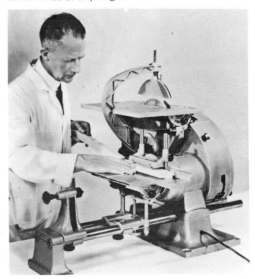

As a fret saw, it will cut out the most intricate shapes.

As a jig saw, it will cut out sections in awkward and bulky work pieces. It will cut solid timber, plywood, chipboard, plastic and aluminium.

By adding a moulding attachment and the wide range of cutters, a variety of profiles and grooves can be obtained.

For tool grinding, a wheel is screwed on the motor driving shaft. Drills, knives, cutters, chisels and other tools can all be ground.

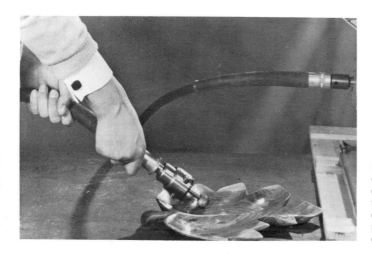

By adding a flexible shaft direct to the motor drive, you can add to the range of jobs that can be undertaken—more difficult sanding, buffing and polishing, drilling in tight corners, etc.

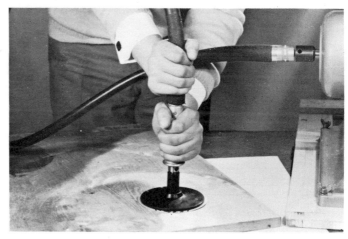

For enthusiasts who want the ultimate, there is the combined planer and thicknesser attachment. It has a planing width of 8″ and, as a thicknesser, will take boards up to $2\frac{1}{8}$″ thick.

As a belt sander, it is ideal for sanding down long boards and fillets. It will sand dovetail joints and others, and the job can be held steady by using the circular saw fence. The sanding belt is made in three abrasive grades—fine, medium and coarse.

The Lathe

The wood-turning lathe, shown below, squeezes a length of wood between two points and whirls it so that sharp chisels can cut it perfectly round, with any desired curves or tapers along the round. The wood is rotated by a spurred drive centre and spins on a sharp cup centre (left, right, respectively, in photographs).

Flat-round objects — like dishes, trays, and lamp bases—are attached to a face plate for turning. Chisels do not take paring cuts (as with between-centre turning) but scrape.

The engineer's lathe works on the same principle, but its cutters are clamped into a holder and wound on to the job by means of a cam wheel.

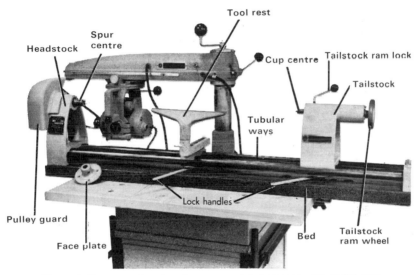

Tool rest · Spur centre · Headstock · Cup centre · Tailstock ram lock · Tailstock · Tubular ways · Lock handles · Pulley guard · Face plate · Bed · Tailstock ram wheel

Some lathes mount on benches, some have special stands; most are individual tools. This one is special accessory for radial-arm saw, clamps onto saw table, takes its power from saw motor.

Skew chisel (best for smooth finishing cuts) is held precisely, firmly based on tool rest for pass from right to left. Best lubrication here is beeswax at point A.

Flat-round objects are turned on face-plate, a flat steel casting with centre hole for mounting on spindle and holes for screws to hold wood. Motor is at right.

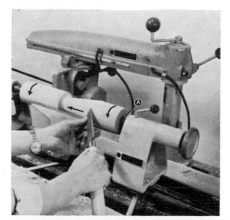

The jig saw

One of the safest tools, one of the easiest to use skilfully, and one of the lowest in cost is the jig saw. It has no precision cutters to keep sharp—only cheap blades to replace.

A jig saw will do a surprising number of things. You can devise jigs and attachments for sawing, filing, and sanding of wood, metal, or plastic; pattern cutting in stacks of paper, cloth, or leather; and straight ripping of long boards.

Basically, the jig saw is a machine that jitters a saw blade up and down. Blades may have coarse or fine teeth, may be as wide as $\frac{1}{4}$-inch or as narrow as 1/64-inch jeweller's blades, but all are so thin that their kerf is little more than a hair-line. A novel blade has a tight-twisted spiral form and cuts in any direction.

An arm of the saw sweeps up and around to hold the upper spring and chuck which fasten to the top of the blade. The lower end of the blade is held in a chuck below the saw table; this chuck is part of the mechanism that moves the blade.

Jig saws vary in working capacity. The smallest will take softwood as thick as one inch; the largest will cut two-inch wood.

Jig saw is safe and easy to use skilfully

A jig saw can have a stand of its own, like this one, or it may be mounted on a bench or table. Castors make the tool portable, increasing its usefulness. A lamp on a flexible arm puts light on the working blade for greater accuracy and ease of cutting. Some jig saws puff air to blow away sawdust and keep the line of cut easily visible, helping you achieve more accurate cutting.

Full-size jig saws are designed so that overarm can be removed to turn tool into sabre saw, in which a relatively heavy blade jigs up and down to cut. Advantages of sabre sawing: There is no limit to size of panel you can cut, nor any limit to twisting and turning as cut progresses. Also, repeated internal cut-outs, like the one in progress, can be made from drilled holes without loosening blade each time.

Jig up for the job

Jigs are special devices that help to make your woodworking projects easier and improve accuracy. With them, you can save hours of tedious shaping, planing, and smoothing.

These photographs show several jigs in use, and the instructions tell how to make them. These are the jigs you will probably need and use most. They are designed by handymen for simplicity of construction.

1 Multiple slots are cut and spaced evenly with this jig. Fasten auxiliary fence to mitre gauge, then mark and cut two slots in timber. Place first cut over blade; mark position for nail in second cut. Nail guides the next ones.

2 Add accuracy to mitre gauge with an auxiliary fence fastened to face of it with screws. The fence gives you bearing surface needed for angled cuts. Also, you can clamp jigs to fence and position timber for multiple cuts.

Cut mitres that fit with this easy-to-make jig

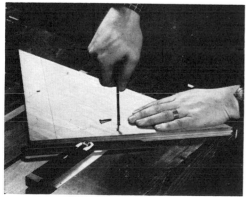

Mitreing jig is triangle cut from $\frac{3}{4}$-inch plywood, with wooden strips that ride in *both* mitre gauge grooves. Bevel gauge set at 45 degrees is used to position jig at 45 degrees to saw blade.

Get better grip on timber you are mitreing by tacking two small blocks of wood to the top of jig for thumb rests. Jig lets you make right and left cuts at the same time for perfect fit.

How to make a tapering jig for your table saw

2 Stop block pushes timber to be tapered through the saw. With tiny brads, tack it to cutting side of jig. Trim block to fit flush with the bottom edge of jig member. This will prevent tilting, and throwing off taper setting.

1 Hinge one end of two battens of the same size and about 24 inches long—or any size you can handle with ease on saw table. Hinge should be slightly undersize, so jig will lie flat and slide against rip fence. Bradawl punches pilot holes for screws. Use seasoned timber for the jig.

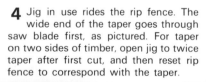

4 Jig in use rides the rip fence. The wide end of the taper goes through saw blade first, as pictured. For taper on two sides of timber, open jig to twice taper after first cut, and then reset rip fence to correspond with the taper.

3 To set taper, first scribe line 1 foot from hinged end. Then translate taper wanted into amount of taper per foot. Example shown is 1 inch of taper in 1 foot. Now tack on scrap to lock jig in position. Hint: Make the exact taper on scrap, and set the jig to conform to it.

Here are some tricks that will give you uniform cuts

Auxiliary rip fence adds needed bearing surface. Also use it when you are working with extra-wide timber. Cut timber to fit length of rip fence and fasten it on with wood screws driven through back. Most fences have holes bored in them you can use. Make the fence out of a level true board that is well-seasoned.

Precision cuts and moulding jobs are easy with saw slotted "spring stick" jig like this one. It keeps timber pressed against the rip fence. To make it, space saw cuts about $\frac{1}{4}$ inch apart in 1 x 4 board, and round end slightly. Then just position the jig against the timber and clamp the jig to saw table. Be sure that the clamp is holding securely.

Tenoning jig slips over rip fence like saddle goes on horse. The top spacer should be *exact* width of the fence; sides are fastened to it. Handle must be at *right angles* to the saw table if you want to get precision in your cuts. The timber rides in front of the handle. For the best results and to speed sawing, it is best to cut the tenon shoulders first.

Drill and saw through rounds and squares with this jig

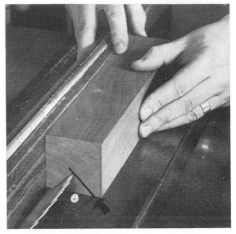

V-block eliminates clamping set-ups and awkward holding positions when you are drilling into cylindrical objects such as dowels. For added accuracy, centre-punch timber to accept the tip of the drill or lead screw of the auger bit. A notch cut in one end of the block will give support for drilling into the ends of round word of any type of timber.

Hardwood square about 3 × 3 × 8 inches is most suitable material and size for V-block jig. Determine centre of square and cut out notch so sides form 45-degree angle. Adjust rip fence for tiny shoulders (arrow). In addition to holding round timber, V-block will keep square timber in position for diagonal cuts. Notch in block lets you work close to blade.

Stop blocks aid drilling operations

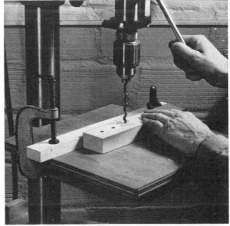

Bore duplicate holes in several pieces of wood with this trick: Tack stop block to the edge of the fence, as shown. Then butt timber you will use against the fence and block. Align fence on drill-press table so tip of drill centres on the spot where you want the hole to be, and clamp both ends of fence to the table. Make a test run on scrap, and adjust.

Stop pin lets you bore series of holes accurately in one piece of wood. Fasten plywood top to drill-press table. Then clamp auxiliary fence to it at correct distance from drill. Drill first two holes in timber and leave drill in second hole. Drive nail through first hole (left of drill) into plywood top. Nail remains there as stop pin for spacing rest of holes.

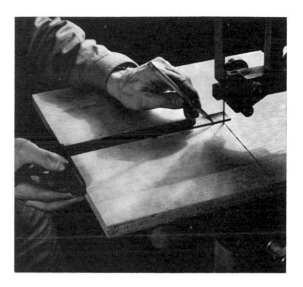

Pivot-type jig for cutting out large and small circles is simply an auxiliary plywood table mounted to your band- or jig saw table. To make it, first pencil a line at right angles to the saw blade after you saw a slot about halfway through the table, as shown in the photograph. Then clamp the jig top to the saw table. Use a plywood section that is smooth or one with the rougher edges sanded off, so it will lie flat on the table.

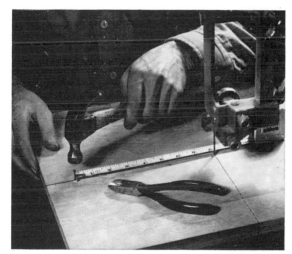

Determine radius of the circle you want, and measure down the line you have marked from the saw blade. Then drive in a small brad at the required measurement and clip off its head with side cutters. For perfect circles, brad must be at *exact* right angle to saw blade and in line with the edge of its teeth. Otherwise, the circle you saw will be out of round. Be sure you drive brad far enough so it will not pull loose at first pressure.

Mark radius of circle on job and make initial cut into it (arrow). When blade reaches line, turn off saw and seat pivot point. Job rotates on point as you feed it slowly into the blade with one hand, and apply slight downward pressure over the pivot point with your free hand. If you measured correctly in setting pivot point, you will get a perfect job.

Know the timber you buy

The next time you visit your timber yard, save time and money by remembering these points:

1. Determine the amount of material you need. You can calculate this in feet and inches and then transfer this measurement into board feet.

2. Determine the grade of timber you need. Do not buy the best grade if a lower one will do.

3. Determine the type of timber you need. If in doubt, tell your dealer what you want it for—he will help you solve the problem at less cost.

For general construction work, softwoods are usually chosen, such as pine, fir, spruce, cedar, redwood, or hemlock. For floors, cabinets, or furniture, you may decide to use either softwood or one of the hardwoods, such as oak, maple, mahogany, ash, walnut or beech.

Timber can be cut to almost any size, but generally it is not possible for do-it-yourself shops to keep every size. If you want a particular size, then it is wise to go to the nearest timber yard.

Non-standard sizes cost more simply because a larger board is planed and cut down to the size you require—you pay not only for the larger board size but for the machining. When planning a construction, you will find it cheaper to work with available standard sizes.

Timbers in general supply are in the following thicknesses: $\frac{3}{8}''$; $\frac{5}{8}''$; $\frac{3}{4}''$; $\frac{7}{8}''$; $1''$ $1\frac{1}{4}''$; $1\frac{1}{2}''$; $2''$; $2\frac{1}{2}''$; $3''$ and $4''$; and the width increases by $\frac{1}{2}''$ up to $6''$, and then by inches up to $12''$. These sizes are for rough sawn timbers.

There is also a wide selection of planed square edged (P.S.E.) timbers. The British Standards specification allows $\frac{3}{16}''$ for planing, but most P.S.E. timber will be only $\frac{1}{8}''$ under size. For instance, $1'' \times 2''$ P.S.E. will finish at $\frac{7}{8}'' \times 1\frac{7}{8}''$.

Tongued and grooved floor and match-boarding also conforms to this rule, but the laid width will be $\frac{1}{2}''$ to allow for the tonguing and grooving.

Usually timber is charged for either by "foot run" or "foot super". The former is a price fixed according to width and thickness. Most do-it-yourself stockists work to this method. In the latter, the price is fixed by thickness and square foot or foot super. The cost of this method is calculated by multiplying the square feet required by the foot super.

These illustrations show the amount of $\frac{3}{16}''$ allowed to be planed off according to the British Standards specification. When ordering timber, state whether rough sawn or planed square edges (P.S.E.) is required. For obvious reasons, rough sawn is cheaper.

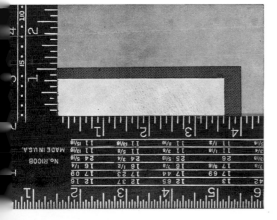 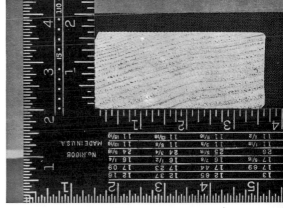

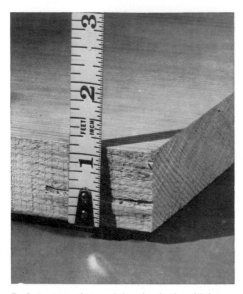

Before starting a job, check the thickness of the timber to be used. This could save a lot of time and trouble when working out and cutting the joints needed. The cost of timber is determined by grade as well as size. The better the grade, the more it costs. Building boards and finish timber are graded by defects—knots, decay, checks and splits.

Plywood, hardboard, and other "sheet" materials are sold by the square foot. Standard size is 4 × 8 foot sheets (32 square feet) in variety of thicknesses. There are various other standard sizes in these materials, so check which size of board is best suited to the job planned. The smaller size boards could save a lot of tedious cutting.

Mouldings and dowels are sold by the running or lineal foot. Shingles are sold by the "square"—enough in each square to cover 100 square feet or surface. Lath is priced by the thousand, though it is put up and sold in bundles of 50. Most timber yards stock a full selection of pre-cut mouldings to cover any job.

For many jobs, you can buy a variety of pattern timber with special edge joints and shapes. Take care measuring up a job when using this type of board. Make the necessary allowances for tongue and grooved boards and the overlap on plane-lapping boards.

Size, grade, and grain direction affect cost

Structural timbers are graded thus:
First grade: free from all defects.
Second grade: small round knots and defects allowed.
Third grade: a larger number of knots and small defects.
Fourth grade: having dead knots and wavy edges.

This is a general guide to grading, but in Europe there are not any laid down grades such as there are in Canada and the U.S.A. Each mill has its own standards. Timbers are also graded according to strength. This includes moisture content, measurement of knots, shakes, splits, wave and slope of grain.

One of the most serious defects is the shakes. This is a fine wavy hair-line running across the grain and is very difficult to detect. Timber with this defect will break at the slightest knock.

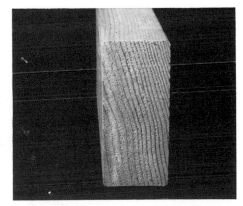

The way wood grain runs is another factor in grading. Timber that is vertical-grained (left) while weaker than flat-grained, produces a wavy pattern—often a basis for selecting boards for appearance. Timber with large cell openings, like oak, is termed open-grained; with small cell openings, it is close-grained.

What to know about plywood

Plywood—those big, laminated boards that every timber yard or do-it-yourself shop sells—is probably the most versatile wood that you can buy. With it, you can build boats, furniture, doors and literally hundreds of things.

There are various grades of plywood, and the chart on page 99 will help you select the grade needed for the job. Ply is expensive—so do not buy the best when a lower grade will do.

Hardwood-faced plywood comes in various finishes, such as oak, mahogany, walnut, etc. When buying this type of board, look at the finish carefully.

In pictures 1 and 2, the veneer is free of knots and the grain has been matched up. The veneer joints are also invisible. In picture 3, although the face is free of knots, the veneers have not been very well matched. And in 4, the veneers do not match and there is discolouration which will be impossible to erase. Picture 5 shows the cheapest and poorest—knots, splits and very uneven notching of veneers.

Plywood is sold by the square foot, but a job will work out cheaper if you buy it by the sheet and cut it in your workshop. So before planning your project on paper, visit the do-it-yourself shop and see what sheet sizes are available. Sizes vary from 48″ × 48″ to 108″ × 48″ and 96″ × 60″, with thicknesses ranging from $\frac{1}{8}$″ to 1″. In some places the thickness is measured in millimetres from 3 to 25 mm.

For special work surfaces, it is possible to obtain aluminium or stainless steel faced boards.

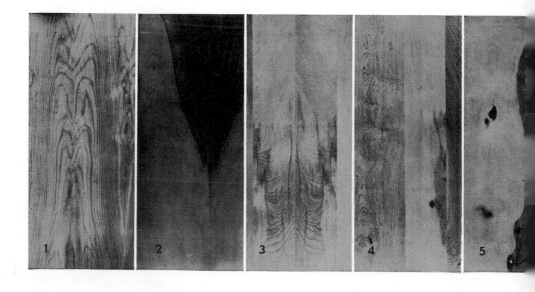

1   2   3   4   5

Imperfections determine the grade of fir plywood

Fir and birch plywood is graded according to the quality of face and back panels. There are two types of board — exterior and interior. The exterior is waterproof. On the right are examples of two grades of ply. The top picture shows the knotty reverse side of the grade one, clean face, knotty reverse, and the lower picture illustrates the plugged side of one clean face, plugged reverse.

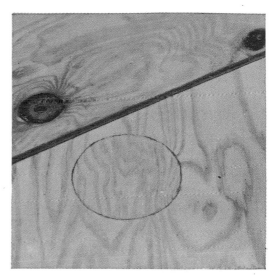

Grades of plywood and their uses

AERO	A perfect board, clean both sides	For good furniture making, etc.
MARINE	Waterproof — with two perfect sides	For boats; both real and model; and for exterior work
TWO CLEAN FACES	Both sides clear of knots	For furniture and cabinet work generally
ONE CLEAN FACE, PLUGGED REVERSE	Knots on reverse side have to to be taken out and plugged	Backings for furniture and for jobs that require only one good face
ONE CLEAN FACE, KNOTTY REVERSE	Knots and splits on reverse	As above
PLUGGED BOTH SIDES	Knots plugged on both sides	For jobs that are to be painted or veneer work
FACE SIDE PLUGGED KNOTTY REVERSE		As above
KNOTTY BOTH SIDES		A cheap grade — use for backings where not seen. Will take laminated plastic surface

Below and on the opposite page are some of the surfaces which have a plywood base. Usually they are sold in sheets 8′ × 4′ or by the square foot—at slightly higher cost.

The panelled effect shown in picture 1 can be used either vertically or horizontally. This type of board finish, together with those shown in pictures 3 and 4, is used mainly to panel walls.

Picture 2 shows two examples of the smooth surfaced version of the boards shown in 3 and 4. The smooth surface board should be used in kitchens in preference to the 'rough' surfaced which tends to collect dirt and grease and is difficult to clean.

Picture 5 shows a good grade of ply—it can be used for unit tops and in general cabinet work. Can be painted or stained and polished.

Picture 6 shows laminated plastic bonded to ply. Use for working surfaces and table tops.

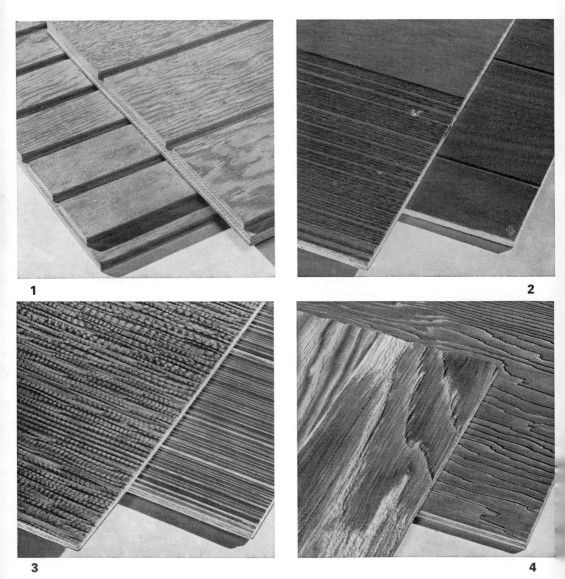

1   **2**

3   **4**

5

6

The plywood core consists of a series of laminated wood veneers—each alternating at right angles to one another. This kind of construction makes a very strong building board which will stand bending and moulding. The number of plies (in this case, five) affects how panels will be used on the job. As a rule, the more plies there are, the stronger the board.

Blockboard is a series of narrow wooden strips specially bonded to equalize the stress of the panel. This core is faced both sides with ply. Used primarily for furniture, built-ins and where edge treatment is needed, core can be dowelled, splined.

Chipboard core—sandwiched between pieces of thin veneer or laminated plastic. It is also used without the veneer or outer plastic layers. As a core material, it requires no crossbanding, and both sides are good. Material can be machined with regular woodworking tools and methods—eliminating the need for special power equipment.

These different edge treatments add variety to your jobs

Butt-edging. Keep edges square; use matching strip of solid wood.

"Mitred" butt-edging. Use glue and brads to fasten the strips on.

Single tongue-and-groove edging. Glue alone may be adequate here.

Splined edging. Variety of mouldings can be used with this joint.

Fluted edging. Stock screen mouldings available can be adapted.

"V" grooved edging is easy to cut on power saw. Glue, brad it on.

Butt-edging sandwiched between top and bottom veneers of wood.

Special filler you can buy makes a smooth, attractive edge for chipboard cores. It is about the consistency of soft putty or patching plaster. To apply, spread filler on edges evenly, let it dry, and sand smooth. Or you can fill the edges with a cellulose filler. Apply it, let it dry, sand, and finish to match colour of top veneer.

Plywood edging tape is real wood that has been coated with adhesive. To use it, strip off paper backing, press to core edge, and run warm iron on face of strip to set it firmly. There is also a wide range of plastic edges.

Working with plywood

Go in both directions with a plane. This keeps the ends from splitting when the plane blade is dragged off the end of the board. Run the plane half-way across the edge—then reverse it and go the other way. Hint: Cut a tiny bevel on each end of the board first to prevent splintering. This trick is the most useful when you have wood to spare. Use fingers to help guide plane at right angle.

Bore holes easier and quicker—without the danger of splintering the board where the bit or drill comes through—by clamping a piece of scrap wood on back of the piece you want the hole in. The scrap accepts the lead screw of auger or expansive bit or tip of drill and helps pull cutting lips through board.

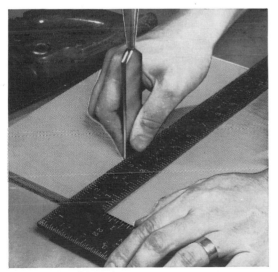

Before sawing plywood, score both sides of the sheet with a sharp chisel or jack-knife at the cut-off point. Scoring should be deep enough to separate the top layer of veneer. This helps prevent splintering and splitting of wood. Another way to prevent splitting: Press a layer of adhesive tape along cut-off line on bottom side of wood. Run saw from top. A fine-toothed saw is best for cutting plywood.

Hardboards are manufactured in a number of thicknesses with sheet sizes up to 12 x 4 feet. These thicknesses—plus special surfaces—give you dozens of variations from which you can choose one that is precisely suited to your needs. Standard hardboard is cheapest; tempered has very high resistance to moisture and wear.

How to work with hardboard

Hardboard—a brown, sometimes greyish material that is usually glassy-smooth on one side and impressed with a screen pattern on the other—is an all-round workshop material.

Like the best of sheet materials, hardboard is versatile. A dense wood product, it can be used for wall panelling, counter tops, doors, drawer bottoms, floors, workbench tops, and other around-the-house projects.

Hardboard has many of wood's characteristics. It can be cut with hand or power saws. It can be nailed, screwed, drilled, routed, planed, beveled, and sanded. You need only ordinary tools for these jobs.

The material is entirely free from grain, and will not split or crack. It also boasts qualities of dimensional stability, rigidity, and high moisture resistance.

Gently rounded curves are possible with hardboard, too, for it will bend around a framework or take self-supporting bends. Radius of the bends depends on its thickness. Cold dry bends may be made on a radius as low as 12 inches with $\frac{1}{8}$ inch hardboard. With heat, moisture, or pressure, make smaller bends.

Generally, any finish that may be applied to wood may also be applied to hardboards.

Cut it with the smooth side up. When using a handsaw, use crosscut or combination blade. With power saws, use crosscut, combination, or carbon-tipped blades. Drill it with a twist drill, rather than an auger bit.

Because of its lack of grain, you have to nail or screw *through* hardboard *to* wood. Hardboard, itself, will not hold the nail or screw.

Prefinished hardboards have plastic surfaces in excellent simulations of marble, popular cabinet-wood grains, tile, structural glass, and plain colours to match any decorative plan. One variety, known as pegboard, is punched with holes for use with hooks as a hang-up board. It is widely used for the panels in cabinets and storage units. While hardboard looks and feels different, it is a true handyman's material— tough and dependable and very easy to handle. Tempered $\frac{1}{4}$-inch hardboard can be used on exterior jobs— if sealed, it will remain in good condition.

Handle hardboard with woodworking tools

First thing you will notice in working with hardboard is its dark surface which hides your pencil marks. For marking purposes, you will find it easier to use a coloured pencil. A wax pencil mark will also show up well. Keep mark thin, though, for more accuracy when you cut.

Smoothest power-saw cut comes from a low-set blade with just two or three teeth showing. Hold board down with the flat of your hand. Work with smooth side up.

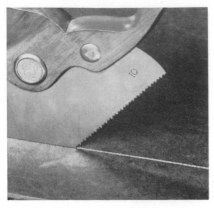

Fairly fine-tooth saw (12 points to the inch down to no fewer than 8) cuts best. Hold the saw at a flat angle for easier and more accurate cutting. Bend hardboard slightly to overcome saw "buckle".

Smooth the edges with a very sharp, shallow-set plane, holding it at a slight angle so that the shearing cut is downward from the surface of board. This method will help eliminate fuzziness.

File or rasp works grainless hardboard to a smooth surface. Hold it true and square and stroke it lengthwise, as shown, rather than across edge.

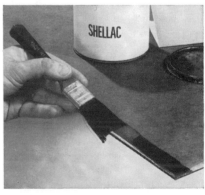

Hardboard may tend to fuzz up slightly under sandpaper—especially standard-grade board. Control this with a thin coat of shellac before final dressing. Do not sand the surface of panel.

Round edges are easy with a plane. Use a shallow set to work round into a nearly final form, then sandpaper it. With lots of rounding to do, you get a start by cutting bevel along edge first.

About boards

TYPE	THEIR USES	SHEET SIZES
Standard hardboard	Cupboards and built-in fitments; floor-covering; furniture and door panels; carpentry generally.	4 ft. and 5 ft. 3 in. widths × lengths up to 12 ft. Also 5 ft. × 8 ft. and flush door sizes.
Tempered hardboard	Where a particularly hard or moisture-resisting surface is required, e.g. floor-covering, outdoor work, caravans.	4 ft. width × 6 ft., 8 ft., 9 ft., 10 ft. and 12 ft.
Medium hardboard	Walls and ceilings; carpet under-lays; coachwork; pin-up and chalk boards.	3 ft. and 4 ft. widths × 6 ft., 8 ft. add 12 ft.
Perforated hardboard	Interior decoration; pegboard; vent covers; surfacing to acoustic materials.	4 ft. width × 6 ft., 8 ft., and 12 ft.
Enamelled hardboard	Walls and ceilings, especially in bathrooms and kitchens; doors and furniture; splashbacks; bath panels; shelving.	4 ft. wide × 6 ft. and 8 ft. Also bath panel sizes and tiled panels 2 × 2 ft.
Plastic-faced hardboard	Working surfaces in kitchens; splash-backs; bath panels; shelf-panelling.	4 ft. wide × 6 ft., 8 ft. and and 9 ft. Also 5 ft. 6 in. × 8 ft. 4 in.
Moulded or embossed hardboard	Panelling; furniture; handicrafts; and wherever a built-in decorative pattern is called for.	4 ft. widths × 8 ft. and 9 ft. Also 4 ft. 3 in. × 7 ft. 5 in.
Fibre insulating board	Wall and ceiling linings; plaster base; thermal insulation; sound insulation; acoustic correction.	2 ft., 3 ft. and 4 ft. widths × 6 ft., 7 ft., 8 ft., 9 ft., 10 ft. and 12 ft.
Wallboard	Panelling walls, ceilings or partitions; underlay for floor coverings.	3 ft. and 4 ft. widths × 6 ft., 7 ft., 8 ft., 9 ft., 10 ft. and 12 ft.
Acoustic boards and tiles	Acoustic correction and noise reduction.	Squares of 12 in., 16 in., and 24 in. Other tiles 12 in. × 24 in. Boards: 4 ft. × 8 ft.

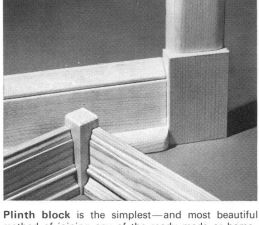

This joint has end of the moulding shaped to match face. For perfect fit, make a back-cut mitre first. Then use the coping saw to cut carefully along the edge formed by mitre cut. Saw to leave *all* of the moulding face on.

Plinth block is the simplest—and most beautiful method of joining any of the ready-made or home-built mouldings at corners. There are no mitres to cut, no difficult joints to fit. You simply cut the plinth blocks and nail them up; then butt the square-cut mouldings against them for perfect fit.

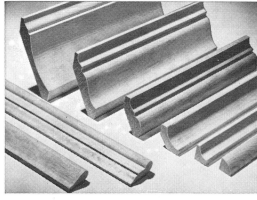

On flat surfaces joints can be finished or plain surfaces dressed up with one of the many shaped beadings available—some are made of plastic.

Mouldings from core to quarter round. Cove and bead mouldings give beauty to ceilings. There is a wide range of sizes and shapes to choose from.

Some more types of mouldings. The corner moulding (right) is ideal for making a neat job of outside corners.

Inside corners can be coped (top) or mitred (left), but all outside corners must be mitred, as shown. Corners will fit easiest if you cope or mitre the ends of two pieces, then cut the pieces to length with a square cut between corners. Butt the square edges together for the appearance of a continuous strip.

Aluminium—metal you can whittle

Metalworking with a few basic tools is easy using soft-alloy aluminium.

Available in sheets, rods, bars, angles, and tubes, it is soft enough to smooth with a woodworking plane, but sturdy enough to use in conjunction with projects you will want to build.

Remember that aluminium sawdust is hard, so when you machine it on power tools, wear safety glasses.

Another word of caution: there are various grades of aluminium. Some are hard and cannot be worked safely, either with saw, plane, scissors or brace and bit. When you buy the metal, be sure you get the correct grade.

For drilling, use a twist drill in bar, angle, tubes, or rod, but you will cut a cleaner hole in sheet with an auger bit. Taps and dies meant for steel will cut it easily. Coarse threads are best.

Handy aluminium shapes include (left to right) edging, $\frac{3}{8}$ inch rod, $\frac{1}{8} \times \frac{3}{4}$ and $\frac{1}{4} \times 1$ bar, 1×1 angle, $\frac{5}{8}$-, 1- and $1\frac{1}{4}$ inch tube, and 36×36 sheets, plain or embossed. Rivets, screws, bolts are aluminium, too, to aid in joinery when you work metal.

Smooth edges fast with ordinary plane, on sheet or bar. Set plane for fine cut; bear down to minimize chatter. Clamp sheet between boards for rigidity. Soft alloy cuts easily with power- or hand-operated woodworking tools, but avoid hard alloy.

Scissors cut sheet aluminium easily and smoothly, in more intricate curves than tin snips would allow. Be sure that all of your tools are sharp; blunt edges tend to tear the soft metal. Mark cutting line on surface of aluminium with awl or crayon, as shown.

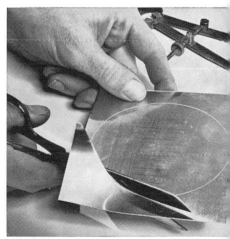

Fine-tooth saws work best, and a coping saw makes an ideal cutting tool for this metal. Make this joint in tubing by cutting paper pattern of tube end. Scribe it on tube, saw it out, then make a final fit with a half-round file. A wood plug driven into the end of the tube takes a screw to hold joint tight. Note that cushion (piece of rubber tile) is used to protect work from vice.

Power saw gives accuracy to straight cuts in sheet aluminium, and to cut-offs and mitres on tube, rod, bar, or angle stock. The metal tends to slip on a mitre gauge, so hold it firmly. If the sheet rises from the saw table, hold it down with a strip of wood, as shown in the photograph. (However, use your blade guard for safety.) Cut slits in tube or rip bar against the ripping fence.

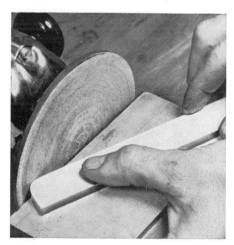

The disc-sander attachment on a portable drill (shown) or on a table saw will round corners and smooth saw cuts on aluminium, just the same as it will with wood. Select the medium and fine-grit abrasives. The coarse paper will leave the metal rough, so it should be used only for fast cutting. After final sanding with the finest grit, use buffing wheel to restore polish of aluminium.

Wire wheel in drill kit or on a grinder will smooth rough cuts and can be used to achieve a satin finish. The wheel cuts the aluminium fast, so use a fine brush. Keep the metal moving for a satin finish. Let the wheel cut more, and you will get a pebbled surface. Wire wheel quickly removes burrs left by cutting tools and saws. Insert dowels into short tubing for a better grip.

Mitred corner is easy to cut in the soft alloy if you drive wooden plug into a tube before you make the 45-degree-angle cut. Use either a simple mitre box or a table saw for the cut. Hold the stock firm. A screw combined with glue makes a good, strong joint. Light work, however, may be strong enough with glue and no screw. If plug is hardwood pre-drill for screw.

Make corners in angle stock in either of two ways. Make an overlapping corner by locking the angle in a vice and cutting one side of it square. One half then overlaps the other as the right-angle bend is made. Secure the joint with a rivet. A mitred corner in angle stock has a 90-degree V cut from one side (on bench). When bent, it forms mitre.

Join bar ends with a cleat of the same metal or with a long-taper splice. Use rivets or bolts to secure either joint. Put one rivet or bolt in place first, then drill for the others through both bar ends at one time. Cut the long taper on your power saw, or grind it on disc sander, for smooth fit. A wide range of nuts, bolts, rivets, screws, also made of aluminium, are available.

To join tubes, cut short scrap and saw $\frac{1}{4}$-inch-side slit in it, as shown. When you squeeze this "sleeve", it slips inside the tubes, and springs back to hold them together. Use self-tapping screw for any permanent joints. Joint can be made invisible by finishing on a wire wheel. A dowel inserted in the ends of the two pieces of tube will also make a good joint.

Aluminium rivets serve as fast and tight method of joining sheet to angle or bar-stock aluminium. First you lock assembly with two or three rivets, then drill the remaining holes.

Rolled edge for sheets is easy to obtain with simple jig you can make by sawing slot along a piece of dowel. Slip edge of sheet in slot and twist dowel, while holding roll right. Use dowel slightly smaller than desired roll.

Join rod to bar with the self-riveted technique, and joint will barely show. File end of the rod into a round "tenon" to fit hole drilled in bar. Countersinking on back of bar fills tight when you burr over rivet. File, buff smooth.

Right-angle jig is slot sawed in board or two pieces of timber clamped on edge of metal. If you plane inside surface of jig at an angle, the bend you make is more than 90 degrees. Return to angle you want for a square corner.

Hand bending works well. Make jigs for slightly smaller radius than desired bend, to allow for spring-back. Tube bends (on larger curves) call for regular bender. Or pack tube with wet sand so that it bends without crushing.

Sheet-to-tube joints are made by sawing a slit in the tube and inserting the sheet. Then bolts can be put in through both the tube walls and the sheet. Or double-hem metal sheet and squeeze up tube over it, as shown.

Moneysaving tips for the handyman

Use lower grades of timber, hardboard and plywood to cut costs of job. Lower grades often meet job specifications, especially where material will not show. Use lower grades of timber and plywood for built-ins and cabinets which will be painted. Holes can be filled and sanded. Cheaper, standard hardboard is for interior use; tempered is moisture resistant, withstands heavy wear.

Loose knots need not prevent you from using a board. When you find one, push it out, coat the rim with clear cellulose adhesive, and press the knot back in place. Wipe away any adhesive that squeezes out, and allow at least an hour for drying. The adhesive forms a colourless bond that will hold the knot permanently in place. Before staining the wood, sand away the glue on the face of the board to permit the stain to penetrate.

Warped or bowed board can often be straightened. Support the board at both ends and pile weights on the centre. Do not weight the board too heavily, and give it plenty of time to straighten. If board will be nailed to rigid frame or wall that will hold it flat, it is not necessary to straighten it first. Just force it into place, then nail it down. If an end is badly warped, you may have to cut it off, and use the good section.

Bowing. This board has become bowed, forming a gutter-like hollow from one end to the other. Often you can correct such a defect by wetting the concave side and covering it with damp rags. Leave rags in place overnight, in a warm room; swelling may flatten board.

Twisting. Timber that is twisted out of shape, like piece at the right, can be difficult to work. If the piece is thin enough to be somewhat flexible, and joins another board with tongue-and-groove, you may be able to force it back into shape as you nail it in place. But usually you have to discard a part of the piece, and use only the best portion.

Checking. Cracks like this are called checks. Unless they are deep enough to weaken the timber seriously, do not worry about them. For a smooth painted finish, fill such checks with plastic wood or a gap filler made of glue mixed with fine sawdust. It is a good idea to fill checks and let the filler harden before final smoothing job is done.

Grade marking. Look at the end of the timber you are buying. Besides revealing any bowing and the depth of any cracks, the end often bears the grade stamp, in number or in symbol. Timber is graded at the mill, long before it reaches the wood-yard. However, do not select by grade alone; a load of any grade will contain some pieces that are better than others.

Timber, materials storage

Every man planning a project should first prepare a list of materials so accurate that, when the job is completed, there are hardly enough scraps left to start a fire.

Unfortunately, it never works out that way. Every job results in odds and ends of wood that look too useful to burn or throw out.

Then, too, there are times when you come across a good buy at your timber yard. This makes it a double problem of storage, because you will have various sizes and shapes of wood to find storage for.

What to do with those useful-looking scraps, and how to store that stock of new timber can be solved by using the space-saving ideas shown here. The simple, low-cost racks are easy to build and keep your materials off the floor and out of the way.

Another plus for these storage racks is their design, which holds timber and sheet materials in such a way that warping and bowing are kept to a minimum. Proper installation of the racks is of great importance in keeping boards flat and straight. Follow these instructions carefully for best results.

Three-level timber rack separates different kinds and sizes of boards, reduces fairly large supply to three easily handled piles. Stock lifts off edgewise, so no space is needed at ends of rack. Mounted high on wall, it leaves room below for operation of tools.

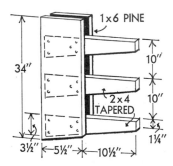

Add a support like the ones shown here for each additional 4-foot length of timber to be stored; 16-foot needs four supports, 12-foot needs three supports, and so on. Build one unit, then assemble others on top of first so they are all identical. The horizontal arms should have a slight upward tilt.

Vertical members are 1 × 6s, horizontal arms are 2 × 4s. Use 2½-inch nails. Tapered brackets increase storage and handling space without reducing strength. You can use inexpensive timber for units if knots are not loose.

Install the supports by straddling ceiling joists with top of vertical members. Keep them tight against the wall. Install the end units first, then stretch a string tightly between them for aligning remaining units.

For ideal plywood storage, sheets should lie flat to guard against warping. This, of course, is impractical in most shops. Alternative is to stand them on edge as vertical as possible. Rack holds six sheets with room for timber above.

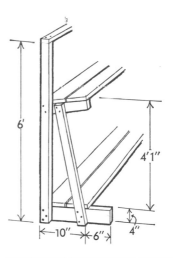

The sheet materials rack is built of 1 × 2, using 2-inch nails clinched at back. Be sure to make one right- and one left-hand side. Ends are 4 feet apart to give best support for full sheets of plywood, hardboard, other materials.

To allow sheets to be stored in a nearly vertical position without danger of falling forward, screw a turn button to the ends of shelf supports.

HOME WORKSHOP owners agree on these suggestions for preventing an accumulation of scrap around the shop . . .

Throw away most scraps of ordinary 1 × 1 and 2 × 1 timber. Its common use continually produces more pieces you will be able to use.

Throw away most scraps from cut-off sawing. They are difficult to work with and seldom prove useful.

Save larger scraps for cleats, nailing strips, and so on. They may save your ripping a good board.

Save scraps of plywood for use as corner braces and for other uses where its two-way strength makes it essential.

Save nearly every scrap of the expensive cabinet woods. The larger pieces can make attractive accessories.

Save useful lengths of mouldings, especially types you have used in the house. They will simplify matching for repairs to existing mouldings.

Store small scraps of ordinary lumber in a tall cardboard carton. When the box is full, burn it, scraps and all, and start over again with a new, empty box.

Nails, screws, and bolts

Know-how makes any job easier — even a job as simple as driving a nail or a screw. The professional tricks shown here will help you do better work with these basic holding devices.

The basic types of nails are wire, ovals, panel and veneer pins. Common wire nails are used mainly for heavy work. Ovals are thinner, and are valuable where a common nail might split the wood. Panel and veneer pins have thin heads that can be set below the wood's surface. For special uses, you will find nails of other types and other metals. It is impossible to describe them all here, but a selection of the various types is shown in the following pages.

Common screws include the flat-head, which is set flush with the wood's surface; oval head, more decorative and often brass; and the roundhead, which does not require countersinking. Large coach screws have square heads, are driven with a wrench instead of a screwdriver.

When buying screws, you will find the length designated in inches, the diameter of the shank designated by a gauge number, usually from No. 0 (about $\frac{1}{16}$") to No. 24 (about $\frac{1}{2}$"). For other gauge numbers, see the handy chart of nails, screws and bolts on the following pages.

Steel screws should be used on heavier construction jobs. But do not forget that steel rusts so, if the job is an outside one, consider galvanised or coated screws. Brass or copper screws do not rust but are not quite so tough as steel.

Most nails are sold by weight, irrespective of size, the smaller of course the greater the number of nails per pound.

Screws are packed in gross boxes but can be bought singly or by the half-dozen. The handyman who has insufficient storage space, or uses a small number of nails and screws, can purchase them pre-packed and in quantities for the job in hand. If possible, it is wise to keep a small stock of nails and screws — it does obviate a trip to the hardware shop every time you start a job.

There are important reasons why you should know what you are getting when you ask the hardware man for what is commonly and casually called a "nail". Not everything with threads on it is intended for the same purpose. In the picture an adjustable wrench (left) is correctly used to tighten nut on a bolt, while a screwdriver is used to drive a screw (centre), and a hammer is used to drive a nail (right). Each of these three basic fasteners — bolts, screws and nails — is made to do specific jobs. Points to remember: Holes drilled for bolts should be the correct size — over-size holes result in slack joints, and under-size holes tend to split wood because the bolt has to be forced into them. Always tighten a nut on to a washer and not direct on to a job. Pre-drill holes for screws — and, in some cases, it is wise to pre-drill for nails.

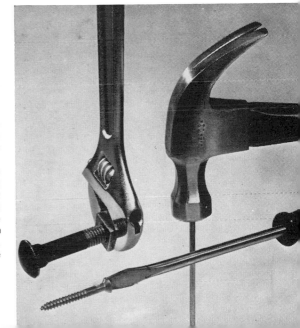

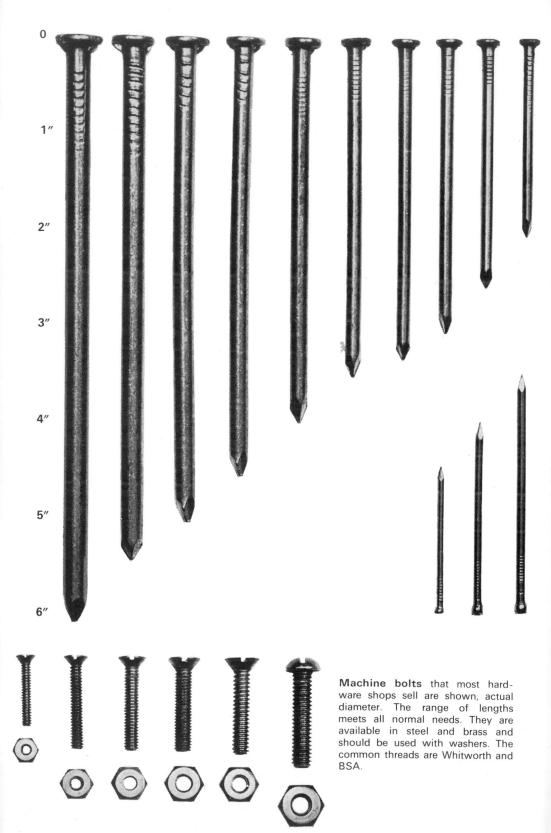

0
1"
2"
3"
4"
5"
6"

Machine bolts that most hardware shops sell are shown, actual diameter. The range of lengths meets all normal needs. They are available in steel and brass and should be used with washers. The common threads are Whitworth and BSA.

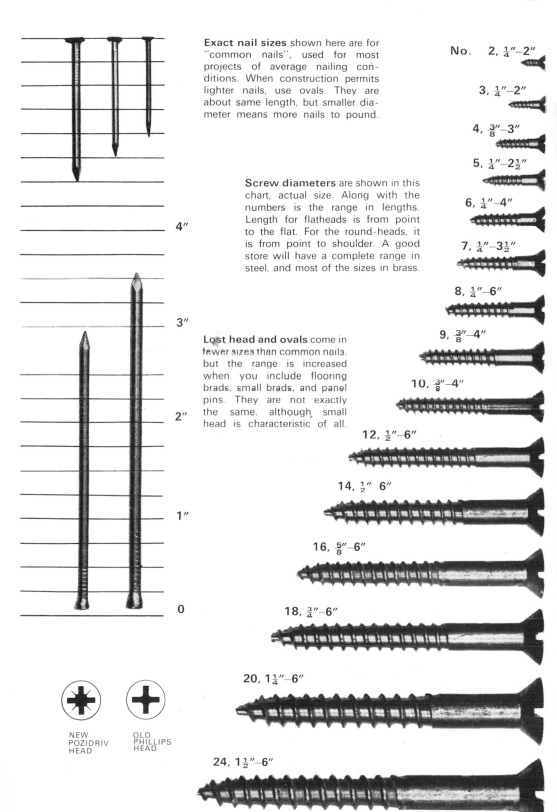

Exact nail sizes shown here are for "common nails", used for most projects of average nailing conditions. When construction permits lighter nails, use ovals. They are about same length, but smaller diameter means more nails to pound.

Screw diameters are shown in this chart, actual size. Along with the numbers is the range in lengths. Length for flatheads is from point to the flat. For the round-heads, it is from point to shoulder. A good store will have a complete range in steel, and most of the sizes in brass.

Lost head and ovals come in fewer sizes than common nails, but the range is increased when you include flooring brads, small brads, and panel pins. They are not exactly the same, although small head is characteristic of all.

4″

3″

2″

1″

0

NEW POZIDRIV HEAD

OLD PHILLIPS HEAD

No. 2, $\frac{1}{4}$″–2″

3, $\frac{1}{4}$″–2″

4, $\frac{3}{8}$″–3″

5, $\frac{1}{4}$″–2$\frac{1}{2}$″

6, $\frac{1}{4}$″–4″

7, $\frac{1}{4}$″–3$\frac{1}{2}$″

8, $\frac{1}{4}$″–6″

9, $\frac{3}{8}$″–4″

10, $\frac{3}{8}$″–4″

12, $\frac{1}{2}$″–6″

14, $\frac{1}{2}$″ 6″

16, $\frac{5}{8}$″–6″

18, $\frac{3}{4}$″–6″

20, 1$\frac{1}{4}$″–6″

24, 1$\frac{1}{2}$″–6″

Common screw heads: flathead (brass shown), roundhead (blue, brass, nickel shown), cheese head (nickel shown). Flatheads are countersunk.

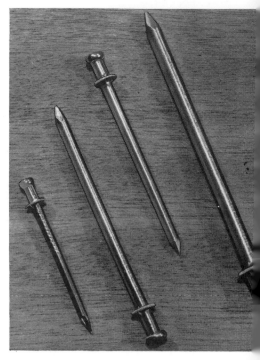

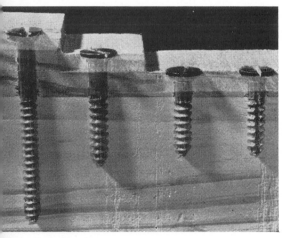

Double-headed nails are used for building temporary structures that will be dismantled. Nails can be driven to depth of lower head to hold work. Top protrudes for gripping with hammer claws when the structure is dismantled.

Length of screw depends on thickness of bottom board and the strength required. Smooth shank should reach through top board. Groove in screw at right helps it penetrate hardwood.

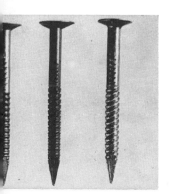

Hardboard nails have tapered threads and flat head for better holding. Will hold fast where movement is present.

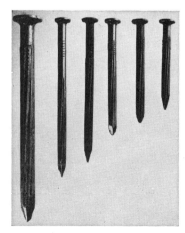

Some masonry nails are threaded. These are made of high-carbon steel. They are excellent for anchoring items to foundations, walls, and so on.

A **hexagon bolt** (you buy the nut separately) costs about three times as much as a machine bolt. But it is of better steel and worth the extra amount when used in a position where strength is very important.

Machine bolt has head; carriage bolt has square collar that locks it against turning in wood. Use latter in wood; former in metal— or in wood with a washer under the head.

Coach bolt and screw have square heads for wrench, and coarse threads for pre-bored hole in wood. Use it when you cannot bore through. Bolt, when feasible, makes a stronger joint.

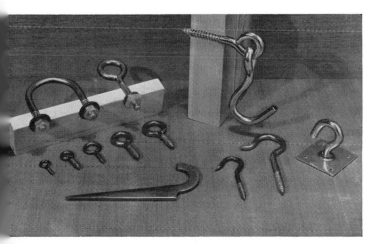

Hooks and eyes have a variety of uses

Both screws and bolts come in hook-and-eye styles. A U-bolt is the strongest "eye" you can install. The screw eye and hook in the piece of 2 x 4 will support a fair weight. The hook which is fastened with four screws (lower right) can be used for a number of jobs. The one that does not screw into place is a spike hook, which you drive into place with a hammer.

Washers. Screws hold best when washers are used for a "snowshoe" grip. Under roundhead screw (left) is a flat washer. Cup washers, shown with the flathead and cheese-head screws, add to neatness of job and can be removed without marking.

In plaster. Fastening in plaster or hardboard is a common problem. For light work, use a plaster screw (right). Use toggles and anchors for greatest strength. Just insert flange into a pre-bored hole and tighten the bolt. Tightening bolt spreads arms of flange so that they bear against the back side of the plaster, hardboard or plywood walls or partitions.

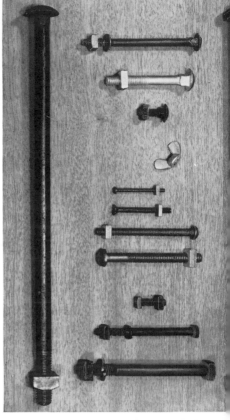

Bolts. The range is so wide that it is impossible to show them all. Some are made with a thread taking up the entire length of the bolt. Others have threads for three-quarters of their length and less. All can be fitted with the large assortment of nuts and washers available—some of them made for special uses.

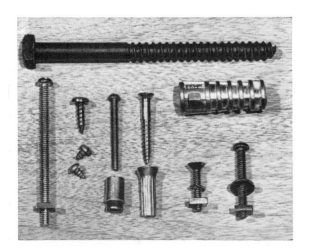

Screws can be fastened to metal and masonry

The three small screws are self-tapping for use on sheet-metal. Machine bolts (one far left, two far right) look alike but have different threads for use with metal. They fasten with nuts. Two screws in centre are for masonry. Plugs (below them) can be of lead, rubber, nylon, or fibre, and are inserted in holes drilled in masonry. At top is coach screw with lead anchor for masonry.

Wood joinery methods

The first problem a handyman faces whenever he starts to build something is the technique of fastening two boards together . . . the selection of a kind of joint adequate to the job's needs in beauty, strength, and speed.

There is no sense in "overjoining" a simple project, and there is no wisdom in "underjoining" one that demands rigidity and greater permanence. The right joint is just as important as the right wood.

Here is the cardinal rule in joinery: *Make the joints fit.* Even with a simple butt joint, fit is important in a square cut end. More complex joints will be stronger and better only if they fit. Take time making any joint, whether you work with power or with hand tools. Remember, the job is only as good as its joints.

Bolted butt joints can be made with just a brace and bit. Bore holes for the nuts first. Use a square placed over the nut holes to locate the path of the bolt and the point where you will bore into the upright member. Holes for nuts and washers should be half the horizontal member's width in from the end.

Toenailing can be used in light or heavy construction jobs if you wish to leave the face unmarred. Let nails on one side force the frame out of line (arrow). Back-nailing returns the piece to position.

This method for butt joints gives you maximum strength against shear stress (arrows). Fasten it with screws through face, or with angled nails. Drive them from bottom so they are hidden. Glue alone gives good joint.

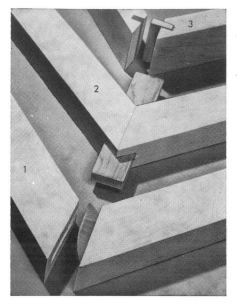

These are neat, strong corner joints for light materials

Strongest mitre needs additional "glue line" plus physical support. Hidden spline (1) has a groove cut along face of mitre, with spline shaped to fit. Make "through" spline (2) by continuing groove along full length of the mitre face. Trim the spline when the glue is set. The groove is crosswise for the cross-spline (3). All three of these joints have great strength.

Cleats strengthen butt joints for stress in all directions. Use them when you need strong joints for light members and appearance is secondary. Nail ½ inch from edges so wood won't be so likely to split. Hardboard and plywood make good cleats. The cross-grain lamination in ply resists stress in all directions. The nails need not go clear through, but if they do, clinch them on other side for the most strength with this type of joint.

Half-mitreing permits a surface fastening technique on back (1), with the mitre's neatness on the front (2). Cuts you make (3) are simple, and with glue on all surfaces, a fitting half-mitre is a strong joint.

Mortise and tenon (1) is common in windows. Open mortise (2) is easier to do, has great strength when glued and pinned. Single dovetail (3) is self-locking, decorative. Half-joint (4) has good gluing area.

Techniques for edge joinery

Joining boards edge to edge requires additional support—glue alone does not make a strong enough joint. Dowels (1) inserted into both edges to be joined is a popular method, but be sure that you drill the holes dead centre in the edge and also at right angles to the edge.

In (2) a plywood spline is glued into two grooves cut into the edges of the board to be joined together.

In a third method, corrugated fasteners are hammered across the join of the boards on the wrong side. Boards joined by this method should be weighted down on a flat surface while glued edges set.

Steel or brass mending plates screwed across the join is a fourth method of joining boards together. Before screwing the plates to the boards, the ends of the plates should be bent slightly upwards from the middle and the boards should follow this line.

A fifth method is to use wire nails instead of dowels. Undersized holes are drilled and the heads of the nails cut off. This joint is strong, but it has to be an accurate fit.

End cleats add strength, discourage warping of edge-glued jobs. You can tongue-and-groove them (1), or use nails or screws and glue (2) at ends of boards. Both methods eliminate problem of finishing the end grain.

Use a cleat screwed to back (right) or a strip dovetailed into the back to reinforce the edge joints. Snug-fitting dovetail with glue needs no fasteners. Both techniques help control swelling and warping of timber.

Mortise and tenon; dowel joint

Mortise and tenon (1) is classic joint for strength and good looks in furniture. Half-joint (2) is simpler if joint shows from one side only. Glue and clamp these joints to get strength without any other fasteners.

Integral dowel for dowel joint is turned on end of square to fit bored hole, with wedge to tighten. Slot in round end is same shape as wedge, but smaller. Thus wedge exerts pressure along full length of the dowelled end.

Two ways to make half-joints

Cross joint is easy, neat, convenient, for a cross joint on a flat plane. Lay members at right angles, scribe widths. Then saw half-way through each. Clean out between the cuts with a chisel, then use fasteners or glue.

Opposing butts are false cross lap, useful if you need many joints—as in egg-crate designs. Corrugated fasteners front and back secure joint, and can be set, filled, and painted. Beware of splitting if you use hardwood.

Heavy-duty construction comes from the fitted joints, fastened with bolts. These two joints are simple to make by scribing width of the cut from the actual crosspieces. Clamp the members in position, and drill through both at the same time for a perfect-fitting and tight joint.

Making drawers, you gain strength and simplify assembly by using butt joint plus small rabbet (arrows). Corner reinforces drawer against loosening when it is jerked open or slammed. Cuts for either overlapping (left) or flush drawer speed assembly of drawers.

Short corner blocks (2 inches or so), on back side of many joint types, provide extra glue surface plus bracing when other mechanical means of strengthening might be unsightly or unfeasible. They must fit tight since they are not clamped. Glue the main joint first.

Joining ends to increase length is easy with tapered splice (1), lapped ends (2), cleat (3), or long lap (4). When splice, cleat, or lap is long, you get a big glue area, and these joints can be stronger than the individual members if they are properly cut, fitted, and fastened.

Join rounds to flat by treating them as you would dowels, as this cutaway model shows. Wedge (1) is sanded flat after it's driven. Blind joint (2) has part way hole. Angled joint (3) is easiest as a butt joint, and is best fastened for permanence with screw (shown).

Reinforce joints with metal

Mending plates—pieces of metal with screw holes already drilled in them— are a fast, dependable means of adding strength to new or old wood joints.

They are cheap, and available in many shapes, sizes, and angles . . . and you can bend and twist them to fit your project.

Mending plates can be added to a joint with ease, as these pictures show. Only the simplest hand tools are necessary for the job.

Generally, you will want to use metal plates where they do not show. In some cases where the metal reinforcer *will* show, it is available in a decorative finish that will not detract from the appearance of the job in hand.

A flat plate can be mortised into the wood, too, so that it is hidden. Step-by-step instructions for mortising a plate are on page 133.

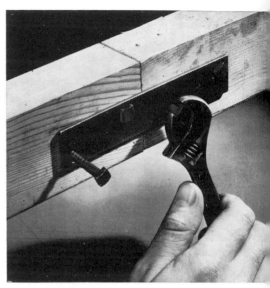

Heavy mending plate forms a strong joint by itself. Make the joint still stronger by adding strength of small lag screws or carriage bolts. Plates are heavy-gauge steel, and come in various lengths and widths. It is possible for you to get extra-large and heavy ones tailor-made.

T-plates, like other mending plates, take work out of difficult joining jobs, give you professional look at same time. Vice holds brace for "tight" bending jobs— like this one. If you want to increase the joint strength, use lag screws to attach.

You can buy metal reinforcements for almost any kind of joint at your d.i.y. shop. Such mending plates, like these right angle and T-shaped plates for corners, form strong joints by themselves, and are even more effective as strengtheners for glued, screwed, or nailed joints.

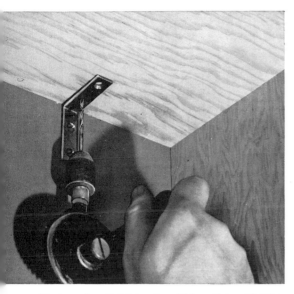

Shelves for light loads will hug the wall when fastened on with angle brackets. First, plug the wall, then screw the braces to the plugs, being care ful not to damage the plaster. Place shelf frame on braces; drill the screw holes.

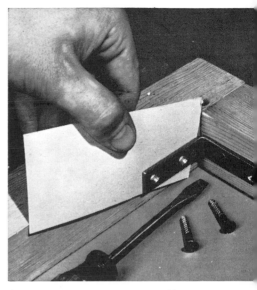

Pull joints tightly together in this way: Insert a thin piece of cardboard between angle bracket and the frame. Fasten bracket to side member, then remove the cardboard, and run the other screws in.

Small angle brackets are ideal for fastening the bottoms of chairs to frames, among many other of their strengthening uses. Position one bracket in the centre of each side, holding the bottom tightly to the frame to ensure the proper alignment.

Table-top fastener screws to under-side of top, while lip of fastener slips into saw cut around apron. (Or do job with corner blocks.) To avoid stress from shrinking and swelling, do not use glue

Wide corner brackets are designed for heavy-duty work where regular corner bracket is not strong enough to support weight or pressure. Brackets can be positioned to fit almost any situation, as on stepladder here.

More strength for inside corner joints is furnished by still-wider bracket—big brother to the one used for the stepladder. Position and drill pilot holes for wood screws—or small coach screws, for exceptional strength.

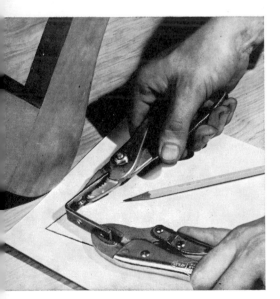

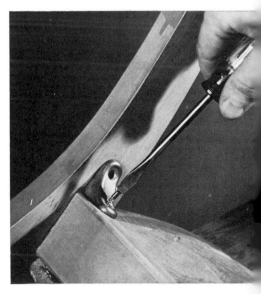

Regular angle bracket or mending plate is bent to fit curvature of chair and table frames. Trace curve you want to duplicate on light cardboard placed behind frame. Then bend bracket with pliers to match it.

Copper-plated brackets—they are especially designed for tables, chairs, other furniture pieces, and boxes—are very lightweight, yet strong. Dull finish makes them attractive if they must be used where they will be seen.

Here is how to mortise in a mending plate

1 Repair splits in chairs, chair bottoms, table tops with mending plates mortised in for more reinforcement and a neater job. Scribe outline of plate on surface with sharp knife, bridging it across the split.

2 Chisel out mortise after making cuts —about $\frac{1}{8}$ inch apart—to depth you want. Now smooth bottom by holding chisel flat, bevel up. Guide blade with fingers so it will not jump and mar back.

3 Screw plate in place. It should be about $\frac{1}{8}$ inch below surface. You may have to make several smoothing cuts in mortise with chisel so plate fits snugly without rocking on uneven bottom. Chisel with grain.

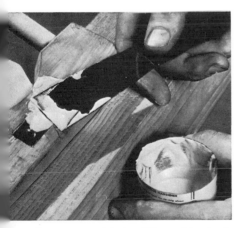

4 Complete job by filling with plastic wood, bringing it to level of surrounding surface. Remove excess. Sandpaper patch smooth. Refinish to match.

5 Reinforce weak corners of windows and doors by mortising in a mending plate across joint. Scribe outline of plate on edge to depth you want. Space saw cuts, and chisel out.

How to work with dowels

Dowels are round rods of beech or ash that for years have been an unexcelled method of lending strength to joints in woodworking.

Standard dowels are made $\frac{1}{8}$" thick, and then in eighths up to 1"—length depends on thickness. Cutting to required length and scoring them is a simple matter.

If you keep several lengths of dowelling in your workshop, keep them on racks so that they will not get broken accidentally.

Think beyond joining jobs when you think of dowelling. Here is a wood that will take beautiful finishes for furniture parts, spindles, pegs, dividers, and a host of other uses.

When the diameter goes above 1", it is not called dowelling. It is classified as timber and goes up to 2" in diameter.

Dowelling costs only a few pence for a 3' or 4' length. Diameter runs from $\frac{1}{8}$"÷1" in graduations of $\frac{1}{16}$th. Wood is beech or ash in these "dowel" sizes. In the case of "rounds", lengths go to 20' or more, and diameters to 2". The wood used for these is mostly ash or pine.

Make dowels from dowelling by cutting to length and scoring spirally with corner of a file. This permits excess glue to ooze out of the hole. Without the groove, glue will be trapped by piston-and-cylinder actions as the dowel is forced home. Rounding the ends helps.

Here are the tricks that will help you do accurate, neat work with dowels

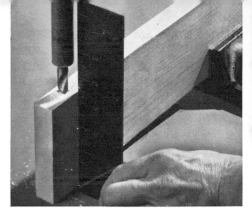

With practice, you can bore fairly true holes by lining up drill with square. Small bits are easier to steer, so bore $\frac{1}{8}$-inch hole first, then dowel-size hole. Simple depth gauge is "sleeve" made by drilling through large dowel.

Holes for dowels must be snug fitting, drilled true. A precision dowelling jig that you can buy holds bits or drills in accurate position. Clamps enable you to position the holes.

Put dowels in place on one side of joint first. Tap snug with hammer or mallet. Wipe glue off protruding part (and gluing faces), unless two parts will be joined immediately. Otherwise hardened glue will hold the joint apart.

A couple of well-placed dowels can be surest guarantee of a good join at mitred corners. Clamp stock in vice at 45-degree angle, then drill on the true vertical or horizontal.

Home-made dowelling jig, for a particular job, is simple to make from scrap. Drill properly spaced holes clear through timber—making them true and parallel. Clamp jig in position, and let its holes steer drill straight.

Glueless joints are possible, but some strength is sacrificed. Saw into end of dowel and insert wedge. This spreads dowel as it is driven into hole. To avoid splitting board, make sure the wedge spread is the long way of the grain.

One dowel has little value, but two or three half-inchers give greater strength to butt joint. Large timber permits big dowel, but do not weaken with a too-large hole.

In repairs, new holes must match old. Dividers give accurate fit; do not guess. Scribe from corresponding sides of the two holes. To find position of dowel, measure from end to edge of hole. Add half hole diameter to mark centre.

Dowels are excellent means of fastening to concrete wall. Hammer dowel home in hole (made by masonry bit or punch), then nail into dowel. Dowel will stay firmly in place.

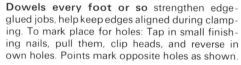

Dowels every foot or so strengthen edge-glued jobs, help keep edges aligned during clamping. To mark place for holes: Tap in small finishing nails, pull them, clip heads, and reverse in own holes. Points mark opposite holes as shown.

Use short slices of dowelling to fill in sunken screw holes, sanding them smooth when glue has dried. Match up grains and colour of wood as far as possible.

How to use glue

Gluing is a fast, easy way to join two pieces of material. Three simple rules will help you get good joints every time:

1. Prepare the joint for glue by removing wax, grease, oil, or paint from surfaces to be coated with adhesive.

2. Determine the kind of glue that suits the purpose best.

3. Clamp joint until glue dries.

A convenient way to group the currently available woodworking glues is under two main headings—glues formulated from materials of natural origin, and the synthetic resin glues.

Glues of natural origin are animal, vegetable, casein, and soy-bean. They come in ready-to-use liquid form and powder. Setting time is from 6 to 8 hours.

Casein glue offers great strength and good water resistance, and sets in about 5 hours. All joints made with these glues must be clamped or otherwise held free of movement for a time.

The synthetic resin glues include urea-resin, phenol-resin, resorcinol-resin, melamine-resin, and polyvinyl-resin emulsion types, plus contact cement.

Of these, the polyvinyl type is most familiar to handymen. It is the white liquid glue that comes ready for use—generally in a plastic bottle. It will set in about 30 minutes at a temperature as low as 60 degrees.

Other synthetic resin glues come in powder or liquid form and must be mixed before use.

Of particular interest to handymen are resorcinol-resin and urea-resin glues, both of which set at room temperatures. The former offers very strong, waterproof joints, and the latter, strong water-resistant joints.

In cases where you want instant bonding of materials, use contact cement. It will make a strong, waterproof bond between nearly any two materials.

Good glue joints require careful planning

Thin coat of glue is best. Spread it out over glue area, and wipe off the surplus after you clamp the job. Most glues work best when temperature is 70 degrees or higher. A clean scrap of wood serves as a spreader, as shown.

Glue area determines the strength of glue job the more surface you coat, the better. Open mortise-and-tenon joint (at bottom) gives glue 8 inches more surface than butt joint. Plan joints so you have most glue area.

When gluing edges, turn alternate sides of stock up to reduce warping. Turn heartwood side up on every other board when three or more boards are used. Plastic-resin glue is resistant to moisture; gives firm bond.

Wood expands more across grain than with the grain when it becomes wet . . . the cause of most joint failures. Assemble the pieces so grain direction is parallel on both pieces (arrow), for the same expansion and contraction.

Make your own clamping jigs from scrap wood

Clamping blocks for mitred corners are just two pieces of scrap stock with notches cut at 90-degree angles for the clamping surfaces. C-clamps are versatile holding devices. They are the least expensive type.

Clamping jig is nothing more than a triangle of plywood with holes drilled through it to accept clamps. Quick-setting glue lets you unclamp job in half an hour or so. It comes in liquid form, needs no mixing, spreads easily.

Adhesives

Type	Resistance to water	Liability to Stain	Shelf Life	Setting Time	Uses
Animal Glue	Poor	None	Indefinite	12 hours	Woodwork, repairs to woodwork and veneers, book binding and repairs.
Synthetic Resin **Type A:**	Excellent	None if iron is avoided	About 1 year	1—12 hours depending on temperature	General and particularly outdoor woodwork
Type B:	Excellent	None if iron is avoided	About 1 year	1—12 hours depending on temperature	Special grade for woo-laminated plastic
Casein	Good	Particularly oak	Unlimited	4—8 hours depending on temperature	General woodwork where staining is not a disadvantage.
PVA	Fair	None	*About 1 year if free from frost	4—8 hours	General woodwork and repairs, paper, fabrics, some plastics, veneers, as a size.
Contact Adhesives (Apply with spreader)	Good	None, but is coloured	*About 1 year	Immediate	Fixing sheet plastics, fabrics, hardboard, etc. Gives flexible bond
Rubber Latex	Good	None, but is coloured	About 1 year	About 1 hour	Bonding fabrics, paper, rug making and repairing, etc.
Epoxy Resin (A 2-part Adhesive)	Excellent	None	Indefinite	Depends on temperature	Metals, glass, china, plastics
Balsa Cement (Cellulose Acetate)	High	None	*Indefinite	1—2 hours	Balsa wood and absorbent materials
Polystyrene Cement	High	None	*Indefinite	2—6 hours	Polystyrene plastic articles

* Keep pot or tube tightly sealed after use

Improvised ways to clamp stock edge to edge

A woodworking vice will hold edge-glued timbers rigid while the glue dries, if the job is not too large for the vice. Centre the material between the vice and bench stops, and tighten up the handle. Do not apply too much pressure, or it may buckle. Use strips of scrap timber to protect edges of work—wide strips supports long joints better.

This clamping jig you can make from scrap timber uses wedge action to lock edge-glued boards together. It works best on jobs that are splined, dowelled, or that have matching tongue-and-groove joints. To make the jig, use 1 × 4 timber fastened with bolts, washers, and nuts. Holes (arrow) make jig adjustable. All holes should be spaced exactly the same.

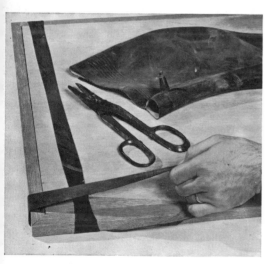

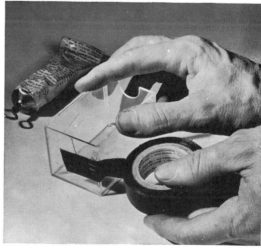

Wide rubber bands cut from old inner tube will produce more clamping power than you think—especially for table-edging projects where dowels or splines are used. Before you place bands, tape edging in position.

Plastic or adhesive tape holds small pieces in place while glue sets. Clamping pressure from tape is light; do not use it for big jobs. It is best to use quick-drying glue so it can set before the tape loses its holding power.

Bar clamps on the front and back of job keep edge-glued wood from buckling. They can be rigged for any length, making them especially handy for wide or long jobs, and where work needs pressure from clamps

Glue blocks reinforce corner joints, and usually require no clamping. Saw them out of scrap stock in triangular shape, as shown. Apply adhesive to glue area on block, and slide it along joint to thin out glue for tighter bond.

Dowel joints make strong glue joints for fine cabinet work, or where a hidden joint is required. Groove dowel pins with pliers before you apply glue. This keeps air from becoming trapped in hole, pushing the joint apart.

Cushion blocks prevent clamps from marking fine jobs, and spread out pressure from clamp more evenly on work. Aluminium foil keeps surplus from sticking to wood. Select your glues with care to suit the job in hand.

How to fasten to any kind of wall

Knowing how to fasten to any kind of wall is important if you are planning to do such jobs as putting up a tool rack or shelves, or hanging pictures.

There are several types of wall fasteners available, and knowing which will do the best job on a particular wall is a good start.

Screws and masonry nails are simplest and easiest where you have something solid to fasten to.

Of course, if the item you are fastening to a wall is light enough, suction cups, paste, or glue may prove to be adequate.

When you are fastening to lath and plaster walls and there is no framework in the proper place, use gravity or spring toggle fasteners. Walls of solid masonry generally require friction-held fastening devices.

The flange-type fasteners, which come in a variety of sizes, have a toggle or flange that spreads on the inside of the wall to hold the mounting bolt in place.

Most fasteners for solid masonry walls are driven into a pre-bored hole and are held in place by expansion after screws are driven into them.

Blind fasteners

Flange-type fastener fans out in back of wall (right) after you insert it through proper size hole and turn the screw in the centre to collapse anchor. Remove screw and slip through fixture to be hung. Then alter screw to anchor and tighten.

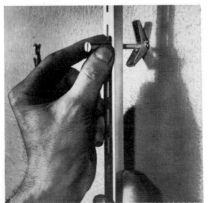

"Wings" on toggle bolt compress, then spring apart at back of the wall for secure mounting in plaster. Thread the bolt through the fixture and part way onto the "wing" section. Push it through the hole, as shown, and tighten with a screwdriver. The spring and gravity toggles come in various sizes.

Fastening to lath and plaster walls

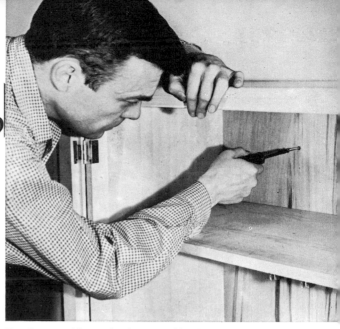

For heavy objects (such as a cabinet), use wood screws driven through the plaster and into the studs. Take time to make sure that the screws you use are heavy and long enough to support the weight of the article you are hanging. Try to drive them into centre of studs for strength.

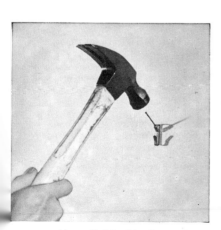

Hang light objects on plaster walls with ordinary picture hooks. Long steel pin slips into hook at angle as shown, increasing weight it can hold.

Bridge studs with a piece of wood when you hang heavy objects between them. Use screws to hold the board to the studs and the object you will fasten to it. If edges of the board will show, countersink screw holes, and fill after you run screws in.

Hold with suction cups, paste, and glue

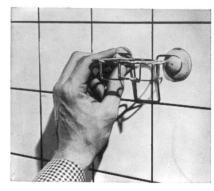

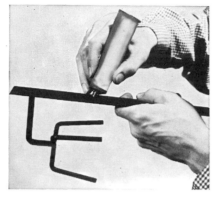

Suction-cup supports—now made with many different kinds of attachments —are stuck to smooth wall surface. For a permanent grip, coat rim of discs with glycerine or with clear nail-varnish.

Contact adhesive cement supports light-weight shelves, plant holders and other small objects directly on the wall. Spread cement on back of object and to the wall. Press to the wall and let dry.

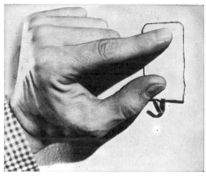

A gummed-cloth hanger will support light-weight pictures, plates. To apply, moisten glue, press to wall. When paste dries, hook is ready to use. To remove the hanger, moisten cloth and peel off.

There are coat hangers and various bathroom fittings which are manufactured with adhesive backs. This backing only has to be moistened to fix it to the wall. For a perfect job, ensure that the wall is clean and free from grease. Better adhesion is achieved if the wall, at the spot where the fitting is to go, is roughened a little.

When gluing, remember that all areas to be glued together must be clean, free of grease, dry, and—for some types of glue—have a rough surface. Most contact adhesives should be spread on the two surfaces to be joined and then left for 15-20 minutes before the surfaces are brought together.

Metallic glue cements any kind of metal to the same or other kinds, in light fabrication. It holds tight if you apply it over relatively large surfaces in lapped joints. For best results, follow the manufacturer's instructions, particularly if you do not always use same kind. There are many types.

Masonry anchors fasten to brick and concrete

Masonry nails are tougher than ordinary nails—are the simplest of masonry fasteners that you can buy. Drive into concrete, mortar joints, brick or breeze walls, etc.

Some tips to follow

When hammering masonry nails into a wall, use a series of lighter blows rather than trying to drive the nail home in two. This type of nail is made of tempered steel and will break rather than bend, so hit head squarely.

When making holes with a hand punch, a series of lighter blows will produce a much neater and more accurate hole. Rotate punch as you hammer—this helps the fluted blade to clear away waste and give correct size hole.

Always use the right size plugs—undersized plugs, if used for heavy jobs with a lot of strain, will eventually pull out. On the other hand, if you use over size plugs, it becomes very difficult to drive the screw right home because—in forcing the plug into the hole—the pre-drilled screw hole is closed up. Instead of ready-made plugs, you could use the type of plugging that is mixed into a paste with a little water. While still in its paste state, it is pressed firmly into the hole and the screw hole made with a very sharp pointed tool supplied. This method does allow for slight inaccuracies.

When drilling holes using a power drill, it is wise to use a speed reducer when working on very hard materials. Never use much pressure on drill.

Holes in concrete, brick, stone are needed for most masonry plugs and anchors. Use a punch or carbon-tipped drill in a power outfit. To remove the powdered concrete, twist the drill as you hammer.

Another simple fastener is fibre plug (shown) or lead anchor inserted in hole. Thread ordinary screw through object and run screw into the plug. Drill the hole *exactly* as deep as the plug is long.

Carbon-tip bit in an electric drill will drill accurate holes in masonry in a hurry. Will drill concrete, brick, stone, and similar hard materials. Use slow speed.

Non-electric. This iron has a heavy copper tip, is usually heated in a blow-torch flame.

Electric. Self-heating, this type comes in several sizes. Get size to suit jobs you have in mind.

Pistol-type. This new self-heating gun delivers heat seconds after trigger is pressed.

Soldering metals together

The number of repair jobs you can handle around your home is very limited if you do not know how to solder. Whenever you have to join two pieces of metal, soldering will give you a stronger, safer, easier joint. But to get best results, you must follow the rules.

First, make sure the iron itself is at maximum heat, with the tip clean and well tinned with solder.

Second, make sure the material being soldered is absolutely clean. The correct flux, applied before or with the solder, cleans away oxide and prevents more from forming, thus

Solders and fluxes. With solder, you must use a flux. There are two main types. Rosin flux and non-corrosive paste are used for electrical work and on easy-to-solder metals like tin and copper. Acid flux, for more difficult metals like galvanized iron, has greater corrosive effect, and must be washed away after soldering. Stainless steel requires a special flux. Handy core solder has the flux in the centre of a solder ribbon; it is applied at the junction of the iron and the work. Solid bar solder is applied after a flux is brushed on the work.

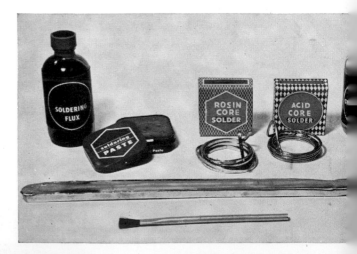

1 Filing the iron. Plug in the iron, and while it is heating, check the soldering tip. If it is not smooth, clamp the iron in a vice, and file the tip lightly.

2 Proper shape for iron. Remove corrosion, but do not file to a nubbin. Properly filed iron has this modified chisel shape, with slightly blunted point.

helping solder get into the pores of the metal you are working on.

Third, heat both metal being joined and solder to temperature above the solder's melting point. Apply heat with the iron point held flat against the metal; do not try to transmit heat with the pointed tip alone. It will not work.

If either solder or metal is not hot enough, you may get a cold joint. Then the solder will look like unstirred sugar at the bottom of a coffee cup.

With rosin flux, lack of enough heat may also produce a rosin joint. Here the rosin coats the metal so that the solder cannot penetrate. The joint must be heated enough so that the flux does its cleaning work and then boils away. Little points of solder sticking up indicate too little heat. Metal and solder were too cold and solder did not take well.

A soldering "don't": Never put a hot iron in flux—the heat will make it worthless.

3 Clean point; "tin" it with thin coat of rosin-core solder (or solid solder with rosin flux). To cover point, rotate hot iron in "bed" of solder. Apply flux before solder, unless using core solder.

4 Preheat metal; it *must* be hot enough to melt solder. Heat metal with point of iron held flat. Use rosin-core solder, rosin flux, or non-corrosive paste on electrical work and metals like copper or tin.

5 Acid flux, generally used for metals like galvanized iron, will corrode. Wash excess off when finished. A flux cleans surface and keeps heat from oxidizing surface before solder is applied.

With soft solder, join galvanized sheet, brass, and copper

Soft solder works best when soldering area is fairly large. "Tin" surfaces with solder after cleaning to shiny brightness. Join together, reheat with torch or iron. Lapped and bent butt joints (at left) hold tightness with solder.

Interfolded joint, called "stove-pipe seam" by tinsmiths, is easiest of mechanical ways to join metal sheets. Fold metal at ends, interlock, and hammer flat. Make joint waterproof by flowing soft solder along one edge.

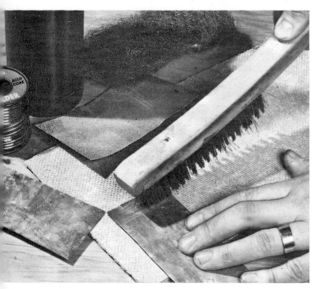

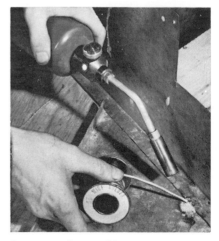

Clean joints stick best. With wire brush, sandpaper, steel wool, grinding wheel, or jack-knife, remove *all* dust, dirt, grease, rust, corrosion, paint, and even fingerprints from surfaces to be joined. Metal should be shiny bright. The difference between a strong joint and a weak one is usually the time you spend in cleaning the metal.

Get more heat with a torch for large soldering jobs or where more heat is required to melt the solder. When soldering "flat" surfaces, tin both pieces after they are cleaned. Then join the tinned surfaces and reheat with an iron or torch, flowing more solder along the seam. You will find that "sheet" metal has a great radiating capacity and its large surface will conduct heat away. Keep torch away from inflammable liquids.

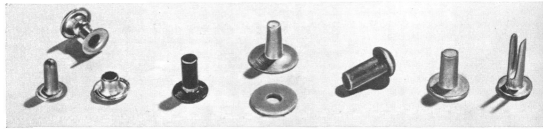

| Two-piece hollow | Tubular | Solid | Split |

Repair it with a Rivet

The next time you are prepared to discard something that is broken around your house, think twice— maybe you can repair it very easily with a rivet or two, and use it again.

Riveting requires no special tools. It takes no special techniques and training. All the rivets you will use in small repairs will not cost more than a few pennies, and any d.i.y. shop will be able to supply the types you need.

Solid, tubular, and split rivets fasten sheet metal, thin wood, and thick plastics very efficiently.

You will find the tubular and split rivets will work, too, on soft materials like canvas and leather. And, for even greater ease in fastening soft materials, there are two-piece hollow rivets that practically put themselves into place. They will hold the pieces being joined with a vice-like grip. Keep some of each type on hand.

Not many tools are needed for riveting. Just two hammers, a block of steel, and a vice top to use as an anvil for the rivet are all that you will need to handle any riveting job.

Tubular rivets

1 Drive rivet with wood or lead anvil.

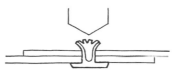

2 Begin curl of rivet end with centre punch

3 Vertical hammer blows spread rivet walls

Hollow rivets, like the solid ones, should project no more than one diameter through thicknesses of materials. Insert in punched or drilled holes, or drive in over a soft block.

With rivet head placed on an anvil begin curl of the rivet end with a centre punch; then hammer. Use washer in thin materials—they are not necessary in thick materials.

Split rivets

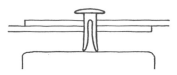

1 Simply drive the split rivet through sheets of material laid flat on the anvil

2 Rivet legs will spread and curl flat when they strike the solid anvil surface

Split rivets come boxed in assorted lengths, generally with special holding tool. Snap rivet into the spring claws of the tool to hold it for starting. Aim it straight into material, then drive it, pull the tool free. You then have rivet started.

With rivet started and driven perpendicular to the anvil, its legs will spread and curl outward. This flattens the rivet and grips it firmly in underside of material, as in belt. Wire-holding tool is shown at bottom of the picture.

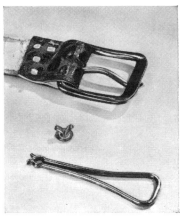

Solid rivets

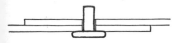 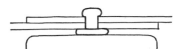 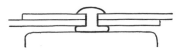

1 Lay one sheet over the other. Drill a hole through the sheets and put rivet in place

2 Press the sheets together. Hammer rivet to shorten it and secure it snugly in hole

3 It is best to round rivet heads by hitting them with slanting ball-peen hammer blows

Rivet for metal should not be too loose in hole, and its end should not project more than one diameter. Use a hammer and a nut (or deep hole in the rivet set, at lower left) to push the sheets tight together to ensure proper seating of the rivet.

In second step, use vertical hammer blows to spread rivet in the hole, and begin its head (rivet at right). Rounded head at left is finished with succession of slanting blows, or it can be moulded with cup on rivet set, whichever you wish.

Two-piece hollow rivets

Easiest of all to use, two-piece hollow rivets are handy for a lot of minor household repair jobs. First step in using them involves punching or drilling proper-size hole in materials. Next, insert the tapered piece from underneath.

1 Push tapered portion of rivet through the material. Slip the hollow portion over it

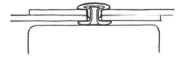

2 Lay rivet on the anvil and drive the two parts together with vertical blows

Place the head of the rivet on the anvil next. Then strike the rivet with vertical hammer blows (see the photograph) until it is flat and secure. A rivet seal like this is very practical and simple, and it will last indefinitely.

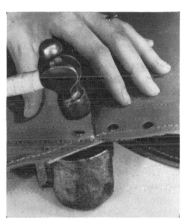

There are many kinds of rivets for metal

Rivets are a cheap, easy way to fasten sheet metal. Countersunk, flush rivets leave smooth surfaces. D.i.y. shops usually stock several types, made in many metals, to meet all your needs.

Heavier iron and steel are joined with solid iron rivets, "set" with a ball-pein hammer. Rivetting is fast, gives strong joints (steel bridges are built with rivets).

Interior Decorating

Preparation

It is a great temptation to avoid the proper preparation before decorating a room. The following notes indicate some of the things that can go wrong simply from lack of a few hours' preparatory work.

Grease is most frequently found in kitchens (near the cooker), behind the sideboard, on doors, up the stairs, etc. Applying paint over grease means slow-drying, poor gloss and sometimes peeling or flaking.

Wax polish inevitably gets smeared on to skirting boards and the bottoms of doors. It has much the same effect on paint as grease, with also a risk of future chipping.

Dust at the very least is likely to spoil the appearance of new paint unless it is removed before painting. At the worst, it may prevent the paint from adhering properly.

If the surface is clean, re-painting stands a good chance of success. It may be necessary to use paint thinner followed by a wash with soap and water or detergent solution to remove heavy films of grease or wax polish. In most cases, however, soap and water or detergent solution alone will do the trick. Rinse in clean water but allow ample time for the water to dry off before starting to paint. *Damp* can cause as much trouble as grease or dust.

Old paint: It is still thought necessary to strip or burn off old paint before beginning to decorate. But this is only vital if the old paint is badly crazed, blistered, perished or flaking. If the old paint is in good condition, you can usually put new paint on top.

Where there are small areas of poorly adhering or defective paint, remove them by scraping back to a firm edge. If there are cracks and other imperfections, cut them out and make good with a filler. Allow the filler to dry completely and then lightly rub down the areas with fine sandpaper to make sure the surface is perfectly smooth, then prime before re-painting.

If the surface to be re-painted has previously been painted with a gloss paint, then—after washing down and while it is still wet—lightly rub down with fine waterproof sandpaper or suitable abrasive. Give it a final rinse and allow to dry thoroughly before re-painting. This process, called "flatting", gives the new paint a surface to adhere to.

Metal surfaces: Some years ago tests were done to find out the best ways of preparing iron and steel for painting. It was found that paint put on to well-prepared steel lasted five times longer than paint applied to badly-prepared steel.

To clean iron or steel surfaces perfectly for re-painting, you really need to grit-blast the surface, and that requires special equipment. So the handyman needs to chip and scrape and use a wire brush. Try to get rid of all the loose rust and scale and leave the surface as clean and bright as possible.

Rust and grease are the enemies. When you are sure you are rid of them both, apply a primer designed for iron and steel as soon as preparation is finished. Remember that rusting is an inevitable chemical reaction between metal and air in the presence of water, so do not leave the job overnight. Any rain or damp will cause further rusting.

Bittiness: Paintwork which seems to be covered with specks of dust or grit—known as bittiness—usually results from working with dirty brushes or raising dust in the atmosphere before the paint is dry. But it may be due to not removing dust from the surface before painting, or bits of skin on the paint which have been stirred in, instead of being strained out before use. If you made this mistake, allow the paint to harden for a few days, then rub it down very lightly with fine abrasive paper, taking care not to scratch the surface. Wet and dry sandpaper is probably the best for this job. It will allow you to wet the surface while rubbing down, which is a less violent method than the ordinary dry sandpaper. Sponge with clean water after rubbing down, allow to dry for an hour or so and then apply another coat of finish, making sure that you have clean brushes and paint.

Priming: The functions of a primer are to stick to the surface and, in turn, provide a key for the undercoat and top coats of paint to stick to. Also, if the surface is absorbent, it will ensure that the primer is absorbed rather than the following top coats. If you do not use a primer, the later coats may not stick. Equally, if you apply the wrong kind of primer, there will be trouble.

It is as well to spend some time considering the surface to be painted, working out what it consists of at the moment, deciding on the correct preparation before painting. The popular misconception that "any old paint will do for priming" is quite wrong. Most paint manufacturers make primers specially designed for each of the surfaces usually found in buildings.

Concrete, asbestos, cement sheets and certain types of plaster, for example, are often highly alkaline when new, so if they are to be finished with an oil-based paint, gloss or egg-shell, they need priming with an alkali-resistant primer.

Wood primers are intended to fill the minute pores in the surface and to help keep the moisture content of the wood at a satisfactory level—not too wet, not too dry. Primers based on white lead or aluminium are generally satisfactory. Whenever possible, wood should be primed before fixing, so that all sides are protected.

Emulsion paint does not generally need special primers. Very poor surfaces, however, should be given a sealing coat of emulsion paint, thinned in the proportion of one part water to two parts of emulsion paint.

Always use the correct primer for the job and remember that the right primer can make an enormous difference to the life of the paint.

Sealing: Different sealers have different qualities. Some sealers are made of bitumen or tar, others have anti-rust properties, others are made specially to prevent powdering and flaking of old water paints.

Do not think the sealer is just the paint manufacturer's excuse for selling more paint. The sealer is designed to play a vital part in several different paint systems. For instance, consider a downpipe. Perhaps bituminous paint was used on it some years ago. Now you want to get rid of the ugly black colour and make it harmonise better with the overall colour scheme of the house. But bituminous paints tend to be active under new coats of paint and to stain badly. Touch in any bare spots with chromate primer and, when it is dry, apply one or two coats of aluminium sealer

overall to subdue the bituminous coating. If possible, leave for a couple of days before applying undercoat or gloss finish.

Preparation Summary

Never apply paint on a flaking or blistered surface, otherwise the new paint will not adhere properly.

Never paint over dirt, grease or wax polish, otherwise new paint will have a poor gloss and take a long time to dry.

Never paint over wet surfaces, or flaking and blistering will result.

Never paint over old, thick, soft paint, otherwise new paint may blister.

Never ignore the skin that forms on the top of paint in already opened tins. If you can, remove it. If the skin becomes mixed in, strain the paint into another clean container. A double layer of old nylon stocking will make a good filter for this job.

Never sweep floors or dust just before, during, or just after painting. The dust will spread to ruin the surface.

Never use dirty brushes, otherwise paint will be bitty.

Paint regularly and the task of preparation is made easy.

Read the instructions on a can of paint. The text has been carefully prepared and provides vital information.

If painting over wallpaper with emulsion or water paint, do a small trial area first. If the pattern on the paper stains through the paint, which is by no means impossible, then use a primer sealer. This will usually overcome the trouble. But remember that sealing the wallpaper will make it more difficult to remove at a later date.

Make sure new walls are completely dry before painting.

Do not apply paint too thickly. It may dry with a wrinkled or shrivelled surface.

The paint for the job

Emulsion paint: It may be used straight from the can to give maximum opacity and freedom from drips or, thinned with water in the ordinary way, to give traditional application and spreading properties. In either case opacity is excellent, the paint is easy to apply and dries quickly to a tough, smooth surface with a pleasant low sheen. There is a wide colour range.

Emulsion paint is recommended for use on all wall and ceiling surfaces, inside and outside, including kitchens and bathrooms; over brickwork, plaster cement, wallboards, previously painted surfaces and wallpaper, where an economical, low sheen, washable finish is required.

It dries quickly and may be re-coated in one to four hours, depending on conditions. Spreading varies according to the nature of the surfaces to which it is applied and the degree of thinning. Its hiding properties are good, and it is lead-free.

Emulsion paint can be applied unthinned to most surfaces. Thinning may be required to provide a sealing coat or to ease application on surfaces of high suction. Before thinning, stir or beat the paint to a smooth consistency, then add the required amount of water slowly while continuing to stir. The following thinning proportions can be used for application by brush or roller:

As a sealing coat: 2 parts water to 4 parts emulsion paint.

For first coats on high-suction surfaces: 1-2 parts water to 4 parts emulsion paint.

For subsequent coats (or first coats on normal surfaces): Apply unthinned or add not more than 1 part water to 4 parts emulsion paint.

It can be applied by brush or roller, both of which should be cleaned immediately after use with detergent or soap and water. When applying unthinned, load the brush fairly generously, apply a full coat and do not brush out too far. When applied unthinned by roller, stir to a smooth consistency before pouring it into the roller tray.

Eggshell finish: It has good flow and hiding power and dries with an attractive "eggshell" sheen. It provides a smooth surface that can be washed frequently, and is suitable for kitchens and bathrooms if a full gloss finish is not liked. It is not suitable for use on exterior wood and metalwork. There is a wide colour range.

Eggshell finish is tack-free in 4 to 6 hours, hard dry and ready for re-coating within 24 hours under normal conditions. Its sheen and colour are not seriously affected by use on heated surfaces up to 82°C (180°F). Above 93°C (200°F), colours tend to become more yellow, and it is not recommended for use on surfaces heated above 150°C (300°F).

Its lead content is safe for surfaces in contact with children—that is, not more than one per cent lead from all sources.

Normally two coats of eggshell finish should be applied over primed or previously painted surfaces. Three coats may be necessary where there is a marked change of colour, or if the surface is strongly patterned. It is supplied ready for use by brush or roller. When brushing, best results are obtained by applying a full flowing coat of finish with the minimum of cross brushing.

Gloss finish: It gives an extremely durable surface which does not crack or chip, is easy to brush, and has good flow, hiding and spreading capacities. It is suitable for all interior and exterior surfaces where a glossy hard-wearing finish is required.

Gloss paint is tack-free in 4 to 6 hours, and dry and re-coatable within 24 hours under normal conditions. One gallon will cover 80-90 sq yds per coat. The gloss and colour are not affected by heating to temperatures up to 82°C (180°F). There may be some discolouration of pale shades above 82°C (180°F). It is not recommended for use on surfaces at temperatures above 150°C (300°F). Its lead content is safe for surfaces in contact with children.

On previously painted or primed surfaces, one coat of undercoat followed by two coats of gloss paint gives good results. If two coats only are used, it is preferable to give two coats of gloss paint. It comes ready for use, but may be thinned with up to one pint of thinner or white spirit to every gallon of paint. It can be applied by roller without thinning.

Paint fast with a roller

In five minutes, you can learn how to apply paint with a roller.

It does not eliminate brushwork, however. Using a brush is the most satisfactory method of "cutting an edge" up against woodwork and for painting around windows.

There is also a certain wall texture preferred by many which comes from the sweep of a wide wall brush. But for the handyman who has never dared tackle a living-room wall, the roller is an easy answer.

Equipment is sold in paint and d.i.y. shops. Roller materials include: wool, mohair pile, plastic foam and sheepskin.

You can use just about any kind of paint. Emulsion paint is the easiest to work with and does not show lap marks. Areas bordering door frames etc. should be filled in by brush.

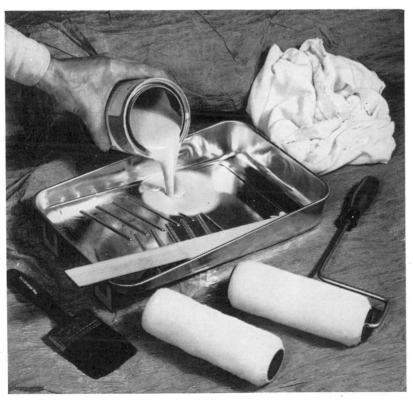

Roller-painting equipment is simple and inexpensive. You need a slant-bottomed pan for the paint, the roller, a regular paintbrush, a wiping-up rag, and a dropcloth. An extra sleeve for the roller comes in handy for quick colour changes. Dropcloth pictured is a big one. It is made of tough crepe paper and can be purchased at most paint shops. Do not paint without dropcloth.

First step: Cut up to edges of woodwork with brush. With emulsion paints which do not show lap marks, do entire room this way—then use a roller.

Fill roller by rolling it into lower end of tray, then smoothing out load on slanted part. Carry as much paint as you can without dripping onto floor.

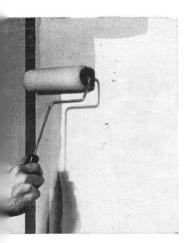

Roll close to woodwork over brushwork, since roller leaves different texture from brush. Some rollers have guards that help prevent smearing of woodwork. Use paint on part of roller so you paint near the woodwork with a dry roller.

Diagrammatic picture shows way to apply paint. Strokes should be made in different directions for best coverage of surface; do not follow a uniform pattern. Avoid moving roller too fast or it may spray drops of paint on floor.

Narrow roller is one of the few "novelty" types you can buy to make it possible to roller-paint any but the most intricate woodwork. Works like big one.

Regular roller now works for panels and for flat surfaces of cross members. Use a brush to paint over (or around) door handles, etc, unless you have removed them.

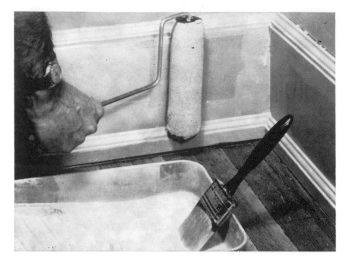

On skirting boards, the paint roller is speedy—thereby reducing the time you must spend in an uncomfortable position. The top moulding was pre-painted with a brush, as preparation for the wall. Then, you brush in the section near floor and use the roller to fill in between. You can buy rollers just about 4 inches wide for this job and for others involving narrow woodwork. Brush is out of the way, but convenient, if you let it rest in the deep end of tray.

Reach the ceiling from the floor (and the upper part of the walls, too) by means of an extension you can buy. Handle of the roller fits in the metal collar which tightens with a screwdriver. You have to cut around the edges of the ceiling with a brush first. Make the pre-painted band fairly wide, and this will compensate for less accuracy with the extension. Make an extension handle yourself, using a broom handle wired to the roller handle. Just be sure it is tight.

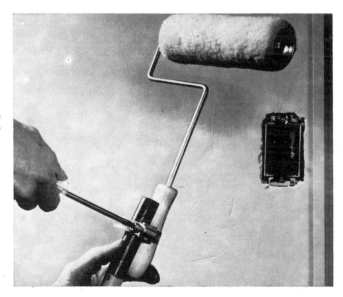

Clean the roller, pan and brush immediately after you have finished with them. Warm water does fast job on emulsion paints. Use turpentine, commercial cleaner, or similar solvents for oil-base paints. Repeat process until it is clean. Then dry out cleaner and wrap the sleeve in aluminium foil to give it protection from dirt and grit.

Use and care of paint brushes

Buy good ones, keep them clean, and use properly

Right brushes to keep your home properly decorated as well as weatherproofed are (from left) 4 inch for flat surfaces, angled sash brush for windows and other narrow surfaces. Use $1\frac{1}{2}$ inch to 2 inch brushes for painting narrow surfaces. You will cover large areas quicker and easier using brushes 3 inches to 6 inches wide. It is wise to invest in good quality brushes. They will give much better results and last longer.

Bristle length helps determine brush's elasticity. Test "spring back" when bristles are slightly bent—they should hang together, not flare out at end. Brush should feel "full of bristles" when compressed. Right is sash brush.

"Flags" or split ends of bristles are key to good quality, animal-hair brushes. The more ends you find split, the better the brush performs. Man-made bristles wear well against rough surfaces, flow paint smoothly, are easy to clean.

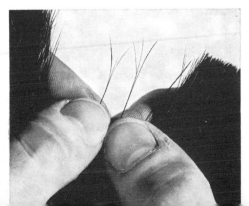

Pre-condition brushes for paint by removing loose bristles and softening the flag ends. Rub briskly on rough surface, and spin in your hands. Soften new brushes in linseed oil at least 24 hours before using them. This soaking will help condition them to accept paint, and help to give bristles longer, more useful life.

Dab the brush tip at loose bristles to retrieve them from the freshly painted surface. Wet paint on the brush will stick the loose brush to it—and makes it easier, and less messy to dispose of them. With a light stroke, re-cover marks the brush left by lifting handle gradually to avoid leaving a thick edge of paint on the surface.

"Stray" bristles—the ones that do not hang with the rest—should be removed with a glazier's knife or a scraper. Place the edge of the tool under the bristle and pull it against the metal ferrule with your thumb, as pictured. Never paint with edge of brush and be careful to remove only the stray hairs.

Dip-and-slap method is a good way to remove the excess paint from the brush. Slowly submerge it in the paint, to about one-third the length of the bristles. Slap off the excess paint against the side of the container, as pictured. Deep dipping wastes paint, leads to accumulation of it in heel of the brush, shortening its life.

Leave your brush in paint if work is interrupted for a short time. Should you be delayed for longer periods, suspend the brush in the paint itself. Use a wire through a hole drilled in the handle to keep ends of the bristles off the bottom of the container. Never store the brush in paint for more than an hour.

Between painting sessions—the days between a weekend job—hang brush in linseed oil or turpentine or paint solvent so ends of bristles do not touch bottom of container. When you are ready to use, wipe out excess turpentine or oil with cloth or rub brush on rough surface. Clean properly for longer periods—see below.

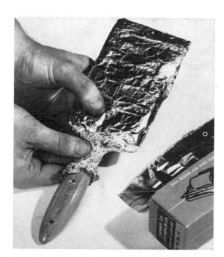

For longer storage clean off brushes with one of the cleaning liquids or solvents, wrap brush in aluminium foil and check that bristles are not pulled out of shape. Double thickness is best protection—twist the excess tightly around the handle, as shown. You can store brushes for ever this way.

Soap-and-water is the final step in getting the brush clean enough to wrap and store away for long periods. First, get out all paint you can with turpentine, thinner, or commercial cleaner. Then wash with cleansing powder until clean water does not show any colour. Wrap in foil, store flat in dry place.

Save that neglected brush

Good-quality paintbrushes represent quite an investment. So if you have any that have become damaged by neglect or improper use, try these methods of restoring them.

Those at left are typical of neglected brushes. At far left is a paintbrush that has been improperly used and cleaned. Bristles are snarled inside; wild bristles on the outside leave marks on work.

The centre brush looks almost hopeless with its bristles stiff and warped by dried paint. At right is a brush in fairly good condition, but "heeled up" with paint deposits at the base of the bristles.

Follow pictured directions for cleaning the second two. For the first, soak brush in linseed oil, then wrap securely in a wedge-shaped sleeve of foil for 48 hours. Clean with turpentine to remove oil. If it is still out of shape after this then it is only suitable as a dusting or cleaning brush.

Soak bristles if your brush is heeled up, as in the third picture above. First soak the bristles in paint remover. If the brush is coated with a dried mass of paint, as in the middle picture, it may have to soak for 30 minutes or longer to soften enough to use.

Comb paint out when the paint is softened to jelly consistency. Remove it with an old comb. Rinse in turpentine, and repeat the combing and rinsing until all the paint is out. Rubber gloves protect your hands from the caustics in the cleaner.

Wash after combing out the loose paint. Use soap and water. Add a cup of turpentine to about a quart of soapy water for washing. Continue with washing until all traces of paint are gone from base of the bristles. Rinse in clear water, and then straighten the bristles and wrap in foil.

How to paint a ceiling

Start a room with the ceiling, of course, whether using brush or roller.

Cover furniture and floor with dust cloths. Two sturdy chairs and a plank can serve as a scaffold

If room needs washing, work part way down walls while doing ceiling; balance of wall then can be reached from floor. Patch cracks while washing to avoid a lot of scaffold moving.

Avoid lap marks when using oil-base paint by painting in narrow strips across ceiling so you can start next strip before paint begins to set.

Paint in strips across narrow dimension of room; keep strips small enough so that you can get back to start next strip before paint begins to set. Wherever possible, paint towards light; glare helps show where you have been.

How to paint a wall

Walls are the easiest part of your job. Most of the time you stand on the floor, and you do not have to reach overhead with the brush.

First, move furniture into centre of room and cover it. Never paint over light switches and power points. If you cannot paint round them then remove while you paint—turn off electricity first.

Do not paint sample smears on wall Experiment on cardboard and tape it to wall if you want to "live with" the colour before applying it.

Begin at upper corner of wall, paint along ceiling several feet. Then move down corner, filling in triangular area between as you go to far lower corner. Method keeps essential "wet edge".

Sweeping stroke evens paint after it is spread with back-and-forth motion. Never put freshly dripped brush on bare wall. Start "in the wet" and work to dry area. Fresh paint softens that on the wall, which prevents lap marks.

Work from small area to broad expanses around doors, windows. Cut close to woodwork, as shown. Level off cutting with brush held edgewise; stroke parallel to woodwork. End stroke by lifting brush away from woodwork.

Woodwork requires special care

Before starting to paint window frames, renew any cracked panes of glass and check that all catches are in good working order—if not, renew.

On sash windows, check sash cords. If there is any sign of wear, renew them all. It will save spoiling newly-painted surfaces in the future. Also renew any broken beading and—if a window rattles—tighten beads by lifting and re-nailing.

Clean all woodwork carefully, taking care to clean out the dust and mould that collects in the corners.

3 Close the sash, but not all the way. Paint the partitions of top sash, then do the rest of the sash and the divider between the windows. Next, do the channel in which the lower sash slides, and the top edge of the lower sash. Last, paint the partitions of the lower sash and frame.

1 Here are "make ready" tools. Hammer, nails, and nail punch are to tighten loose beading. Putty fills nail holes and blemishes. Sponge rinses after washing. Sandpaper will smooth spots where the previous paint or enamel has chipped.

4 Next do the window frame. Paint top, then one side, then other. Switch to a 2-inch or wider brush to speed the work. Finish the enamelled areas with a stroke the length of the painted member. Finish on the sill and underneath it.

2 To start on window, raise the lower sash, pull down upper. Then paint top, front, bottom of "meeting rail" (bottom member of top sash). Then do the strips between panes plus sash above meeting rail for couple of inches.

5 When painting skirting boards, first cut wall edge, then floor edge, then fill in between. Smooth all over. Since dust cloths would be in way, work with rag close at hand. To wipe up drips on floor or wall, use rag folded over a putty knife.

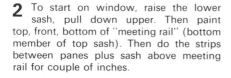

How to paint a door

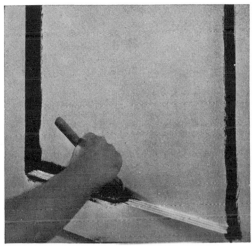

1 Moulded edge first, after door is washed, sanded, undercoated. Start with edge of top panel. After moulding, do centre. Flow enamel on with horizontal strokes and finish with light vertical strokes.

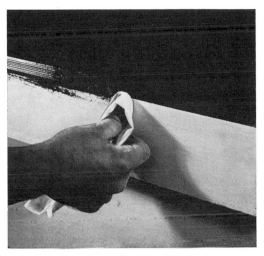

2 Wipe away overlapping edge of wet enamel after painting each panel. Check back for runs and sags, and level throughout with a light sweep of paint-brush. Make corrections while paint is wet.

3 Hinge edge next. Again wipe off ragged edges. Follow by painting horizontal rails (crosspieces) starting at top. Try to cut straight line with brush where rail meets the vertical stile (sidepiece).

4 Vertical stiles last. Complete door, painting side stiles carefully. If over-laps remain and paint has started to set, dip cloth in turpentine to remove overlap or it will show under the last coat.

Tools you may need to paint your home include a selection of paintbrushes, a scraper, a caulking gun, a hammer, a screwdriver, a wire brush, a ladder, and a canvas dust sheet. A 2-gallon galvanised pail will make an excellent container to use for mixing emulsion and cement paints. Plan your painting project before you start. Then buy all the paints and materials, plus any tools you will need. This will save time rushing back to the shop for forgotten supplies once you have begun.

How to do outside painting

Before tackling any exterior painting, check that all necessary repair jobs have been done—gutters and downpipes repaired; any broken or cracked bricks replaced; cracks in pebble-dashed or cement rendered walls filled and made good. And, while you are up the ladder, check on the roof tiles.

The success of an exterior painting job depends about 80 per cent on proper preparation and about 20 per cent on proper application. So do not skimp in getting surfaces ready to paint.

The next most important rule is to use only the best paint—do not be fooled by a bargain price tag. Never apply paint to a surface that is the least bit damp. And do not start painting too early in the morning —wait till sun thoroughly dries area.

Walls that are to be painted with emulsion should be clean, dry and free from efflorescence. Flaking, loose or powdery surfaces should be removed as thoroughly as possible. Where it is not possible to clean off the old surface, a coat of masonry sealer should be applied before the emulsion paint. Emulsion can

be applied by brush, spray or roller.

Follow the same cleaning procedure for walls that are to be covered with a cement base paint. Before application, the wall should be dampened—use a hose if possible. Mix up paint a little at a time because it sets hard quickly.

New wood requires knotting and a priming coat. Otherwise the old paint, if in good condition, serves as the primer.

A coat of paint is about one-thousandth of an inch thick—which is not much. In order to build up a fully effective paint system on a bare surface—or if you have let your paintwork deteriorate seriously— you need to apply four coats of paint!

This costs money and, important for the home handyman, time. So repaint sufficiently frequently to prevent serious deterioration of the old paint. One coat a year for four years is no more expensive, and much less time consuming, than a major effort every four or five years.

You will also have the satisfaction of knowing that the paintwork is always in good trim and the value of your property always kept up.

Scrape off scaling and blistered paint. Then "feather" edges of old paint around spots with sandpaper. A scraper does fast job over large area. Scaling is usually the result of painting over unseasoned or wet timber. After washing down surface, reprime all bare wood.

Wire brush helps remove scaling and blistered paint and dirt and grime collected on weather boarding. Also use it to clean the rust and peeling paint from the metal surfaces. The next step is to prime the metal with aluminium paint, red lead, or a special primer.

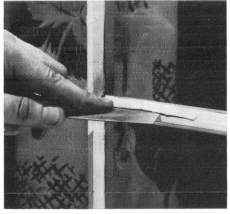

Caulk cracks around the windows and door-frames, where the steps meet the house, under window sills, around pipes, and joints between wood and dissimilar building materials. Trick to using caulking gun: Keep a steady trigger pressure.

Remove broken and loose putty around the windows. If the putty is not damaged, it is unnecessary to dig it out and put it in fresh. Tip of the putty knife inserted between the putty and panel of window helps break the putty loose from the wood and glass pane.

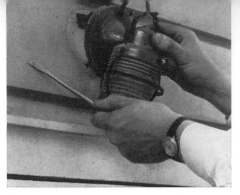

Before painting starts, remove the light fixtures, house numbers, and other hardware. This is much easier than trying to "cut" around them with a paintbrush. Also check wiring in light fixtures. If it needs repairs you had better call an electrician to fix it.

Drive "popped" nails back into any woodwork as you go over the house. Re-nail loose boards, and replace any rotted or damaged ones. Cedar wood facing needs special attention, particularly if boards have lost their colour.

Fill nail holes with putty (not a filler that has to be mixed with water), and remove the excess with the tip of a putty knife, as pictured. Surface of filler should be flush with the surface of the surrounding wood.

Prime bare wood left by scraping process and any new wood which replaced the rotting or damaged boards. This brings new paint film to thickness of paint around it. Use knotting on new wood before priming.

Before you re-glaze window, dust and prime the wood and glass. To give new putty a better bond and waterproof seal, apply the paint to the glass that will be covered by the putty. After window is re-glazed, run a dusting brush over putty to smooth it.

Prime metal surfaces with an aluminium paint, red lead, or a special metal primer after you have thoroughly cleaned off all the rust with a wire brush, steel wool, or sandpaper. Electric drill with a wire brush attached will do a fast job.

Paint troubles you can avoid

Leaves hold water. After rain the undersides of leaves will stay moist for many hours. So it is best to keep plants and shrubbery trimmed back away from the house. If they grow close up against the boards just above your home's foundation, they may cause blistering and peeling of paint.

Cracking and scaling. A poor grade of paint or inadequate mixing often leads to cracking and scaling. Once the paint cracks owing to the inelastic surface, moisture enters and loosens the paint film. The only remedy is complete removal.

Checking. Many fine, hairline cracks, called checking, can usually be traced to insufficient drying time between coats. Undercoat must be dry. Spot fading, premature chalking mean too much thinner, too few coats, or simply a poor-grade paint.

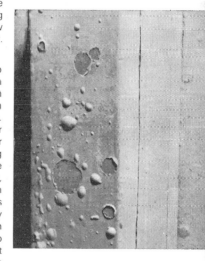

Blistering. Trouble can be due to painting on a damp surface or from moisture seeping through from behind the paint. Often if you open the blister you will find water inside. Perhaps you painted too soon after rain or did not allow enough time for the surface to dry out after washing down. You may have wiped off the water and thought the surface dry, but some moisture may have been absorbed into the surface. Or perhaps the pointing is faulty? Blisters may form when fresh paint is put over an old paint coating, even though no blisters can be seen before new paint was applied. This may happen if the old paint is very thick and soft. The solvents in new paint are absorbed into the old coating causing it to swell and blister. Old paint, if it is very thick and soft, should be stripped off before painting.

Alligatoring. When the checking reaches point where cracks run deep like this, it is known as alligatoring. Besides insufficient undercoat drying, cause may be using too much oil or impure oil as thinner.

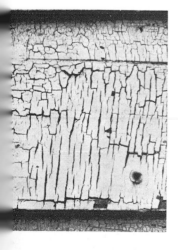

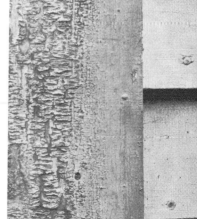

Resin bleeding. To avoid this, knots and pitch pockets should be sealed before painting. In extreme cases of resin bleeding, you may have to cover with an aluminium primer in addition to the knotting.

How to spray paint

Spraying is a fast way of getting paint where you want it. Basically, equipment includes an air compressor with built-in pressure control for uniform air pressure, paint container, and gun.

A spray gun brings air and paint together, breaks up the paint stream into spray, and directs it to surface. The same gun works with attached or separate container.

A bleeder-type gun constantly leaks air so that pressure does not build up in the hose. It can be used with units not having pressure control.

In a non-bleeder type, the trigger controls both air and fluid. It is used with compressors that have automatic pressure controls.

The larger equipment similar to that shown on this page can be hired at a reasonable price. The spray attachment to the power drill or the small electric spray would do most spraying jobs around the house.

The spray attachment on some vacuum cleaners is suitable for general wide area spraying, but the control is not fine enough for the more intricate spraying jobs.

Prepare surfaces as usual, but the surroundings must be more adequately protected from the spray.

Stir paint carefully; strain it if there are any lumps. Some sprayers handle paint of brushing consistency, while paint must be thinned for others. Generally, for use in attached container, it must be thinned.

The paint for this gun may be contained in the pressure feed tank (at left), or attachable container (centre).

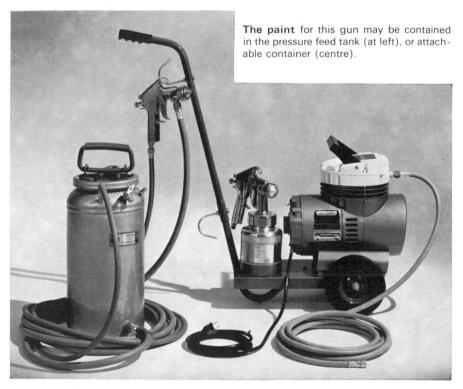

When painting inside with either a spray gun or an aerosol, especially with enamel, spread newspapers behind and under the object to stop any overspray. On narrow objects—like furniture legs—make strokes up and down the length. Aim spurts crosswise, to fill any hollows. Cardboard shield held in your free hand can block most of the spray, but fine particles can drift a long way. If possible, spray in a small, vented booth.

To mix the paint and build up pressure inside aerosols, you must shake the container vigorously. If it is a can of coloured paint, it will probably have a steel ball inside. Shake with a twirling motion until the ball rolls freely on the bottom of the can. While you are spraying the paint, keep the can in motion as much as possible, then take time occasionally to "shake it up" again. Always avoid heating or puncturing the can.

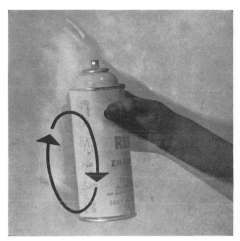

Common problems

SAG

RUN

Sags and runs. Professionals take care of sags (finish laid on so thick it flows down in drapes) and runs (large drops streaking down) by wiping them away quickly with the palm of the hand. Rags are not used because they may leave lint on finish. Bare area is carefully spotted in with short, cautious spurts.

HOLIDAY

Holidays. Fill-in "holidays" (spots left bare) exactly as you repair wiped spots—with cautious spurts. Cure fogging (dull, pebbled surface) by holding the spray gun closer to the work.

ORANGE-PEELING

Orange-peeling. Too thick a paint or too much air pressure will produce orange-peeling (bumpy finish). Thin the paint or adjust gun for less pressure. Repair by wiping and spotting.

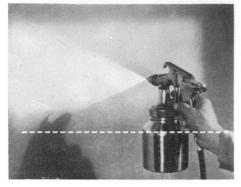

Hold tip 6 to 8 inches from surface so that spray strikes at right angles. On each stroke, begin sweep from point to one side of where you start spray. Press trigger at starting point, release at end without halting the gun.

Lap top fourth of each stroke over lower fourth of preceding stroke, since centre half of each sprayed strip gets thickest coat. Begin at top: work from side to side. Do not change pace: halting causes paint to pile up.

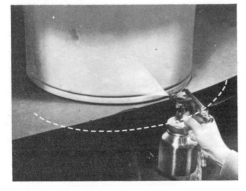

Follow curve as if tip of gun were connected to surface with an invisible link the same length as proper spraying distance. Holding gun too close produces sag or run; holding it too far fogs finish, and produces dull effect.

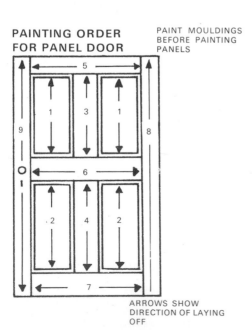

PAINTING ORDER FOR PANEL DOOR

PAINT MOULDINGS BEFORE PAINTING PANELS

ARROWS SHOW DIRECTION OF LAYING OFF

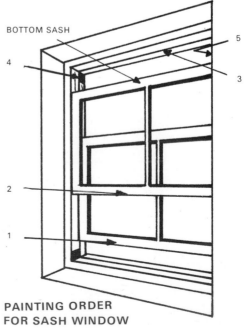

BOTTOM SASH

PAINTING ORDER FOR SASH WINDOW

Popular wood finishes

You can give wood a natural finish with clear varnishes or lacquers to emphasize its grain and colour. Wood can also be stained to deepen its splendid colours and grain pattern.

Another treatment is bleaching. This lightens the colour of the wood without destroying its natural look. It can be coloured with pigment stains which combine natural attractiveness with hues that are not found in the natural colour scheme of woods.

Pages 174 to 177 list procedures for finishing mahogany, walnut, pine, oak, and fir. The finishes apply to furniture and flooring, as well as panelling. The most important step of each procedure is to begin with clean surfaces. The wood must be free not only of dirt, grease, and old finish, but also of sanding particles in wood pores.

Follow these procedures with care when dealing with finishes requiring sealer coats. Without a proper base, finish coats cannot be expected to look right. Also, do not forget to sand lightly between coats to ensure a proper bond.

For professional looking detail on furniture, the ideas listed below can give pleasing results.

Wood bleach can make dark woods almost white, or any shade in between. Brush it on bare wood according to manufacturer's directions, usually in separate applications of two solutions. Use an old, inexpensive brush.

Unfinished pine furniture (below) can be made to look antique by first applying an antique pine stain, and then scarring and denting it. Make the dents by pounding on a piece of wire, then rub wood stain in dents.

On painted furniture (below, right) you get antique look by rubbing on streaks of wood stain right from the tin. Then apply splatter with an old toothbrush. Dip in wood stain, flip with thumb.

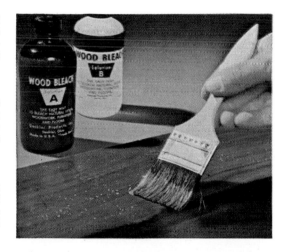

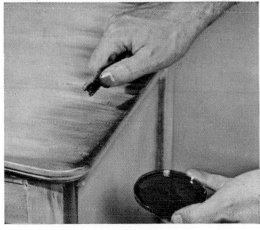

Finishes for 5 kinds of wood

Here are instructions for putting beautiful finishes on five kinds of wood: mahogany, walnut, pine, oak, and fir.

Whether you use solid timber or plywood, the finishing method for each kind of wood is the same—oak ply takes the same finishes as solid oak.

If you are planning to apply an enamel finish to your project, the least expensive of the materials is the one to use, of course. That is plywood, which will take a fine opaque finish as well as those outlined here which let the grain show.

When you are working on any of the finishes listed here, it is a good idea to make your first attempt on a small piece of scrap wood of the same material, or on a hidden spot some-where on the project itself.

When you have mastered the technique on scrap, you are ready to start on your project. And this chart will help you do just about any finishing job you want to do.

Natural mahogany	To maintain original colour, bleach slightly. Rinse. Sand and dust carefully. Apply sealer, which will return wood to natural colour. Fill with filler tinted to wood colour with spirit or water stain. If slight darkening is required, brush on a coat of clear varnish. Use tinted filler. Continue with varnish to final finish. To intensify wood colour and emphasise grain, use stain with sealer without previous bleaching. Fill and varnish. Experiment with wood scraps to determine colour desired.
Blonde mahogany	Use commercially available bleach after final sanding. Mahogany may take two bleach applications. Rinse. Sand when dry. Dust carefully. Use sealer. Fill with neutral wood filler. Proceed with varnish.
Antique mahogany	Sand. Dust. Stain with mahogany stain. Stain lighter by diluting stain and wiping it sooner, to minimize penetration. Or use thinned synthetic sealer before staining. Seal stain with thin coat of shellac. Fill with filler darkened with dark oak stain. Then finish with shellac or varnish.
Natural walnut	Walnut stays light beneath an all-lacquer finish. Rub between coats. For lighter finish, bleach slightly, as with mahogany. Varnish and the clear resin sealers darken walnut. Unless it is exceptionally open-grained, walnut will smooth out under successive coats of varnish or lacquer, without filler. If you use filler, tint it slightly with a darker wood dye.

Stained walnut	Same as for Antique mahogany, except with walnut stain. Walnut not be stained too dark. Keep stain light by wiping quickly, diluting the stain, or applying a thinned coat of synthetic resin sealer before you stain.
Natural pine	This is the easiest finish of all—but the final golden-brown colour does not come until the wood has been exposed to light for several months. Brush on boiled linseed oil. Let it penetrate for an hour or so—then wipe it off. Wax.
Antique pine	Sand. Apply thin coat of button polish. Mix weak wiping stain of light oak in linseed oil. Experiment on scraps until you achieve gold-brown colour desired. Darken slightly if you wish. Brush, wipe off after a few minutes. For walls, use wax. For pine furniture, varnish.
White-spread oak	Sand. Dust most carefully. There must be *no dust in the pores of the wood.* To play safe, use vacuum cleaner. Brush on coat of high-varnish-content enamel—black or dark brown, green or blue. Sand to smooth and scuff. Dust again—just as carefully. Enamel again. *Do not sand,* Mix tiller quite thick, with good-grade white enamel. Brush on. Spread across the grain with a stiff cardboard. Then finish wiping clean with rough cloth—across the grain. Sand very, very lightly to scuff. Apply two or three coats of varnish. *Take care never to rub through initial enamel.*
Natural oak	Oak often runs less true to colour than most woods and may need bleaching for natural oak finishes to equalize colours. After bleaching, sand, dust, and fill with neutral filler. Retain natural look with shellac, lacquer, or varnish. Interesting variation of natural oak: Mix a tint of brown, red, or green in your wood filler, for a grain-toned finish.
Bleached oak	Sand and dust. Bleach. Bleach again if necessary. Sand. Dust carefully. Fill with filler toned white. For maximum blondeness, use a white wiping stain or a white synthetic resin penetrating filler. For average whiteness, follow white filler with varnish.
Pigment-stain fir	Do not sand fir. It is as smooth as you can make it, the way you buy it. Brush on filler—one coat or two, depending on degree of staining desired. Experiment on scraps. Stain with desired colour. Brush on—wipe off. Blend out, wiping selectively, for result desired. Finish with two coats of varnish.

White-stain fir	Brush on white sealer—or dilute white enamel. Then wipe it off. Varnish, if thicker finish is desired.
Medium-stain fir	Seal soft-and-hard grain pattern of fir plywood with resin sealer. Then apply regular walnut-oil stain, wiping quickly to cut down penetration. Varnish to degree of finish desired.
Frosted fir	Brush high-varnish-content enamel of colour desired for background—directly on the raw wood. Most of it will sink out of sight in the soft wood. Re-coat. This will leave small unsealed areas in fir. Brush on white sealer. Wipe, blending "frost" colour as needed for best appearance. Protect frosted finish with a coat or two of varnish.

There are three types of wood 'stains': water, spirit and dyes.

Water	In powder form, has to be mixed with water. Advantage of this stain is that you can wipe off and start again if you make a mistake.
Spirit	Already mixed when you buy it. Can be lightened. Difficult to remove once it has dried out. Will cover and penetrate grease spots whereas water stain will not.
Wood dyes	Check carefully that you have the right colour because these dyes are permanent once applied.

Long-life clear wood finishes

There are two types of synthetic floor coatings that work as well on parquet blocks as on standard strip flooring. One type contains polyurethane, and the other has an epoxy base; both of these finishes form a hard, clear surface that needs no waxing.

   Generally, the polyurethane varnishes dry to a very hard finish—even harder than the epoxies—and stand up well to scratching and staining. The polyurethanes also will keep their gloss, even when used on outdoor projects.

   Epoxy varnishes are outstanding in two ways: they stick tightly to almost any surface—urethanes need careful preparation—and they stay light and clear after application. Epoxy varnishes are also extremely tough when it comes to resisting harsh chemicals.

   Both polyurethane and epoxy varnishes will wear longer than standard varnishes. Some tests show that the very hard polyurethane finishes last three times longer than spar varnishes.

Sand

Dust

Seal
Fill

Finishing points . . .

Sand by machine or hand until you get a perfect surface, finish with very fine paper.

Dampen to raise grain, then sand again—except when you bleach or use water stain, which replace dampening.

Bleach whenever you want a light finish—and bleach mildly in most natural finishes, to compensate for inevitable darkening of the wood.

Seal whenever medium or dark finishes are in order on woods that have "wild" grain, or when you must retard penetration of stains. Use a good sealer.

Stain to darken and intensify wood colours—or to impart other colours with pigment or wiping stains.

Fill open-grain woods with filler used natural or coloured to match wood. (Pigment-filled finishes are not filled until base colour is applied. See main text.)

Sand lightly, to remove "toothy" residue of filler.

Finish-coat with varnish, lacquer, or shellac, depending on your demands for speed, durability, etc.

Scuff-sand lightly on varnish after 24 hours, lacquer or shellac after 4 hours. (Double these times for cool or damp conditions.) Use sand paper to level the surface and provide key for second coat.

Second-coat with varnish, lacquer, or shellac. Lightly sand again, taking care not to cut through finish to the bare wood.

Finish off with as many coats as you need to build up level, smooth finish.

Final surface can be rubbed up with pumice and oil, or fine steel wool followed by two well-buffed coats of wax.

Maintain finish by keeping it clean, applying a good wax polish as needed. A good finish stays bright and clear almost indefinitely, unless it becomes dirty. A gentle wash with mild soap, followed by polishing and buffing, removes accumulated surface dirt, uncovering the finish and allowing the natural wood to show through once more.

Special effect wood finishes

Here are three pages of Cinderella treatments that turn the most hopeless pieces of old, ugly furniture into prized additions to your decorating scheme.

Begin by removing wax and grime with turpentine and steel wool or a commercial paint stripper, and then sand. You do not have to be particular about sanding, because imperfections add to the antique look. Then give the furniture two coats of flat enamel. The finish mellows colours, so choose one that is brighter than you actually want.

To give whitewood furniture an antique look, begin by applying one coat only of an eggshell finish wood sealer or flat white, thinned with turpentine. When dry, sand lightly to let grain show through. Apply edging tape to all exposed edges.

Finish off with the colour you require. Wipe off stain, but let some grain show. Varnish and wax.

Put an antique finish on an old, drab piece of furniture or a new unpainted piece with only a few relaxing hours' work. The materials you will need to use are common and inexpensive, the work is simple and fun—and the results will make you feel like a real professional.

Make shading and streaks with oil colours at the ends of flat surfaces, such as table tops and drawer fronts. Blend colours together on a clean piece of cloth folded into a convenient-sized pad. The procedure for antiquing clear finishes is exactly the same as for painted pieces, except that you apply the clear varnish to the raw wood or to wood you have stained to a desired shade. If you use water stain, check that the surface is free of oil. Apply streaks parallel to the direction of grain.

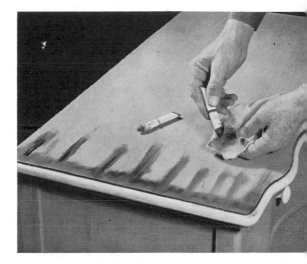

Feather out the shading streaks by wiping from the centre of the piece towards the edge. Lightly sand the centres of the panels to bring out highlights caused by the brush strokes in the base coat of thickened paint. Do not overlook possibilities like the white trim on this chest. Paint on the trim or add stencils after the base coat, then clear varnish with the rest of the piece. Touches like these give an authentic look, but it is best to avoid "overloading" a piece with these devices.

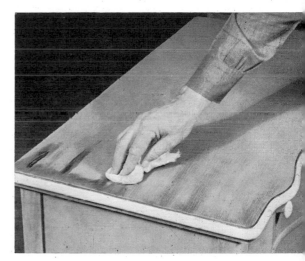

As a finishing touch, you might want to splatter the surface with a slightly darker stain. Use a toothbrush and your thumb to spray on the desired amount. Apply this splatter very sparingly around the edges of the piece, working in towards the centre until you are satisfied with the effect. Do some experimenting first to develop the right technique for applying. After all glaze has dried for several days, rub lightly with steel wool, wipe surface free of dust, then wax.

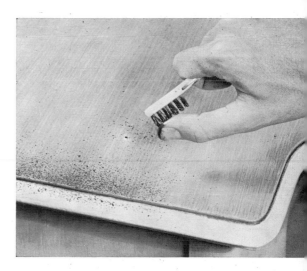

On painted pieces, thicken the first coat of paint to make the brush strokes show up better when you apply clear varnish. Mix in a little plaster of paris until the paint is thick and creamy. Brush on, let it set for a few minutes, then stroke with brush in long, straight sweeps, slightly overlapping strokes.

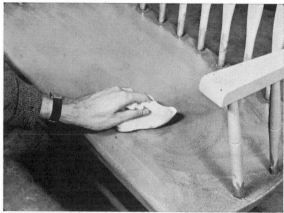

Mix button polish with spirit or oil stains—use a darker colour towards edges. Apply solution liberally with a rag. Wipe off while still wet, working from centre towards ends in flat areas. Use a pad of soft cloth, wiping off most of the glaze in the centre, less at the ends.

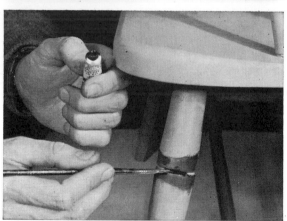

After you apply the over-all glaze, give grooves in legs and joints a special treatment. Rub a 1-inch wide band of dark stain, straight from the tube, around the leg in uneven rings; then brush raw umber into the groove. Treat the joints the same way, wiping and brushing undiluted stain into the extreme corners, crevices, and joints.

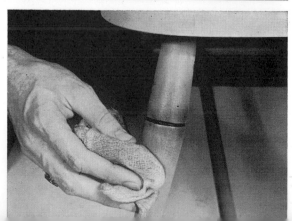

Wipe the colour, working from the outside of the area in towards the centre. Allow colours to blend together. If you do not like the effect, remove while still wet with a turpentine-dampened cloth, rubbing lightly. Rubbing also highlights raised areas of the wood.

French Polishing

General principles:
1. Build up a surface by fairly generous applications of polish, and levelling it at intervals by sanding.
2. Perfect the surface (or film) by using a drier pad.
3. Produce final surface with finisher.
Remember at all times to keep the polishing pad moving—never let it rest on the job. When polishing, work in a warm room with an air temperature of above 60°F.

Materials needed:
Garnet finishing paper; good quality cotton wool; clean yellow duster; soft, thin cotton rags about 7" square (handkerchief material is ideal —shake well to remove any trace of fluff); methylated spirit and cellulose thinner, each in a lidded jar; various grades of glass paper, wood filler, stopping, and stain—these may be required for the initial preparation.

Preparation:
Old surfaces must be free of old polishes. Next, wood sand, using a block, until you have a perfectly smooth surface. Wet with water, then dry off and sand with very fine paper. Always sand with the grain. Fill open grained wood and then brush on two coats (more, if necessary) of lacquer, standard or white for French polish. Two coats of polyurethane clear varnish itself should be brushed on if you use it as a French polish. If a stain is used before polish, test on an off-cut of wood and allow two hours for it to dry before applying finish.

How to polish:
1. To make a pad, moisten a wad of cotton wool on all sides with French polish and squeeze polish into centre of wool. Before making the pad, dip rag in methylated spirit and wring out. Enclose wad and start polishing immediately. (If using polyurethane varnish, use the rag dry or with a trace of thinners).
2. Cover the whole of each flat surface repeatedly with a progressive, even, spiral movement (see illustrations). On small areas,

leave at least for a few seconds between each covering. If using polyurethane varnish, leave for a longer period and never make two turns with the pad in the same place—this removes the varnish film already deposited. Move the pad very quickly over the surface. After twelve coverings, sand down and repeat the whole process until the required finish is obtained. For polyurethane varnish, leave for 4 hours before sanding. Leave French polish for 24 hours before applying the final covering.

3. When rubbing down (between every twelve coverings), do not remove all the polish. Use a slightly coarser grade of paper for the first sanding.

4. Last coverings of polish are given with a drier pad which will leave no wet patches. Give at least twelve coverings without sanding and then, after three hours, polish again until the pad dries up. With polyurethane varnish, do this stage within 24 hours.

5. Finisher (applied 2 to 24 hours after Stage 4) is applied with plain, new layers of cotton wool only, freely moistened. Rub in strips with the grain, exerting pressure back and forth, about twenty times. While the section is still moist, take the yellow duster and rub in the same way—but more swiftly and lightly—until

the polish is dry and brilliant. With polyurethane varnish, more rubbing will be needed and 48 hours should be allowed to elapse before the finisher is applied.

Notes: Never leave the pad exposed to the air when not in use—place in a closed jar. Make a new pad when the polish stops flowing. When re-charging the pad, apply polish to top centre of the cotton wool only—never directly to the rag. Keep spare rags soaking in a jar of methylated spirit. Polyurethane varnish pads must be renewed every 24 hours and, when the rag has been used all over, soak in cellulose thinners (*not* meth) and use again slightly damp.

Before re-charging the cotton wool with finish, peel off the thin coated film from the face of the wool. Add new layers of wool to the dry side and re-moisten the wet side only. When drying off the finish, keep to the same part of the duster—do not turn it over or stop rubbing until the surface is dry.

French-polish repair. In a shellac, varnish, or a lacquer finish, some marks can be removed by French polishing. Use a very fine sandpaper, fine steel wool, or a felt pad charged with pumice and oil to remove the old finish. With rubbing pad charged with shellac and a little linseed oil, work up new finish, blending carefully with old. Finally, blend in the old and the new finish with pumice and oil.

Wood finishing, home maintenance

1 Finishing furniture. If the wood is too dark, lighten with a commercial bleach. Or apply stain to darken. Apply coats with a soft brush, avoiding sags on the curved surfaces. Sand and dust with each coat, then finish with wax. Finally, rub with a fine steel wool or powdered pumice and oil, then apply wax polish. You will find that this technique gives a smooth finish.

2 A steel-wool rub-down. After each coat has dried, rub down with steel wool or very fine sandpaper to remove pin points and other roughness, and then dust with a tack rag, or one damp with turpentine. On curved surfaces such as those shown, steel wool makes it much easier to follow the contours than it is to follow them with sandpaper. Wear an old leather or cotton glove, as shown, so your fingers are protected from abrasions.

3 Waxing. A good wax can be used to produce a lustrous finish on your project. Spread it on evenly and thinly, let it dry for an hour, and then polish. Repeat. For variations, rub with a felt pad charged with powdered pumice stone and machine oil, or you can get the same results with a special rubbing oil. For a less dull finish, rub with a fine steel wool dipped in oil. Remove all the traces of the oil after the desired finish is achieved.

4 Knotty problem. Use "knotting", a special paint for sealing knots and resin streaks to get them ready for varnishing, painting, or any other type of finishing. It will form a firm base for any subsequent coats of paint. When you are sealing knots or resin streaks in this manner, be sure to cover the knot or streak by overlapping by at least $\frac{1}{4}''$.

5 Small scratches. Can be touched out without having to re-polish the entire piece of furniture. In a tin lid or similar container, mix stain until you get the correct match. Apply stain into scratch with a small paint brush. Allow to dry out and repeat if necessary. Wax polish to finish. If scratches are hair line, a good wax shoe polish rubbed well in will cover them up, or you could use a commercial scratch-removing polish.

How to re-finish Furniture

Before beginning to re-finish furniture, all old varnish, french polish and paint has to be removed—particularly in the case of varnish and french polish. Paint applied to these surfaces direct will, of course, crack and peel.

With the liquid varnish and paint removers now available, old surfaces can be removed in a matter of minutes. Awkward spots can be reached and tedious scraping is no longer necessary. Remover is used in conjunction with steel wool and scraper or both. When using a scraper, avoid marking woodwork.

Procedure for use of most finish removers

Use plenty of remover—too little will not do the job and a second application may be necessary. Keep the surface you are cleaning in a horizontal position. If you use a brush, make just one sweep with brush. Or, pour remover on work, spread it with a brush.

Remover has done its job when bubbles appear or you can rub down to the bare wood with a finger. Use a scraper to take off the bulk of the remover and paint. You can use steel wool if the paint is not too thick. Wear rubber gloves to protect your hands.

Steel wool holds just the right amount of water for the wash-away and it gives the gentle abrasion needed. When all the old finish is off, rinse the piece with water, wipe it down with a clean cloth, and let it dry out completely before sanding.

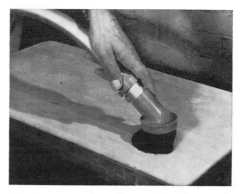

Sandpaper, rasps, and files, steel wool, and specially shaped sanding blocks help to get the wood clean and ready for a perfect new finish. Bad blemishes will require extra sanding and smoothing unless you are "antiquing" the piece. This cleaning up step is important. Use progressively finer sandpaper as you work.

Dust your project thoroughly. After sanding, use a vacuum cleaner to get rid of as much sanding dust as you can. A soft brush will also do the job, but brushing usually leaves fine dust particles in the air. When you put on the finish, work in a room as dustless as possible. Particles almost smaller than you can see will show up when you finish.

Wood stains are now available in every wood colour, plus many non-wood shades. When the exact tone you want is between two colours, you can usually intermix the stains to get the proper effect. Always experiment on scrap of identical wood or on an underside of your project where it will not show to see how much stain to use.

Put the stain on, then wipe it off with a soft cloth. You can darken the colour by permitting the stain to remain on the wood longer. By wiping it off quickly, you can make the colour lighter than normal. Extremely light areas of the wood may need extra treatment. Apply stain to these areas repeatedly, as needed, then wipe it off when the light places look right. Take care to feather and blend the edges of these spots so they will not show up against rest of surface you have stained.

Modern varnishes and brushing lacquers need, to be applied in thin coats. Brush them well, but do not go back over an area previously smoothed or you may leave brush marks. The best smoothing angle to hold the brush is shown here. Be sure to read the directions on the lacquer or varnish you choose; some of the fast drying products require you to work quickly. Also, read directions to find out the correct thinner for the varnish or lacquer you intend to use.

Gentle sanding between coats with a fine grade sandpaper smooths out any high spots caused by dust specks, and scuffs the glossy surface for proper adhesion of the next finish coat. For best results, use a cork sanding block like the one shown here, or glue felt to a wood scrap to make your own. Hold the block so it will not rock over the edges of the piece you are sanding and cut through the finish to the bare wood beneath.

The same high-quality varnishes and paints used for brushing are also available in pressure cans for spraying. Many bright accent colours, especially in enamel finishes, are also sold in spray cans like the one shown. When the job is small, these cans are simple and efficient to use. For best results, hold the can about 10 inches above the work and try to make even, uniform passes. In any case, hold can back far enough so no runs appear.

Plumbing repairs

Small plumbing repairs around the house are not difficult. There are several you should know how to deal with in an emergency.

You should be able to fix a dripping tap, for example. Or a clogged drain. Or repair a lavatory cistern that overflows or will not stop running. Or thaw out a frozen pipe so that your water supply is not interrupted for too long at a time.

Often a simple, early repair will avoid a major repair job or a costly replacement later on. The only cost will be for tools you should own anyway—less than a professional plumber would charge you for a day's work. And you avoid the inconvenience of waiting until the plumber can get round to your little job.

Changing or adding to the home's basic plumbing system is certainly not impossible for the handyman. The system is really very simple, though it looks complex.

If you intend to add to your present system, try to do it with the same materials as those already installed. A point to remember—polythene tubing is not suitable for hot water systems. It softens when it gets hot and melts at approximately 230 degrees F.

Any basic changes you make will have to conform to local building regulations, and the work done inspected by the local authority.

Until you have had considerable

All the tools that you will need are shown here. They will take care of those small plumbing repair jobs that keep your plumbing system operating at peak efficiency and help you avoid major repairs. At top is a plunger, below, wrench and screwdriver, and at right, spring-type "snake" of steel with adjustable handle.

experience in this field, it would be wise to confine your plumbing efforts to the simple repair jobs described in this chapter.

Before you start, acquaint yourself with the layout of the water system in your home. Note where the various stopcocks are situated and make sure they are in working order; check the tap sizes—both hot and cold—and have spare washers handy; check that your hot water system will not be damaged if you turn the cold water supply off at the mains.

Do not give up too soon. Put your plunger in place over the drain, partly fill the bowl with water, and work the plunger up and down vigorously a couple of ·dozen times. To get full pressure on the stoppage, you will have to plug the overflow outlet with a damp rag and hold it in place. When the stoppage clears, the water will rush out of the bowl. A plunger is sometimes successful in clearing a clogged toilet.

How to open a clogged drain

Drain cleaner. If the plunger does not remove the clog, siphon any standing water out of the bowl and try a·commercial drain cleaner. Use cleaner sparingly, especially if you have copper pipes, and follow directions. Do not allow cleaner to touch any porcelain or enamelled surface. Let mixture work several hours or overnight, then flush it away. If drain is not completely clogged, flush with very hot water before using cleaner. Regular use helps avoid clogging.

Cleaning traps. If neither plunger nor drain cleaner does the job, look for a waste plug at bottom of the U-trap. If you find one, unscrew it. If not, take off whole trap, as pictured. (Adhesive tape protects chromium from marking by wrench.) Place bucket beneath trap to catch water. With a piece of wire, rake the drain pipe clean as far as you can reach. If you remove trap, scrub it in hot, soapy water. Put new rubber washers in trap to restore the watertight seal.

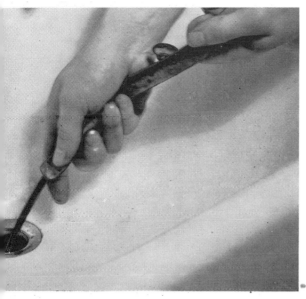

Drain auger. If you have a drain auger with an adjustable, crank-type handle, you can work through the sink opening in removing a clog. The coiled steel spring, known to plumbers as a "snake", is easy to work past the trap and down the drainpipe as you crank the handle, gradually moving it up the spring. A 10-foot auger is relatively inexpensive, and will clear most pipe stoppages.

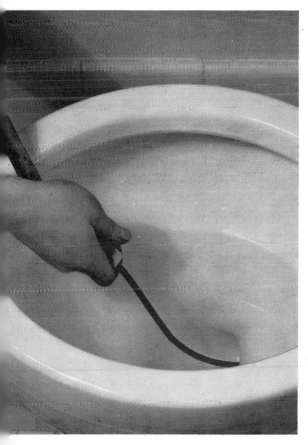

Clogged lavatories. You can also use your drain auger to open a stopped-up lavatory, although plumbers use a special closet auger with a long handle. Push the coiled spring through the large opening at the back of the bowl, and keep cranking until you strike the clog. The hook on the end of the spring will catch some obstructions so you can haul them back up, break up others so they may be flushed away.

How to open a clogged sewer

Sewer lines beyond the walls of the house sometimes become clogged. A common cause of stoppage is the accumulation of grease and waste such as newspaper, polythene bags, etc., so avoid flushing away this type of waste.

The treatment is the same as for a clogged drain, except that you use special sectional sewer cleaning rods. Such sewer rods have an assortment of end attachments to use in boring or cutting through the obstruction, depending on the nature of the stoppage. They are cranked into the sewer through the manhole found near the point where the sewer line enteres the house.

If tree roots are causing the clog, they may be repelled (once an opening is made) by flushing the sewer with a solution of copper sulphate. A more permanent repair, however, is made by replacing the clay pipe with heavy cast-iron pipe—or remove the tree.

In extreme cases it is always wise to call for professional help in cleaning a clogged sewer.

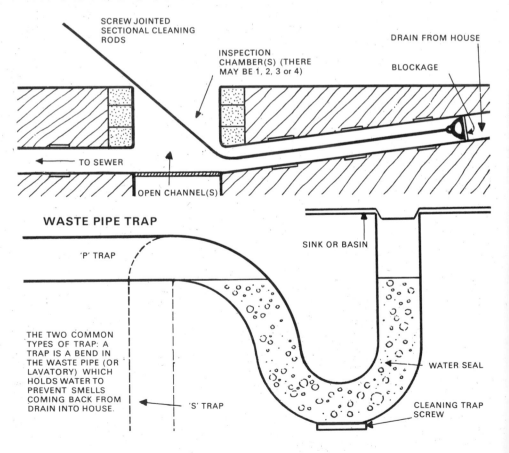

TYPICAL UNDERGROUND DRAIN

SCREW JOINTED SECTIONAL CLEANING RODS

INSPECTION CHAMBER(S) (THERE MAY BE 1, 2, 3 or 4)

DRAIN FROM HOUSE

BLOCKAGE

TO SEWER

OPEN CHANNEL(S)

WASTE PIPE TRAP

'P' TRAP

SINK OR BASIN

THE TWO COMMON TYPES OF TRAP: A TRAP IS A BEND IN THE WASTE PIPE (OR LAVATORY) WHICH HOLDS WATER TO PREVENT SMELLS COMING BACK FROM DRAIN INTO HOUSE.

'S' TRAP

WATER SEAL

CLEANING TRAP SCREW

How to fix a leaky tap

Taps generally give years of trouble-free service. The two most common causes of dripping are either a faulty or worn washer or loose packing. Both faults can be repaired by the handyman.

Water which leaks through the bib is due to a washer fault, and water which leaks out through cap or spindle is a packing fault, or simply a loose gland nut.

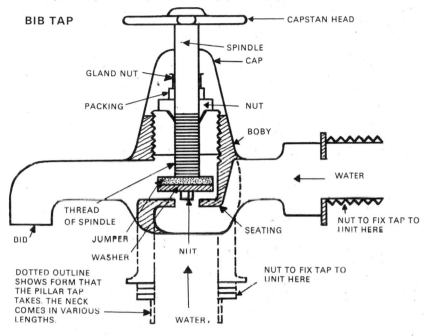

BIB TAP — CAPSTAN HEAD — SPINDLE — CAP — GLAND NUT — PACKING — NUT — BODY — WATER — THREAD OF SPINDLE — SEATING — NUT TO FIX TAP TO UNIT HERE — BID — JUMPER — WASHER — NUT — NUT TO FIX TAP TO UNIT HERE — DOTTED OUTLINE SHOWS FORM THAT THE PILLAR TAP TAKES. THE NECK COMES IN VARIOUS LENGTHS. — WATER

Study the diagram above which shows the common type of bib tap. Turn off the water supply. To renew the washer, turn on tap to fullest extent and unscrew cap which should be only finger tight; then unscrew the nut which holds the spindle, etc, to the body (on some taps the capstan head will need to be removed before you can undo the spindle). Lift spindle from body, unscrew washer retaining unit, and renew washer. Check that the washer is of the correct size and type—there are washers for hot and cold systems.

Re-assemble tap.
To renew packing, remove spindle from body as already described, undo gland nut, take out old packing and re-pack with waxed hemp. Before you carry out this repair, you could try tightening the gland nut a little—it may stop the leak.
A point to remember: Do not turn taps off as tightly as you can. This will split the washer and could damage the seating. Should this happen, a new tap is required. If you fix a new tap, remember to seal it with plumber's mate.

Tank and cistern repairs

In both the W.C. cistern and the storage cistern, water is supplied by way of a ball valve. This valve shuts off the intake of water when the water in the cistern reaches a certain level—this is either approximately ½ inch below the overflow pipe or to the level marked on the inside of the cistern. The three main types of valves and their construction are shown in the diagrams.

To renew the washer, remove the pivot pin

which holds the ball and arm to the valve. On large storage tanks, take care not to drop it in the tank. Undo the caps that retain the washer and renew. If you have to renew the pivot pin (split pin), use brass or copper but *not* steel which will rust and corrode.

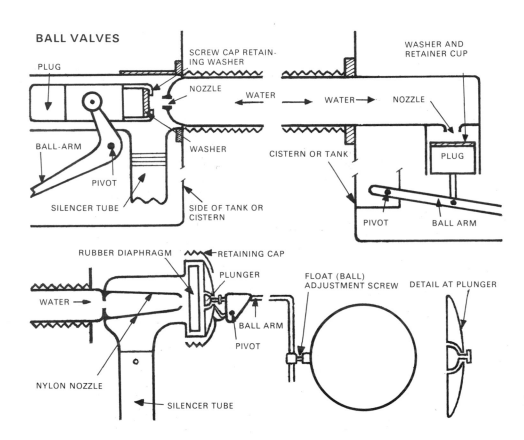

BALL VALVES

PLUG

SCREW CAP RETAINING WASHER

NOZZLE

WATER

BALL-ARM

PIVOT

SILENCER TUBE

WASHER

SIDE OF TANK OR CISTERN

WASHER AND RETAINER CUP

WATER

NOZZLE

CISTERN OR TANK

PLUG

PIVOT

BALL ARM

RUBBER DIAPHRAGM

RETAINING CAP

PLUNGER

WATER

BALL ARM

PIVOT

NYLON NOZZLE

SILENCER TUBE

FLOAT (BALL) ADJUSTMENT SCREW

DETAIL AT PLUNGER

Frost precautions

"Prevention is better than cure" applies especially in the case of frozen pipes or tanks.
Pipes: They should be lagged with particular attention to those exposed to the elements. Lagging comes in bandage form—glass fibre or treated hair felt—or in rigid lengths of poly- styrene, asbestos composition, glass fibre or plastic foam. There is also a self-adhesive sealing tape which can be used—it is a little more expensive than those mentioned above but it needs no tying or strapping. When lagging, do not miss difficult corners and go

right up to stopcocks and taps—it is at these awkward spots that ice forms quickly.

Tanks: There is an excellent choice of laggings which include fibreglass wrappings and blankets and expanded polystyrene coverings—all tailor-made to fit almost any size of tank. Hot water tanks should also be lagged—the heat loss of an unlagged tank is considerable.

If you do get frozen up, do not apply direct heat to the pipes or tanks concerned. The gentle warmth from a fan heater (set on half heat), hair dryer, hot water bottles, or even cloths soaked in hot water and applied to the pipes, will unfreeze them slowly but without causing a burst.

The first sign that there is anything wrong is water coming out of the overflow pipe, either in a steady flow or a continuous drip. As the washers in this type of valve last a considerable time, it is worth carrying out the following procedure before renewing the washer:

1. A piece of scale or dirt may have penetrated between the washer and the seating, so stopping the valve from shutting off correctly. Work the ball arm up and down sharply so that the sudden rush of water removes the offending piece of grit.

2. The ball may be riding too low in the water and therefore failing to shut the valve at the correct time. Check that the ball is airtight. Any water in the ball will cause the valve to remain open. Either fit a new ball or empty water from the old one and re-seal.

3. If the ball is all right, then the arm needs to be bent downwards so that the valve will cut off sooner. Do this by degrees and do it with

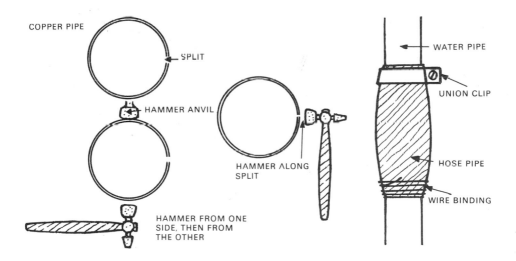

COPPER PIPE

SPLIT

HAMMER ANVIL

HAMMER ALONG SPLIT

HAMMER FROM ONE SIDE, THEN FROM THE OTHER

WATER PIPE

UNION CLIP

HOSE PIPE

WIRE BINDING

care. The ball of the "Garston" valve is adjusted by a thumb screw.

If you do get a burst pipe, turn off the main stopcock and make one of the following temporary repairs:

In the case of lead pipes, gently hammer lead towards the centre of the hole until it closes up. Then bind with sticky tape or a proprietary water sealing strip. The tape should run for at least 2″ on either side of the hole.

Copper pipes split when they burst so two hammers are needed—one to act as an anvil (an old flat iron would do). Following the

diagram, hammer the pipe first from one side, then from the other, until the split closes up. The pipe will now be oval in shape, so gently hammer along the split in order that its lips draw more tightly together. Now bind with tape, as described above.

Another method of repairing a pipe is to cut the holed section away and then re-connect the pipe by inserting a length of garden hose. Use wire binding or Jubilee clips to secure it to the pipe.

Water should be turned on at half pressure or less until a permanent repair can be made.

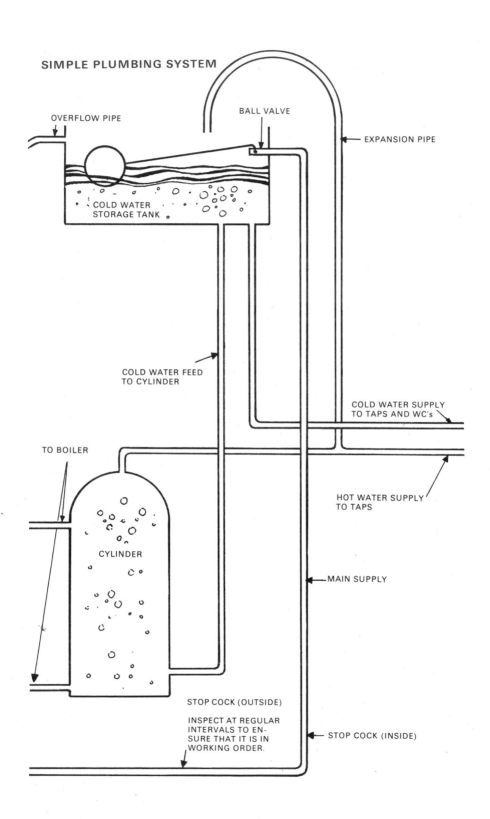

SIMPLE PLUMBING SYSTEM

OVERFLOW PIPE

BALL VALVE

EXPANSION PIPE

COLD WATER
STORAGE TANK

COLD WATER FEED
TO CYLINDER

COLD WATER SUPPLY
TO TAPS AND WC's

TO BOILER

HOT WATER SUPPLY
TO TAPS

CYLINDER

MAIN SUPPLY

STOP COCK (OUTSIDE)

INSPECT AT REGULAR
INTERVALS TO EN-
SURE THAT IT IS IN
WORKING ORDER.

STOP COCK (INSIDE)

Electrical repairs and wiring

It is important for any householder to know that his home has a wiring system that is adequate for carrying electricity to the many appliances and machines which we depend on to help us live comfortably. However, even as a handyman, your part in the job of bringing wiring up to date will probably only be that of recognising deficiencies and knowing what corrections you want. The task of wiring a home is rigidly controlled by local and national regulations, and it must be done by an expert. The regulations are strict because poor work can cause overloading of circuits, which in turn may damage wiring or appliance motors.

SAFETY

You can safely do a number of repair jobs, but it cannot be too strongly emphasised that when working on any circuit, appliance or piece of equipment, it must be completely isolated from the electricity supply, that is, the plug disconnected or fuse removed.

It is not good enough to switch off a piece of equipment by its own switch or by the switch plug, because under certain conditions it may still be live (e.g. TV sets and radios). For example, a switch plug may have been wired up with the leads reversed so that, when it is in the "off" position, the neutral side is switched off but the live side is carried through to the plug and the piece of equipment connected to the plug is therefore still live. **So—pull the plug out altogether.**

HOUSE WIRING SYSTEMS

With the advent of new regulations all power and lighting points must be earthed even if they are plastic. An earthing terminal and earthing conductor is now required to run through any power or lighting circuit (this is known as earth-continuity conductor—e.c.c.). There are two main systems used in house wiring: separate circuits and "ring" circuits. Figs. 1 and 2 show typical wiring installations.

SIGNS OF FAULTY WIRING

1. Lights dim or flicker when appliances go on.
2. Appliances are slow starting, slow operating.
3. Fuses blow or circuit breakers trip too often.
4. Radio fades or is scratchy when appliances go on.
5. Television pictures shrinks. (This may be due to a cut in voltage from the electricity supply).
6. Outlets and switches seem scarce when you need them.
7. Switches or plugs are overheating.

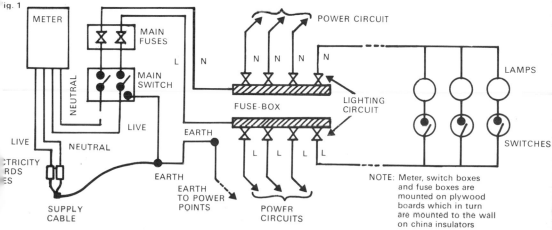

ig. 1

METER

MAIN FUSES

MAIN SWITCH

NEUTRAL

LIVE

LIVE   NEUTRAL

CTRICITY
RDS
ES

SUPPLY CABLE

EARTH

EARTH

EARTH TO POWER POINTS

L   N

FUSE-BOX

L   L   L   L

POWER CIRCUITS

N   N   N   N

POWER CIRCUIT

LIGHTING CIRCUIT

LAMPS

SWITCHES

NOTE: Meter, switch boxes and fuse boxes are mounted on plywood boards which in turn are mounted to the wall on china insulators

Fig. 2

HALL 2 WAY SWITCH

HALL   LOUNGE

MAIN SWITCH
LIVE
NEUTRAL
EARTH

FUSE BOX

SWITCH

SWITCH

SWITCH PLUG

SWITCH

ONLY ONE POWER
POINT SHOWN BUT
USUALLY ONE OR TWO
PER ROOM

KITCHEN   DINING ROOM

BEDROOM 3   BEDROOM 2

SWITCH
HALL 2 WAY SWITCH

SWITCH

BEDROOM 1

LANDING

LANDING AS PER
HALL LIGHT WITH 2
WAY SWITCHES AS
SHOWN FOR HALL
LIGHT

SWITCH

SWITCH

BATHROOM

LIVE WIRE   SWITCH WIRE - - - - -
NEUTRAL WIRE   EARTH

EVERYDAY EQUIPMENT AND APPLIANCES

The following table lists the most common pieces of equipment in the home, together with plug, fuse rating, flexible cable and house wiring cable to be used.

FUSE BOXES

Each fuse in your fuse box should be labelled showing which circuit it controls. Self-adhesive labels are available—they can be fixed to the fronts of the fuses so that, when the box is opened, you can see at a glance which fuse covers which circuit. In the new ring main fuse boxes, space is provided on the lids opposite the fuses concerned.

FUSES—WHY THEY ARE USED, AND RATINGS

Fuses are fitted in house circuits as well as in many pieces of equipment to protect you and your property against shock and fire damage, which might well occur under faulty conditions. Always replace fuses with the correct ampere rating—failure to do this can cause trouble (see Fig. 3).

TYPICAL USE	FUSE RATING	FLEXIBLE CABLE				PLUG	HOUSE WIRING CABLE		
		CABLE SIZE	CORES	CURRENT (AMPS)	APPROX LOAD (KW.)		CABLE SIZE	CURRENT (AMPS)	APPROX LOAD (KW.)
BEDSIDE AND STANDARD LAMPS, RADIOS, RECORD PLAYERS, TV SETS, RAZORS, ELECTRIC BLANKETS, CLOCKS, DOOR CHIMES, FISH-TANKS	2	14/·0076	2	3	0·5	2 or 3 pin 2 amp	1/·044	5	1·0
SMALL FIRES, IRONS, REFRIGERATORS, SMALL POWER TOOLS, SOLDER-ING IRONS, SMALL BATTERY CHARGERS, VACUUM CLEANERS, TOASTERS	5	23/·0076	3	6	1·0	3 pin 5 amp	3/·029	10	2·25
TWO-BAR FIRES, KETTLES	10	40/·0076	3	13	3·0	3 pin 13 amp 15 amp	7/·029	20	4·5
LARGE FIRES AND HEATERS, WASHING MACHINES WITH WATER HEATERS. WASH BOILERS	13 15	70/·0076	3	18	4·25	3 pin 13 amp 15 amp	AS ABOVE BUT FOR 7/·036	ABOVE LARGE 28	EQUIP'T. 65

Fig. 3

ELECTRICITY BOARD S
FUSE 10-40 AMP
DEPENDING ON YOUR
REQUIREMENTS

FUSE ADEQUATE FOR
AREA SERVED

LIVE

NEUTRAL

EARTH

POWER STATION

TO OTHER HOUSES

HOUSE

15 AMP
15 AMP
10 AMP HOUSE
5 AMP   CIRCUITS
5 AMP

From the diagram (Fig. 3), it can be seen what would happen if a high rated fuse is put in a lower rated position, such as a 2″ nail instead of a piece of 5 amp fuse wire (this has actually been done!). If there is a fault—say a dead short between two wires—there is a risk of damage being done to wiring due to over-heating, causing a fire, and possibly more trouble by blowing the Electricity Board's fuse as well as your own.

There are different values of fused plugs, and some have been coloured coded to assist identification. The square 3-pin plug fuses are coloured as follows:

Blue:	2 amp	
Grey:	5 amp	B.S. 1362
Yellow:	10 amp	
Brown:	13 amp	

Clock sockets:

Green:	1 amp	
Yellow:	2 amp	B.S. 646
Red:	5 amp	

Round pins:
(15 amp)

Yellow:	10 amp	
Grey:	5 amp	B.S. 1361
Blue:	2 amp	

Similarly, cartridge type fuses are coloured as follows:

Yellow:	500 milliamps ($\frac{1}{2}$ amp)
Green:	750 milliamps ($\frac{3}{4}$ amp)
Blue:	1 amp
Purple:	2 amp
White:	3 amp
White/black:	5 amp

Fuse wire usually comes in three sizes—5 amp, 10 amp and 15 amp. Keep a supply with a small screwdriver, plus candle and matches, in your fuse box so that it is at hand if a fuse needs replacing. To renew, loosen the two screws, remove the bits of old wire, secure the new piece of wire under one screw, thread wire through fuse holder (not too tightly), secure other end making sure not to leave any long ends. Before replacing the actual fuse, check that the cause of its blowing has been repaired or removed from the circuit. (See Fig. 4.)

TYPES OF PLUGS AND THEIR RATINGS

There are many types of plug in use today. The most common are listed below, together with the rated current and approximate load:

2 pin	2 amp	450 watts (0.45 kw)
3 pin	2 amp	
2 pin	5 amp	1000 watts (1 kw)
3 pin	5 amp	
2 pin	10 amp	2000 watts (2 kw) (Seldom used because it it has no earth pin, and any piece of equipment carrying such a high load must be earthed).
* 3 pin	13 amp	2900 watts (2.9 kw) (Known as a D & S plug; has the fuse incorporated in the live pin which screws into the plug).
* 3 pin	13 amp (flat pins)	3400 watts (Has fuse incorporated within the plug. In some cases the plug top has to be removed, or the fuse snaps in a position adjacent to the live pin).
3 pin	15 amp (old type)	3400 watts (3.4 kw)

* Indicates fused plugs. Fuses lower than the maximum rating shown can be used with them.

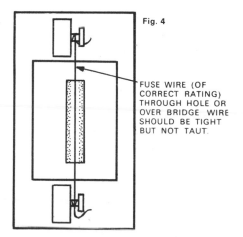

Fig. 4

FUSE WIRE (OF CORRECT RATING) THROUGH HOLE OR OVER BRIDGE WIRE SHOULD BE TIGHT BUT NOT TAUT.

Fig. 5

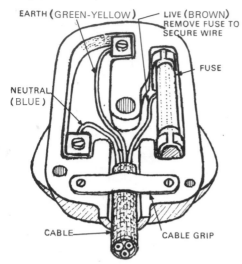

EARTH (GREEN-YELLOW)
LIVE (BROWN)
REMOVE FUSE TO SECURE WIRE
FUSE
NEUTRAL (BLUE)
CABLE
CABLE GRIP

HOW TO WIRE A LAMPHOLDER

Switch off at main or remove fuse. Remove the old wire by unscrewing the ceiling rose, then undo the screws which hold the wire in the rose—note which holes they come from. Now unscrew the top of the lampholder and remove the wires from it by releasing the screws holding them.

Cut away about $\frac{1}{2}''$ of the insulated covering on each wire of new flex, twist the wires to tighten, then thread the flex through the top sections of the holder. Undo the terminal screws, fold the ends of the wires back on themselves, leaving about a $\frac{1}{4}''$ strip of bare wire to insert into the terminals. Tighten the screws, pass the flex round the shoulders of the holder and tighten the top. This grips the flex in the holder so that it can take the weight of your lampshade.

Now refix into the ceiling rose, but do not forget to thread the cover of the rose on to the wire before you do so. Fig. 6 shows the recommended four-terminal ceiling rose.

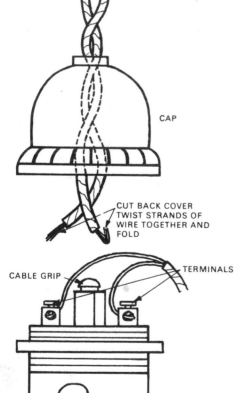

CAP

CUT BACK COVER TWIST STRANDS OF WIRE TOGETHER AND FOLD

CABLE GRIP
TERMINALS

LOCKING RING FOR SHADE

Fig. 6

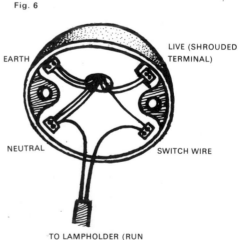

EARTH
LIVE (SHROUDED TERMINAL)
NEUTRAL
SWITCH WIRE

TO LAMPHOLDER (RUN EARTH TO HOLDER IF IT HAS AN EARTH TERMINAL)

HOW TO TAKE CARE OF PLUGS, POINTS AND CABLES

Check the plugs of your iron and vacuum cleaner for tightness. Make sure the wires have not pulled away from the cable grips or from their terminals—holding by a single strand of wire will *not* do. If you discover frayed wire or broken insulated covering, cut the wire well back and make fresh connections as follows. Place the new end of the cable into the plug and mark where the cable grip falls after allowing enough for the coloured wires to reach their terminals. Now cut back the outer cover to the required spot, and cut the coloured wires to the correct length. Cut away $\frac{1}{2}''$ of the insulating covering on each coloured wire, twist the strands of wire together and then fold the end back on itself.

Follow Fig. 5 for wiring a standard 3-pin 13 amp plug or a conventional round 3-pin plug. The pins are labelled N–BLUE, L–BROWN and E–GREEN-YELLOW. When repairing, take care to put blue wire to N, brown to L, and green-yellow to E. Finally, check that all screws holding top and cord grip in position are tight

HOW TO TAKE CARE OF AN ELECTRIC FIRE

Never run a fire off the lighting circuit of your home it is not built to run this type of appliance.

All new electric fires will have guards. If you own an old fire, arrange for a guard to be fitted at your local electricity showroom or by the manufacturer.

Before attempting to clean or do any small repair to a fire, it *must* be isolated from the electricity supply—pull the plug out of the socket.

You will obtain maximum heat from a radiant fire if you keep the reflector clean and polished —a dirty reflector will absorb heat instead of pushing it round the room.

Never light cigarettes, paper, etc. from the element. It is dangerous and you could also break the element. Before replacing a burned out element, switch off and pull the plug out. Remove the guard, then unscrew the old element and lift from the spring supports. Insert a new element of the correct voltage and wattage. Tighten the terminal units and replace the guard.

Beware of frayed flex because it could give you an unpleasant shock. See **How to Take Care of Plugs, Points and Cables** for repairing a frayed flex.

EXTENSION LEADS

Never connect anything in such a manner that is likely to be a danger. For example, suppose an extension lead for a loft light or power tool is made up in two parts—see Fig. 7:

Fig. 7

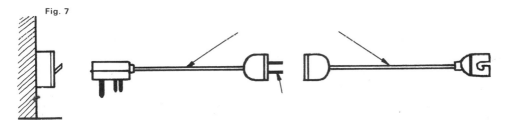

This, of course, is very wrong. Connected in this way, it would mean that if the centre connection was pulled apart the two exposed pieces of the two-pin plug would be "live". The extension should have been made up like this:

Fig. 8

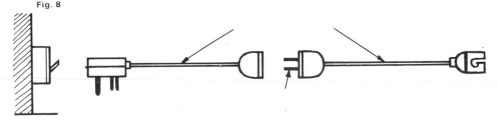

If in doubt about any wiring, consult a qualified electrician. Always check that the plug and wiring are not overloaded. Never run flex or wire under carpets or lino to extend a point or lead.

TWO-WAY SWITCHES

Some installations are separately fused downstairs and upstairs. Others use junction boxes for switch wires, while others carry the live wire to all switches or use the four terminal ceiling rose. It is recommended that the ceiling rose be of the new type which combines joint box and rose and is of a four terminal type (see Figs. 6 and 9). A safety point of this type of rose is that the live terminal is shrouded.

The old type of two and three plate rose can still be used but must have terminal mounting behind the base of the ceiling rose—a two terminal type in case of two plate to carry live and earth and one terminal in three plate to carry live wire.

Older installations have a fuse in both live and neutral wires, whereas modern systems have a fuse in the live side only.

In the case of older installations which employ separate joint boxes the arrangement will be as in Fig. 10. This shows two way switching but can be made one way by fitting a single one-way switch.

All cables used should be 3/.029 p.v.c sheathed.

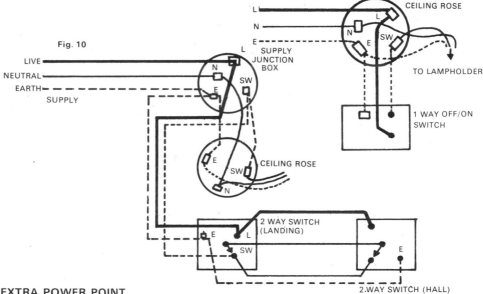

Fig. 9

Fig. 10

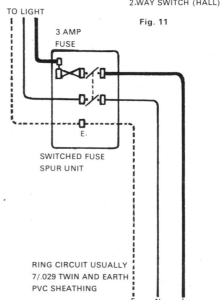

EXTRA POWER POINT

When an extra point is added to a system of separate circuits, an extra three-core cable must be run from a spare fuse in the fuse box to the new position. If no spare fuse is available, it may be necessary to fit an extra fuse box. Do not overload an existing fuse. Check that the plug and cable are of the correct rating for its use. Table 1 will help you, but—if uncertain—consult an electrician.

There is now available a switched fused spur unit which can be used to run in extra lighting points for standard lamps, wall lights, spot lamps, table lamps or bedhead lights. This spur unit carries a 3 amp fuse and the cable feed to the lights should be 1/.044 or 3/.029 twin with earth p.v.c. sheathed (see Fig. 11) This can be used if your system is of the ring-main type.

CHECK LIST OF ELECTRICAL TERMS

Alternating current. The direction of flow of current alternate (generally 50 times a second).

Ampere (amp). Denotes volume of flow, and corresponds to the number of gallons flowing in a water pipe. Watts divided by volts gives amps.

BThU (British Thermal Unit). This is measurement of heat and is the quantity of heat required to raise the temperature of 1 lb of pure water by 1 degree Fahrenheit. 3412 BThU = 1 kw.

Direct Current. As opposed to AC, direct current flows continuously in one direction. Certain products cannot be operated off DC.

Kilowatt (kw). The common unit of electrical power. 1 kilowatt equals 1000 watts. The number of kilowatts is obtained by multiplying the volts by the amps and dividing by 1000.

Ohm. The unit of electrical resistance denotes the resistance of the wires to the passage of electricity. Ohm's Law is the basis of electrical calculations:

$$\text{Amps} = \frac{\text{Volts}}{\text{Ohms}}$$

$$\text{Ohms} = \frac{\text{Volts}}{\text{Amps}}$$

$$\text{Volts} = \text{Amps} \times \text{Ohms}$$

Unit. The normal charge for electricity is measured in units. For example, a 1 kw fire uses one unit in an hour or half a unit in half an hour. A unit is 1000 watts (1 kw) of electricity used for one hour.

Watt. The basic unit of electric power. 1000 watts equal 1 kw. See Kilowatt.

Lighting in the workshop

Lighting in your workshop must be arranged so that any job you undertake is sufficiently well lit for you to work without strain or irritation. Bad lighting leads to bad workmanship but, more important, could be the cause of an accident.

There should be enough power points to operate the various power tools and they should not be extensions from points in the house. The points must be earthed according to the Electricity Board's regulations. Below are some ideas on workshop lighting.

A track light for your workbench is made with two wooden hangers and a length of conduit. Hang the cord to the light from clip-type curtain rings on the conduit. Use half loops as shown for self-storing cord.

Concentrated light for close-up jobs will save time and eye strain. Use a gooseneck lamp —bought new or made from an old desk lamp. Clamp the lamp to the bench.

A floodlight bulb in a photography clamp light is an inexpensive light source. Use it as a light source for power tools to overcome stroboscopic effect of the fluorescent lights.

For general illumination, make a sliding fluorescent fixture as you did track light. Bear in mind, however, that these lights can cause moving power tools to appear stationary.

Centigrade. To convert Centigrade to Fahrenheit, multiply by 9, divide by 5, add 32, e.g. 100°C = 100 × 9 = 900, 900 ÷ 5 = 180, 180 + 32 = 212°F. Fahrenheit. To convert Fahrenheit to Centigrade, subtract 32, divide by 9, multiply by 5, e.g. 212°F = 212 − 32 = 180, 180 ÷ 9 = 20, 20 × 5 = 100°C.

−15°C	=	5°F
−10°C	=	14°F
−5°C	=	23°F
0°C	=	32°F
5°C	=	41°F
10°C	=	50°F
15°C	=	59°F
20°C	=	68°F
25°C	=	77°F
30°C	=	86°F
35°C	=	95°F
40°C	=	104°F
45°C	=	113°F

FUTURE DEVELOPMENTS

Electrical equipment will continue to improve and the use of transistors, automatic equipment, control gear, solid state conductors, together with improved appliances, will make household installations more efficient and less costly. Switch plugs will probably have time switches incorporated in them.

Fuse boxes as we know them may eventually disappear and be replaced by automatic "cut outs" so that, in the event of an overload or short circuit fault condition, the cut-out will "drop out" and disconnect the supply. When the fault is repaired, all that will be necessary to restore supply will be simply to push the cut-out back in again.

Wall-papering

Wall-papering a room need not be a difficult, tricky task. Once you have grasped the basic principles, you can tackle the job with confidence.

The photographs in this section show the professional's approach to wall-papering — measuring walls, cutting paper, and matching patterns.

Your retailer can calculate the number of rolls you will need if you give him the dimensions of walls, windows and doors.

Remove electrical switch plates, if possible, or use the method shown on page 206.

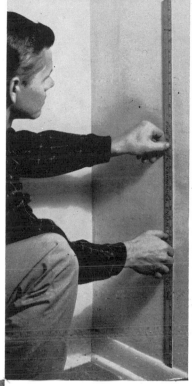

Determine length of the first strip, measuring distance from height you want paper to skirting board. Size newly-plastered walls, and sandpaper walls that were previously painted. At same time, fill any cracks with quick-drying filler.

Gather all materials and equipment for papering before you begin work. They include: pasting table, steel straight edge, wheel trimmer, seam roller, and a paper hanger's brush. You will also need sponge, scissors, rule, paste, brush, string chalk line, and bucket.

1 Use a plumb line to get first strip straight on the wall. It is best to begin in a corner, or at a door or window casing, working to the right. Chalk the line and tack it to the wall near the ceiling or moulding about one inch less than width of the paper. Hold end; snap string for line.

2 Many papers are made with a knock-off selvedge. If not, the wall-paper shop will trim the paper for you when you buy it. If you have to trim it yourself, use knife or scissors.

3 Unroll paper on table for measuring and cutting. Allow extra on length for trimming at skirting, ceiling, and for matching pattern. After first strip has been measured, cut with scissors or by "snapping" it (see picture) on edge of a yardstick.

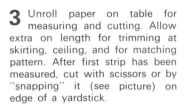

4 Unroll next strip; move it to edge of first and match pattern or "join" points printed on selvedge (arrow). Cut. Stack second strip on top of first, pattern side up. Repeat for other strips.

5 Mix wallpaper paste, adding *paste to water*, to thickness for weight of paper. Stack strips so that the first you cut will be the first you paste. Apply paste evenly along two-thirds of length. Fold strip from its edge to the paste line.

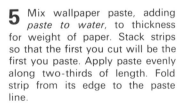

6 Paste remaining one-third of paper to point about an inch from end. Fold strip until unpasted end overlaps other cut end of strip. Keep edges even. Do not crease folds; leave slight "roll".

7 To hang first strip, hold un-pasted end of short fold in one hand and apply at top of wall. Pull out fold with other hand. Be sure right edge follows chalk line. Smooth out the paper with brush.

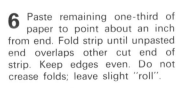

8 Hang second strip, butting edges so pattern matches. Brush air bubbles out from centre of strip to edges. To trim paper, crease at skirting board (as shown) and ceiling with back edge of scissors. Cut on crease. Paste and hang next strips in the order that they were cut. Or use a wheel trimmer, see 11.

9 To insure tight butt joints, edges of strips should be rolled with seam roller. Begin at top where edges touch and roll towards the floor. If the paper pulls apart, you can usually slip it with your free hand (as pictured) to cover any noticeable error in joining.

10 Next to door or window, measure from strip to casing; take widest reading and add inch for overlap. Split strip to desired length. Save off-cuts for piecing. Do same in corners where paper continues on adjacent wall, particularly if corner is not a perfect right angle.

11 Brush edge of strip to moulding. Brush from centre to the edges to work out wrinkles. With scissors, cut slit at top and bottom where paper overlaps. Wheel trimmer gets in close to cut off excess. When hanging paper next to doors, windows—trim it this way, or leave paper to dry out and trim away waste with sharp knife.

12 Use up off-cuts above and below window frames and for the reveals. If using a washable paper, wipe off excess paste with sponge and clean water. On non-washable papers, wipe away excess paste with dry cloth.

13 Plan your last strip of paper to hang in a corner or behind a door so that any discrepancy in pattern (through having to fill with a strip narrower than the original) will not be so noticeable.

14 To paper round a light switch or wall socket, hang the paper in the normal way, but do not brush out. Find centre of switch or socket, make diagonal cuts away from centre to edges of switch, gently ease paper over switch and brush out. Leave to dry out and then trim off waste.

15 Papering ceilings is more difficult than papering walls. The first steps are similar: make a line to which the first piece is to be hung, paste as for walls, but fold as A above. Hold folded paper on spare roll of paper, put to ceiling and slide into position on chalk line—both the ceiling and paper can be pasted to get maximum slide. Move across ceiling, letting paper unfold as you go, and at the same time brushing it out. Go back over piece and brush out all air bubbles.

How to remove old wall-paper

This is a messy job so have a sack or cardboard box handy into which the strippings can be put straight away.

Cover carpets, floor coverings, block or any special floor finish with dust sheets or newspapers. This is particularly important if one of the commercial stripping solutions is used. Spills or drips from these solutions will mark permanently.

Stage 1: Using a distemper brush, soak the wall two or three times with warm soda water. Alternatively, use one of the commercial solutions made for the purpose.

If ceiling is not to be stripped, then it would be wise to knife through the wallpaper at the point where it meets the ceiling **before** wetting the walls.

This will stop any ceiling paper being pulled off with the wallpaper.

Stage 2: Scrape off old paper with scraper, using an upward movement. Do not hesitate to use more water if scraping is difficult—give water a chance to soak right through paper to wall.

While waiting for water to soak through paper, begin to wash down paintwork—the same soda water or stripper used for the walls would do, but **only** if the paintwork just needs washing. If the paint needs stripping, it should be done after the walls have been stripped of paper.

Stage 3: Wash down with clean water. When dry, rub wall down with sandpaper to remove bits.

If you are removing a varnish or plastic covered paper, then score with a wire brush at frequent intervals before soaking. This allows the soaking to go on behind the surface of the paper.

WALLPAPER CALCULATION TABLE																		
Height in Feet from Skirting	Distance round the room in Feet																	
	30	34	38	42	46	50	54	58	62	66	70	74	78	82	86	90	94	98
7 to 7½	4	5	5	6	6	7	7	8	8	9	9	10	10	11	12	12	13	13
7½ to 8	5	5	6	6	7	7	8	8	9	9	10	10	11	11	12	13	13	14
8 to 8½	5	5	6	7	7	8	9	9	10	10	11	12	12	13	14	14	15	15
8½ to 9	5	5	6	7	7	8	9	9	10	10	11	12	12	13	14	14	15	15
9 to 9½	6	6	7	7	8	9	9	10	10	11	12	12	13	14	14	15	15	16
9½ to 10	6	6	7	8	8	9	10	10	11	12	12	13	14	14	15	16	16	17
10 to 10½	6	7	8	8	9	10	10	11	12	13	13	14	15	16	16	17	18	19
Number of Rolls required																		

Using the tools above, you can make good smooth and level patches.

Quick repairs in plaster

Helpful tools

(Pictured left to right)

Smoothing trowel

Chisel

Wall scraper

Sanding block

Cold chisel

Pointing trowel

Wire brush

Hammer

How to patch holes in plasterboard

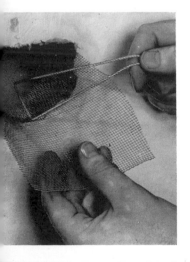

1 Insert wire mesh in hole after you have cleaned out loose and soft plaster. A heavy cord threaded through wire mesh keeps it in right position. Holding onto string, wet the break, adjacent areas for good bond, so that patch will last.

2 "Butter" edges of break with patching material. Wall scraper is best tool for this because it is easier to handle than large trowel. Level and smooth patch as much as possible, keep mesh pulled tight against back of wallboard.

3 Keep wire tight against back of wall while "rough" patch dries. Bridge break with a piece of 2 x 1 batten. Tie string to wood, pulling it tight. When patch dries, remove batten and cut string flush with surface of the patch.

4 Apply "second" coat of patching material, trowelling it smooth. Before you go over patch for last time, wet it to prevent material from sticking to trowel face. This ensures glassy-smooth job. Let patch dry thoroughly before painting.

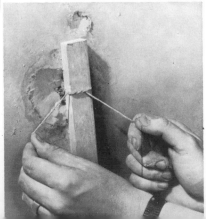

How to patch small cracks in walls and ceilings

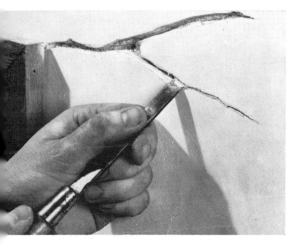

Clean crack first. All loose plaster should be removed. Then widen crack enough to accept filler. Hairline cracks should be opened up a little to ensure they will take filler. By digging away solid plaster about an inch past ends of cracks and under cutting the edges of good plaster to form a V, you will prevent the crack that you are patching from cracking open again.

Run wet brush through crack and moisten small area around it. Water helps provide good bond between filler and wall. It also removes any excess dust and pieces of broken plaster which stick to surfaces of cracks and hinder smooth finish.

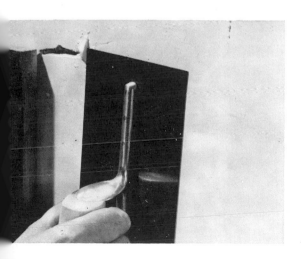

If the crack to be filled is deep, then do it in two stages. In stage one, fill hole to about $\frac{1}{8}$ inch short of the level plaster, score with trowel point, and leave to dry out. Stage two—wet crack and fill to level with the existing wall surface. When trowelling off, keep the surface of the trowel wet. It is better to over-fill cracks because they can be sanded down when the filling has dried out. This method of filling should be used when filling nail holes, but press the filler down into the hole as far as possible. *Never* try to fill a crack over loose plaster.

1 Cut plaster back until you reach good solid plaster or cut right down to breeze or brick.

2 When you have reached clean solid plaster, cut a V-shape under the edges. An old wood chisel will do this quite well.

3 Wet the area, particularly in the V, and cut under the edges of the plaster. Re-moisten if work is held up.

4 Lay an undercoat of filler first pressing it well into the breeze or brick and into the V-edges. Sand surfaces and allow to dry out.

5 Wet area again and trowel on top coat of filler. For a smooth finish, run a wet brush across patch followed by trowel held on edge.

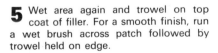

6 Any slight over-filling can be sanded off when filler has dried out.

If the wall is very badly damaged, and you have cut away a large area, it is better to use a cement undercoat of the following proportions: 1 cement: 4 sand: 1 lime followed by a plaster top coat. If necessary, pin wooden battens of the appropriate thickness in the area to be patched—they will help you to keep level with the original wall surface. Fill areas where battens were pinned as before.

Tiling a wall

Instructions for plastic or metal tiles

These step-by-step instructions show how to apply plastic or metal tiles. For ceramic tile, see page 215.

Plastic tile gives a durable, light-weight wall surface. Each tile is coloured all the way through.

Standard tile sizes are 6" × 6" and 4" × 4".

No special tools are needed for these tiles—other than an adhesive spreader. A tennon saw or coping saw will cut the tiles to shape.

Begin by finding the low spot in a room. Measure up *each* wall to tile height wanted (longest measurement from the floor is lowest point). Figure height by placing bottom tile on low wall at least an inch below the bottom line. This gives you room for later fitting.

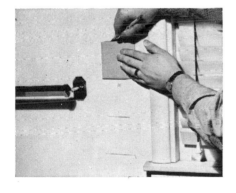

1 Mark off numbers of rows needed, starting little below line at lowest point. Include feature strip in measurement (if it is to be used), but not cap strip, which is installed last. Pencil line up wall for vertical guide; figure rows with a tile.

2 Pencil a horizontal line completely around the room at tile height, starting at the perpendicular line. Use level. Cap strip extends above the line. Scrap plywood was tacked onto the level in picture, giving a longer edge for marking.

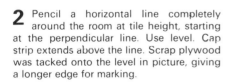

3 From centre of wall, mark vertical guide lines with tile. Start flush to centre line; mark to corners. If *less* than half the tile width occurs at either corner, *centre* tile on the centre line and mark.

4 Patch all cracks and holes, especially around bath and lavatory. Make sure patches are completely dry before you start tiling. Run a straight-edge over the wall to find the high spots, and mark them. Rub these down with sandpaper.

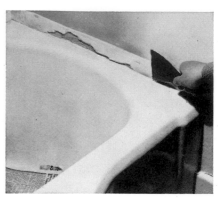

5 Spread mastic with notched spreader, and comb out in vertical lines. Poor bond occurs when too little mastic is used. Ridges will flatten and fill up back of tiles when they are pressed onto wall.

6 Start tiling where vertical and horizontal guide lines meet. Lay two vertical rows, then two horizontal. Slip tile off bevelled edge of adjoining one (picture) to get a tight joint. Press to wall.

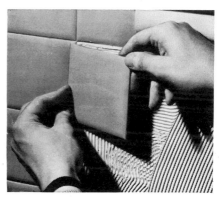

7 Level mastic ridges below row of tiles you have just laid. This smooths out excess mastic and gives clean horizontal joints. Do not slip the tiles up, down, or sideways in the mastic as you apply them.

8 For fitting, hold tile to be fitted on top of full tile it joins. Put another tile over area to be covered, so it overlaps tile to be cut. Scribe along edge of the top tile onto the bottom one; cut it to the line.

9 Outside corner (use moulded corner tile) goes on first; then work toward inside one. Always put on tile with joining edges tight against each other. Tile pushed against another ploughs up mastic. Tiles "float" if too much mastic is used.

10 Clean joints carefully with pointed stick or corner of tile. Regular cleaner removes hard mastic; fresh smears come off with soft cloth. When you have laid a field of tile, clean off excess mastic.

11 Undercut plaster around bath and lavatory so mastic fills the crack and assures a tight seal between tile, plaster, and bath, or lavatory. Thoroughly clean crevice before you apply the mastic.

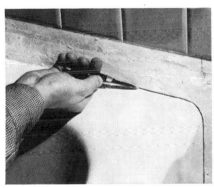

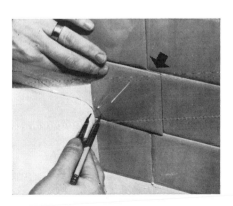

12 Fit around bath by scribing cut with pencil compass. Points are set to width of overlap of tile (arrow). Holding compass horizontal, let steel point follow rim of tub where it joins the wall.

13 Make circular cuts for fitting plastic tile with coping saw. Plywood jig here has cut that allows space for blade. Line up saw with slot; turn tile for cutting.

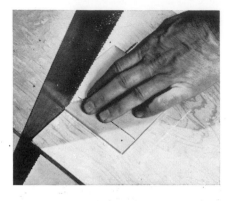

14 Straight cuts on plastic tile are easy with fine-tooth saw held at flat angle with jig. Use hacksaw same way for straight cuts in metal. Use a regular plane for smoothing edges of plastic tile or for final fitting after it has been sawn.

15 Tile around fixtures that you cannot remove from wall, by first cutting away plaster around them with knife or chisel. To get closer fit, bevel edges of tile that will adjoin fixtures. It is best to remove the fixtures whenever you can.

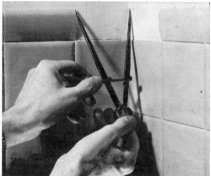

16 Cap strip completes the tiling job. Scribe for mitre cut on outside and inside corners with dividers. Measure from cap strip that mitred piece will adjoin to corner of wall. Transfer measurement to piece to be mitred. Saw on line.

Flexible plastic wall tile comes prepasted

1 Flexible plastic tiles are pre-pasted and ready to apply to ceilings and walls of plaster, plywood, plasterboard, hardboards, and so on. Tiles are 9 x 9 inch size. Patterns are deep-textured, in colours or in simulated wood grain.

2 Application to walls is easy due to flexibility. Tiles can be bent and cut to fit any area, such as in bathroom around bath, lavatory, and flush tank. Complete installation instructions are furnished by dealer who sells you the tile.

How to cover walls with ceramic tiles

For tiling walls with ceramic tile, you may want to use the same precision measuring techniques that are described in the preceding plastic tile section on wall tiling (see page 211).

Either determine the low point in the room and start measuring from there, or set the first tiles around the top rim of the bath.

If you want to start with whole tiles around the edge of the tub, you may save yourself some trimming; the only row that will have to be cut will be tiles next to the floor line.

Materials you will need for setting ceramic tile include the tile and accessories, tile adhesive, wall primer, grout, notched adhesive spreader, glass cutter, pliers, plastic sponge, and a paintbrush. Consult your dealer about any special tiling problems.

1 Start tiling around bath after you have levelled the walls, sanded down any rough spots, and primed walls with a sealer. Be especially careful to keep the first row of tiles level. So that the adhesive does not dry before the tiles are set in place, spread it over small area. Keep it fairly thick—or about the amount which flows from the applicator. Use a twisting motion of your hand to press the tiles in place. As in any tiling job, a level, smooth walls is necessary for good results.

2 To tile away from the bath, mark a straight line out with a level (as shown) and tile from that line down to the floor. This method keeps all tiles that have to be cut next to the floor line. With glass cutter cut tiles to fit around the rim of the bath (arrow). Protect the finish of bath and other bathroom fittings with newspaper or cloths; this will save a lot of cleaning up.

3 Scribe for fitting by overlapping tile to be fitted over edge of next. Mark cut-off point on back of tile; transfer to face of another. Then cut on line.

4 To cut tiles, score face with glass cutter. Place tile over a 2- or 3-inch nail so nail is in line with cut-off, and press down on edges.

5 Tile around pipes and other permanent fixtures this way: Slice tiles in half and nibble out semi-circle in centre of the pieces with pliers or nippers.

6 Soap dish is installed after the tiles. Remove two tiles, apply adhesive to wall and back of fitting, and press in position. Cut and fit tiles around edges.

7 Cap strip and corner tiles go on after field tiles are at height you want. Avoid smearing adhesive above cap strip. If you do, wipe it off immediately.

8 "Grout" joints after the adhesive sets a day or so. Wet joints first with water (about 4 gallons for bathroom) to keep tiles from drawing water from grout.

How to lay mosaic

This method of decoration can be used in many ways—for coffee table tops, bar tops, flower pots, wall plaques, table lamps, bath surrounds, fireplaces, and on walls and floors.

Mosaics come in separate pieces of varying sizes and shapes or in sheet form, about 1 ft square, which can be laid as a whole or cut to suit a particular space or shape.

LAYING METHOD (for level surfaces)
On this type of surface, the mosaic can be fixed direct with an impact adhesive. If laying round a fireplace or hearth, ensure that the adhesive you use is heat-resistant. Grouting is then spread into the gaps between the pieces. Use a rubber spatula, and wipe the surface of the mosaic with a damp cloth or sponge.

LAYING METHOD (for uneven surfaces)
Brick walls: The surface should be covered with a $\frac{1}{2}$ inch cement screed (mix: 3 parts cement to 1 part loam sand). Bed mosaic pieces into the mix. Then fill the gaps between the pieces with grouting material, and clean surface.
Screeded walls: The surface should be wetted with a neat cement grout and then a coating of the following mix laid on $\frac{1}{4}$ inch thick: 3 parts sand: 1 part cement: $\frac{1}{4}$ slaked lime. Butter the backs of the mosaic sheets with a thin coat of neat cement mix and then place in position. Grout the joints as before, and clean the surface. Leave for two days and then mix with a 20 per cent solution of spirits of salts. Then wash off with clean water.

Floors (concrete): Thoroughly clean the floor and then wet it well and apply neat cement grout. Lay a semi-dry mix of 4 parts sand to 1 part cement to the required depth. Butter mosaic sheets with neat cement and lay. Leave floor 24 hours to dry out and then apply grouting. Clean off in usual way.
Floors (wooden): Cover entire area with expanded metal and pin to floor. Then apply cement mix as specified in *Screeded-Walls.* Lay mosaic sheets and allow to dry out for 24 hours. Then grout.

TOOLS REQUIRED:

Trowel; sponge or rags; rubber spatula; metal spatula, shove; watering can with rose; corbiloid-tipped tile cutters; notch adhesive spreader; spirit level; container in which to mix grouting material.

Trowel grout into joints, let set a few minutes, and wipe off excess. Then wipe tiles dry with soft cloth. Let job set a few days before using bath or sink.

How to panel with plywood

Hardwood plywood panelling is easy to install, and in standard sheets it quickly covers an old wall or forms a new one. The panelling is made with a number of surface textures.

Most of the plywood panelling materials are available in pre-finished form, leaving only the preparation of walls and installation of panels to you. And the unfinished panels are made smooth by the manufacturer, so that all you must do is remove surface dirt with fine sandpaper, install the panels, and finish them.

Step 1 is preparation of the wall. Check that it is level, and be certain to fill all holes or cracks. Panels may be applied directly to an old wall, but it is generally desirable to use 2 × 1 battens to fix them. The battens are generally fixed about 24" apart, and vertical strips "let in" where panel joints occur. If the wall appears "hollow" in spots, pack out the

Install panels over battens

2 × 1 battens make ideal "framework" for panelling, which can be applied over virtually any wall surface, and may be packed out to correct wall defects.

Nail strips horizontally about 24 inches apart, and vertically at joints in the panelling.

When fixing 2 × 1 battens to an uneven wall surface, use a spirit level to obtain correct horizontal and vertical positions. Pack where necessary with strips of hardboard or off-cuts of timber.

Fix to the wall either by masonry nails (much the simpler method) or by plugging the wall and then nailing or screwing through the battens into the plugs. If the wall is of plaster-board or lath and plaster, use either a spring or gravity toggle (for fixing instructions, see page 142).

Allow air to flow behind the panelling by cutting a series of V-shaped notches in the 2 × 1 battens and by allowing $\frac{1}{8}$ inch gap between ceiling and top of panels. Fix any insulating material to the battens before the panels are placed in position.

Note the position of the battens so that any shelf or other fixtures can be fixed through the panels directly into the battens.

battens. Where needed, a moisture barrier should be applied to the walls before fixing the battens.

Step 2 is laying out the job. Place the panels about the room to plan sequence for desired grain and colour effects. For most interiors, it is practical to start in one corner and work round.

Step 3 is application of panels. Many of the panelling materials are manufactured with tongue-and-groove joints already so there is no problem in joining them. Others butt together and are prepared so that they form a simple V-joint. Some are joined together with a metal fixing plate.

Where panels are butt jointed, make sure that they are fixed together as tightly as possible. They may be fastened with panel pins which are later set, and the holes filled with plastic wood.

This application is almost nail-less

Plywood panels may be installed direct onto a sound wall with contact adhesive and nails. Do not install panelling over old plaster if it is in bad repair.

Adhesive cement makes a good, waterproof bond that needs reinforcing by nails only at corners and where panels meet doors and windows.

Wall and panel back must be coated with adhesive. There can be no second guessing about application; once the two-coated surfaces are in contact, they are bonded permanently. Use paper buffer between panel and wall if you wish to juggle a little for position.

Apply contact adhesive to back of plywood panel (foreground) and to bare wall with old paintbrush. Let adhesive become tacky before you apply the panel.

Fit the panel carefully into place, and press it to the wall—allowing $\frac{1}{4}''$ clearance at top, bottom. Entire piece must be pressed firmly for good contact.

Reinforce bond by nailing to wall with masonry or panel pins. Use measure so that pins are equidistant; this gives a professional look to the job.

Some manufacturers make an entire "kit" which includes wood panelling or planks, battens, and special fasteners to attach panelling.

For inside corners, the most common procedure is to use a simple butt joint, covering with a cove or quarter-round moulding. For outside corners, panels should be cut to fit flush to edge of the 2 × 1 batten.

"Finish" the edge of pannelling and the side of the 2 × 1 batten by covering with two lengths of half-round beading or a strip of panelling cut to the right width to cover the panel edge and the 2 × 1. Finally, finish by one of the methods shown on page 221.

Kits have all materials for panelling

Some panelling—such as these pre-finished plywood planks—is available in a kit which contains everything necessary to cover a specified area.

Planks have grooved and lipped edges into which metal clips fit to hold planks to battens. Wall battens, in turn, are grooved to hold metal clips. When joined, planks cover the clips, presenting a neat V joint.

Battens are nailed to walls horizontally. Clips are inserted and nailed in place to hold planks. If being used to partition a room, a backing of plywood, wallboard, or similar material should be applied to partition supports before battens are fixed.

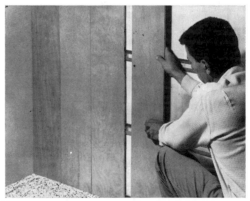

Planks slip into place so that clips engage bottom lip of plank. Top lip covers clips, forms V joint with previously applied plank. Face nail planks at top and bottom where they will be covered.

Ordinary tongued and grooved matchboarding can also be used to panel a room. Fix 2 × 1 battens to the wall as already described on page 218. Fix battens vertically if the boards are to run horizontally round the room or horizontally if the boards are to be fixed vertically. As far as possible, avoid joining boards together in the middle of a run—it not only looks ugly but it is sometimes difficult to fit the next board because the tongues and grooves may vary slightly.

Fix boards to battens with panel pins—heads punched home and holes filled. Or make a feature of the nailing by using copper nails—if the latter method is chosen, seal boards quickly before the copper heads dull.

Corners, etc. can be finished with mouldings—see methods and styles described on page 221. Note the position of the 2 × 1 battens so that any shelf or other fixture can be supported through the boards into the 2 × 1.

Any electrical alterations necessary should be carried out before the panelling is fixed. Support holes cut for sockets and switches with short lengths of 2 × 1.

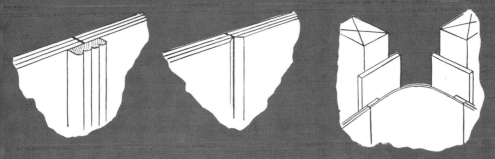

Joints and corners of plywood panelling can be handled a number of different ways. *Butt joint* (left) is covered with a moulding strip. The moulding covers any gaps that may develop in the joint. *V joint* (centre) is one of the most popular joints. The bevel at the edge of each panel is obtained with a sharp plane or with a sanding block. Do not cut deeper than face veneer. At right is a *veneer corner strip*, a smooth inside corner made from a thin strip of matching veneer resting on thin strips of packing. It is bent around the corner and tacked into place onto the wall battens.

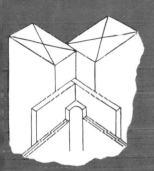

Inset cover moulding (left) gives rounded corner at less expense than veneer corner strip. Join corners with strips of ordinary cove moulding. Set moulding in place first, then butt panels against it. *Cove moulding over the joint* (centre) is another way of finishing inside corners. Butt panels, then cover joint with stock moulding. Leave some space between panels for expansion. Moulding will hide the gap. *Butted panels* (right) is the simplest way of all to turn an inside corner when panelling with plywood. This method provides a joint that is clean and square—and easy to make.

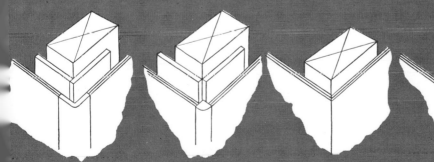

Outside corners may be done these four ways. *Corner strips* (left) will do the job neatly. Another way is to set *quarter round* (second from left) at corner and butt panels of plywood tightly against it. If you have access to a power saw, it is a simple matter to *mitre the edges* of meeting panels (third from left). This style matches butted joints on inside corners. *Butted and sanded edges* (right) are a fourth way of treating outside corners. First butt the two panels, then use sandpaper or plane to flatten the sharp corner edge, as shown in illustration.

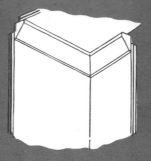 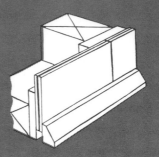

Triangular ceiling moulding produces a heavy effect. Choose design for ceiling lines and bases for harmonious appearance. Triangular moulding (right) matches.

Triangular floor moulding goes well with similar-type ceiling moulding. Trim off the sharp edges with a plane or sandpaper to eliminate possibility of splintering.

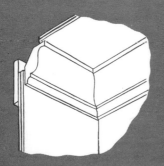 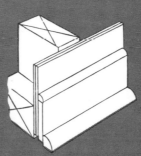 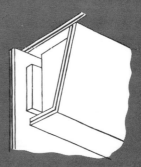

Crown moulding at ceiling offers decorative details at those joints. Match with *plywood moulding at base* (centre) You can build up plywood, quarter-round base.

Cornice at ceiling line (right) is a simple decoration to build. You will probably have enough scraps to make it. Match it with an angle strip at the base (see lower left).

Angle strip at floor matches ceiling cornice. Build a simple angled moulding around base, blocking it in well so that it will hold up under normal wear and tear.

Quarter-round moulding at ceiling line (centre drawing) and at base (lower right) is simplest method of concealing joint between panelling, floor and ceiling.

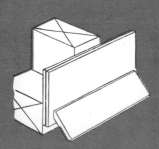 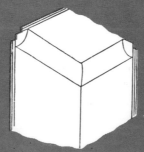 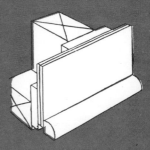

Panelling with hardboard

Pre-finished or unfinished hardboard panels are an ideal wall covering.

The pre-finished material is generally tempered hardboard with a tough, plastic surface in solid colours or in simulated marble or tiles. It is also available in perforated sheets—there are various designs—and reeded. The latter should be matched at the grooves while the perforated sheets should be cut so that the pattern matches.

Pre-finished material may be installed with adhesive, adhesive and pins, or pins alone. Undecorated hardboard may be applied and decorated.

Most hardboards can be fixed to the wall battens by using special pins, the heads of which go below the surface of the sheet when hammered home—this avoids a lot of tedious punching. Pin sheets at intervals of not more than 6″ apart, particularly round the edges.

To avoid marring surfaces of pre-finished boards (left), you can apply them to old walls or in new buildings by using adhesive. Where it is necessary to "follow" uneven walls or to overcome any curve in the sheets, brace with battens across to the opposite wall

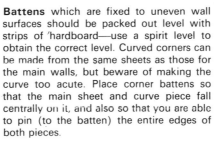

Battens which are fixed to uneven wall surfaces should be packed out level with strips of 'hardboard—use a spirit level to obtain the correct level. Curved corners can be made from the same sheets as those for the main walls, but beware of making the curve too acute. Place corner battens so that the main sheet and curve piece fall centrally on it, and also so that you are able to pin (to the batten) the entire edges of both pieces.

Upholsterer's gimp in leather or artificial leather of harmonizing colour makes an attractive joint treatment for hardboard panels (see lower left-hand photograph). Alternatively, use one of the many plastic edgings available.

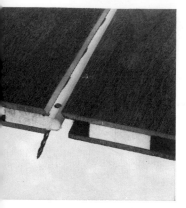

Hardboard panels can be made into tongue and grooved sheets by adding lengths of 2 × 1 down each edge to be joined (see photograph). The panels are fixed to the wall through the tongue while the groove is pinned to the tongue. Note that the underside strip of hardboard on the groove edge is a little narrower than the width of the tongue—this is to allow for the fixing nail and to ensure that the face edges butt up tightly.

See page 107 for chart giving sizes of hardboard, etc. It is advisable to "condition" undecorated sheets either by dampening the backs (rough surface) or by leaving in the room in which they are to be fixed for about 48 hours.

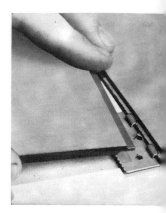

Building a partition wall

Many handyman projects include building a wall to divide rooms or to enclose utilities. Before beginning work, it is wise to study the construction of your home and in particular the room you wish to divide.

Note how the inner wall(s) are made and whether they continue through to upper or lower floors. Ceilings are most likely to be lath and plaster or plaster-board with a skim of plaster. Walls will be of brick, breeze or building blocks, or lath and plaster. If the wall is the latter type, then the possible position of your partition is rather limited because the upright studs will be at 16" centres and the partition must be fixed through the plaster into one of these studs.

Draw a plan of the room to scale (1" to 1′) so that traffic, furniture, door position, etc. can be studied before the partition is erected. Other details to watch when planning a new room are electrical points—both power and lighting; direct daylight; or borrowed light.

When you have decided on the location of the wall, mark its position on existing walls, ceiling and floor, and make sure that this is done accurately and that all lines are square.

Use good quality materials and beware of short cuts. The new "wall" can be made up in sections (see photograph) or in one piece. All fixing holes should be drilled in the studs which will be fixed to walls, ceiling and floor. Erect sections singly but bolt together as you go. If a door is being inserted in the partition, then use a standard size door.

When the partition has been fixed in position, and before covering with either hardboard, plasterboard or panels run in any electrical wiring and fix any insulating material.

Place door in position, mark out hinge and door stop positions. Cut mortise for hinges—use a sharp chisel (see photograph) and temporarily fix the door in the opening. Check door stop position and fix. Check door for opening—do not forget to allow for floorcovering. Cut and mitre door mouldings and fix—these should be set back about $\frac{1}{4}$" to $\frac{1}{2}$" from the edge of the door frame (see photograph).

Fit the door lock and keep when you are satisfied that the door is hanging correctly (see page 262 about locks).

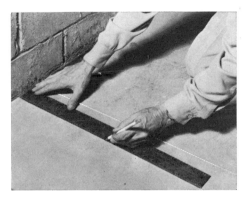

Mark out on the floor, walls, ceiling, the exact position of the partition. A plumb line will give the correct vertical on the walls. Join up across floor and ceiling. On the ceiling note the position of the joists so that the partition can be fixed to them. Note also any unevenness of any surface in case the partition framework needs to be packed out to keep it square.

The partition framework is made up from 2 x 2 or 2 x 3 timber. When making up frames, ensure that they are square. Frames can be made up in one or more sections according to the size of the partition. Whatever course you adopt, keep the upright studs at a standard distance apart. This avoids guessing at a later stage when various fixings—coat hooks, picture hooks, wall lights, etc.—need to be made.

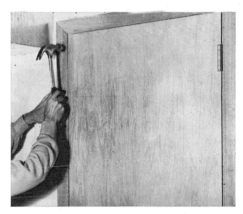

A very sharp chisel is needed to cut the rebates for door hinges. It is better to cut them under size rather than over because the under size rebate can always be enlarged.

Check that all the beadings are at equal distances from the frame. Avoid marking beading with hammer by punching home nail heads. It is easier to knot and prime beadings before fixing.

Installing plasterboard

A quick and economical way to finish a wall is with plasterboard. The plasterboard comes in standard 8′ × 4′ sheets.

The standard material has a tough paper surface on both sides of a gypsum core. As shown in the pictures below, you can cut the board simply by scoring the paper covering and then snapping the core.

After you have cut and sanded the plasterboard, nail to studs and joists. Nail with equidistant galvanised nails. Allow the last hammer blow to make a slight dimple in the board. Fill the dimples with filler. There are several ways either to hide or accent the joint between sheets. One method which conceals the joints completely is given on opposite page.

Plasterboard is low in cost, is easy to work with, and fireproof. Another advantage is its smooth, strong surface which can be finished easily with paint, wallpaper or plaster.

One side of the board is prepared for plastering, the other for decorating —so fix it the right way round.

A sharp knife cuts plasterboard to the required size

1 Score-and-break is a good method to use for making straight cuts in plasterboard. Use a saw if you want L-shaped or irregular cuts. Run sharp knife along a straight edge in order to cut paper covering on one side.

2 To break the panel, slide it over so the scored line comes just at the edge of panels stacked underneath, and then snap down. If the scored line is diagonal, set a board edgewise under panel and snap down.

3 Cut through paper on back, following the crease formed by folding broken end over at right angles. Normally, broken end hangs down and you cut the paper from underside. Sand edges of board until the core is smooth.

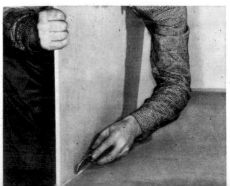

These easy-to-make T-braces serve as "helpers" for you

T-braces effectively support plasterboard panels against the ceiling joists. Short diagonal pieces from leg to the crosspiece are used to add extra rigidity and strength. Two braces of this type are usually required to give the necessary support to the plasterboard panels. Wedge the T-braces against the floor with crosspiece set under the panel and joist, as pictured at right.

Covering joins

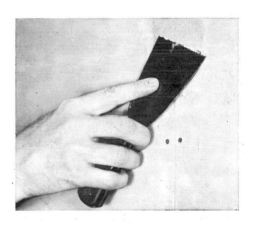

1 Spread plaster or filler in shallow channel formed by two adjoining tapered edges of plasterboard. Use a wide scraper. The filler should be slightly thinner than normal.

2 Imbed tape and centre it over joint after you spread plaster or filler down joint recess for several feet. Tape has tapered edges, and it is perforated to let the trapped air escape.

3 Thin layer of plaster or filler over tape is next step. Spread it out and "feather" the edges. After it is dry, apply a second surfacing coat. Then sand the joints to remove bumps.

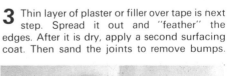

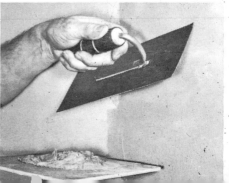

Inside and outside corners are taped like other joints

1 Eliminate cracks at inside corners by using perforated tape, fill same way as at flat joint. Crease tape along centre, apply filler. Use two or three surfacing coats.

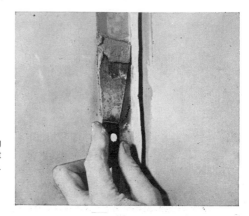

An alternative finish (after filling nail heads in the normal way) is to pin a length of $\frac{3}{4}''$ or $1''$ quarter round beading into the corner. At ceiling level, expanded polystyrene coving can be used.

2 Where pipes go through plasterboard, cement two pieces of tape to wall around pipe, notching each piece to fit around half of it. Imbed tape, finish job like flat joints.

Reinforce openings made for electrical switches with wooden blocks glued to the back of the plasterboard. These blocks will take the fixing screws of the switch plate. Alternative fixings for cavity walls are described on page 144.

If shelves are to be erected, then the fixing screws must pass through into the upright support timber.

If you use metal foil for insulation, it must be pinned to the support timbers *before* the plasterboard sheets are fixed. This applies also to hardboard and other forms of panelling.

Keep out the damp

Dampness in the home is unpleasant and unhealthy. It is impossible to store things with safety, non-stainless metals soon rust over, mildew is quick to form, and decorations are disfigured in a matter of weeks.

To the inexperienced handyman, the cause of dampness may be difficult to find. Here are some of the causes:
1. Condensation
2. Rising ground moisture
3. Rain penetrating walls
4. Faulty guttering and/or down pipes, door and window frames
5. Vegetation growing against walls
6. Broken damp-proof course or no damp-proof course at all.

Of these causes, condensation is the primary offender. If you are in doubt as to the cause of your particular problem, consult a professional builder. But first do some simple checking yourself.

A. The simple solution may be that the gutters or downpipes have become blocked with leaves. Check all gutterings and downpipes for leaks, which you may find at roof level and not at the actual point of the damp patch on the wall. This is because the water has run down the outside of the downpipe until it has reached a fixing which has then diverted it on to the wall.

B. Water getting in through porous and/or damaged roof flashings, tiles or slates, could cause damp patches on walls at ceiling level. These leaks could well be quite a distance away from the actual damp patch. This is because the water runs down the under side of the roof until it reaches a projection of some sort, from which it drips and causes damage. This type of leak should be looked for while it is raining. (See pages 286-7 for gutter and roof repairs).

C. Earth or rubble stacked against an outside wall will allow moisture to bypass the damp-proof course.

D. If a path or garden level is too high, rain splashes "jump" up the wall and above the damp-proof course. If this is allowed to continue, water will eventually get through. The damp-proof course should be at least 6" above ground level.

E. Sheds or lean-to's butting to walls may be without flashings to take the rain water away from the wall.

F. A badly fitting window or door frame would allow water to get in between frame and brickwork.

CURES

A. Repair damaged gutter and downpipe. Allow inside wall to dry out. Treat with one of the silicone waterproof liquids and re-decorate.

B. Repair damage and treat walls as (A).

C. Remove pile of earth or rubble, clean wall by washing, then leave to dry out.

D. If it is not possible to lower the path or garden, then the wall should be treated with a silicone water-repellant liquid.

E. Flashings should be fitted at least two courses of brick above the roof of a shed or lean-to.

CONDENSATION

Black or brown spots of mould growth on a wall are a sure sign of condensation. A simple check is to stick a square of aluminium foil (6" to 9") on the wall where it is damp. If it is condensation, then little beads of moisture will appear on the surface of the foil—dampness from any other cause could not penetrate the foil.

CURE

Try to keep rooms at an even temperature —sudden and rapid warming at night of rooms kept cold all day is asking for condensation. Ventilation is important and, if possible, an outward flow of air should be arranged. The intake of air should come from hall or landing and not directly from outside. Ventilation should be as high as possible. Extractor fans reduce condensation considerably.

Avoid painting bathroom or kitchen walls with gloss paint—this asks for condensation to form with the steam.

Cold walls (around lavatory cisterns) should be lined with expanded poly-styrene sheeting, and ceiling tiles also help to reduce condensation. Wash off all black or brown marks, rinse down with clean water, allow to dry out, apply polystyrene sheeting (it comes in rolls $24\frac{1}{4}'' \times 30'$) and then re-decorate. Plasterboard or insulating board fixed to walls will also cure condensation.

Window condensation can only be cured by double glazing (see page 365).

In older type property where rising damp occurs, cure by dig-ging a trench along the offending wall and applying liquid bitumen to the wall above and below ground level. With a wide scraper or small trowel, remove the dirt that has stuck to the masonry. Get the surface as clean as possible; time spent here will pay off in a lasting repair job.

Use a pail of water and a stiff bristled brush to scrub and rinse the surface thoroughly—use of a spray from a hose will make the excavation too muddy. Chisel or rake out faulty joints and repoint. If the crack is less than $\frac{1}{8}$-inch wide, you will not need to fill it. The liquid bitumen will fill narrow cracks or openings easily.

When the wall surface has dried out, paint on liquid bitumen, ensuring that it is well brushed into all the small cracks and crevices. If necessary, apply another coat. It is important that no hair line cracks or holes are left in the "skin" that the liquid bitumen forms because water will find this blemish and the problem will recur.

When liquid bitumen has dried out, the trench should be re-filled with shingle or ashes or clinker. This allows water to run away from the wall. When re-filling the trench, be sure not to puncture the liquid bitumen skin with either stones or shovel. If shingle and clinker is not available, then fill the trench with earth that has a high content of stones.

How to waterproof exterior walls

A coat of silicone water-repellent liquid prevents rain water from entering brickwork, but at the same time allows the wall to breathe. It can be applied to brick, cement, stone, rendered walls and similar masonry materials. It is colourless so that surfaces treated can be decorated in the normal way.

Apply liquid only after wall(s) have been washed down (plain water), all cracks filled and any defective pointing made good. Seal can be applied with a wide soft brush, starting at the top and working down; or by spray at low pressure. One application is normally sufficient but a second coat may be applied six hours after the first. Do not attempt to thin down these liquids—they must be used neat.

Cement-base masonry paint helps stop moisture

Dampen wall with water before applying paint. Wall should be only damp, not soaking wet; large brush (shown) is handy way to moisten masonry.

Apply paint with brush as you would any other paint. Work quickly and only mix small amounts of "paint" at a time. This type of paint goes off or hardens quickly, thus becoming unworkable. It will also cover up small cracks and holes.

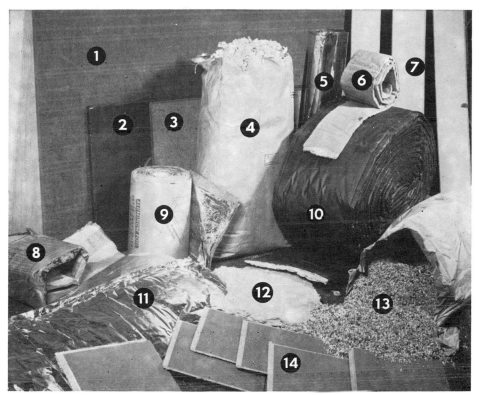

Insulation materials include these products: (1, 2 and 3) insulated sheets generally installed during construction, also used for protecting water cisterns; (4) rock wool, loose fill; (5) aluminium-foil paper in rolls; and (6) fibre- glass pipe lagging; also (7) rigid polystyrene; (8) blankets for storage tanks; (9) reinforced building paper; (10) fibre-glass blanket; (11) foil-covered mineral-wool blanket; (12) mineral wool batts; (13) loose fill, (14) tiles.

How to insulate your home

Most of the insulating materials manufactured today can be installed by the handyman, but leave to skilled operators methods of insulation such as laying foam polystyrene (under pressure) in the cavity of outside walls.

In winter, a house which has been efficiently insulated will retain the heat that has been created within. In the summer, insulation provides a barrier against solar heat.

There are many ways of installing insulating materials, but the method employed will depend on the structure of the building concerned. Some methods are shown here, and they can be adapted to suit individual needs.

While insulating walls and ceilings, do not forget to lag pipes and water cisterns, both hot and cold.

Pour loose fill between joists evenly. Do not skimp. A layer of 1½" to 2" will provide good insulation. Make a simple gauge so that the correct depth is maintained over the entire ceiling area.

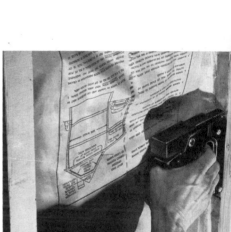

Rock-wool loose fill insulation is easily installed by pouring it between the joists. Both materials can be pushed into the most inaccessible places with the aid of a broom.

Staple edges of blanket insulation to framing. When needed, trim blankets to fit space. Tacks or staples do adequate job. Blanket is fastened to face of framing or to edges, if paper flanges will not interfere with the wall finish materials.

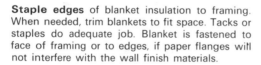

Fasten ends of blanket carefully at the top and the bottom of framing. Cut to fit tightly but only cut when absolutely necessary, otherwise you will get heat loss.

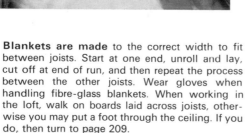

Blankets are made to the correct width to fit between joists. Start at one end, unroll and lay, cut off at end of run, and then repeat the process between the other joists. Wear gloves when handling fibre-glass blankets. When working in the loft, walk on boards laid across joists, otherwise you may put a foot through the ceiling. If you do, then turn to page 209.

Leave air space between single layers of aluminium-foil (reflective) insulation. It is tacked to joists as shown here. Make sure edges are butted or lapped together.

Metal foil can be fixed to the underside of roofing rafters in the same way as to the joists. If there is not any roofing felt under the slates or tiles, then it is worthwhile fixing a single sheet of foil or reinforced building paper to the rafters in addition to that between the joists.

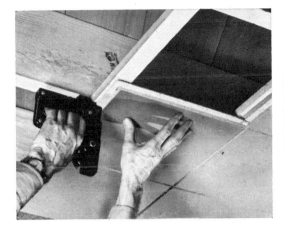

Expanded polystyrene tiles can either be stapled or glued. Photograph shows tiles being stapled to the 2 × 1 battens of a new ceiling. They are equally effective stuck to existing plastered surfaces. Tiles come in various thicknesses, in 9", 12", 18" and 24" squares.

Reinforced building paper or tarred paper fixed to the rafters immediately under the tiles or slates will not only insulate but will give protection against spray from driving rain coming in between the slates or tiles.

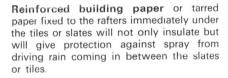

A few reminders on insulation

Whichever type of insulating material is chosen, remember that it must cover the area in question. There is considerable heat loss through any areas left uncovered. If there are any inaccessible spots, it might be easier to use a loose fill which can be pushed into place with a broom, rake or even a stick. Or make a chute so that loose fill can be poured in. Blankets can be pushed into these spots providing that there are no wires or other obstacles which will cause the blanket to pile up on itself.

So, before buying any insulating material, look at the area to be covered and calculate how you can best deal with any problems.

One form of insulation that cannot be carried out by the amateur is filling the cavity between the inner and outer walls of a building with a polystyrene foam. This has to be done under pressure—to ensure that the entire cavity is filled—and at several places along the outer wall. This is done by drilling a series of small holes through the wall and **not** by the removal of rows of bricks.

New floors for old

Old floors of both softwood and hardwood can be restored by sanding off old polish, varnish and dirt. Sanding machines can be hired by the day or hour. They come in various sizes to suit the area of floor, so do not hire a large machine to tackle a small floor area—it does not save time or money.

Before beginning to sand, remove all tacks, nails, old pieces of lino. Any nails or tacks that cannot be pulled out should be punched $\frac{1}{4}''$ below the surface of the floor. Renail loose boards and replace any that are badly split or damaged.

When sanding, work as far as possible along the length of the boards, first with a coarse paper and then with a fine. Do not try and get into corners round door frames—wait until you have completed the main area and then either scrape with a long-handled scraper or use a power drill with sanding disc attachment.

When using a sanding disc, take care not to mark the skirting boards—sand about $\frac{1}{4}''$ away from them. This strip can be cleaned off with a hand scraper later. Use edge of sanding disc only—if used flat, it is difficult to control. For this type of job, it is better to use the metal discs.

Where disc sanding cannot make contact with old finish—close in around woodwork, door frames, steps, etc.—a long handled scraper cleans floor down to new wood. Here it may be necessary to touch up the floor with hand sanding and steel wool to erase scraper marks. Watch so you do not gouge floor with blade.

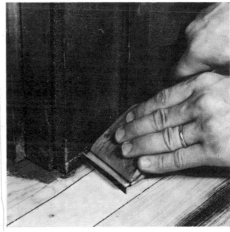

Brush attachment on vacuum cleaner is best for cleaning entire floor area preceding application of finish to surface. Use brush to free corners of any sanding residue. Before final sanding, fill any wide cracks or splits in boards with a plastic wood that matches colour of the floor and sand off after it has dried.

There are many seals suitable for wood floors. They can be applied with a brush, cloth or mop. Apply seal evenly across the grain and then work back along the length (grain) of the boards. Avoid leaving pools of seal. Allow first coat to dry before applying a second, and always make sure that the floor is dust free before applying seal—a softwood floor

may need three coats. The floor should be lightly sanded or rubbed down with steel wool between coats of seal. A rag dampened with seal and rubbed over the floor is a good way to remove dust. When last coat is dry—really dry the floor should be wax polished and, if possible, buffed with an electric polisher.

Another way to finish hardwood floors is to stain them to the desired colour and then hand wax. Rub well into wood and machine polish after each coat. Three coats of wax will be needed to obtain the desired finish. The wax can be either liquid or solid and this type of finish gives the floor more of a natural look.

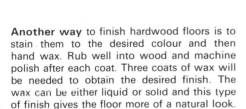

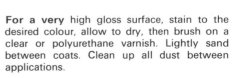

For a very high gloss surface, stain to the desired colour, allow to dry, then brush on a clear or polyurethane varnish. Lightly sand between coats. Clean up all dust between applications.

How to remove a floor scratch

Shallow scratches. Steel wool and a solvent cleaner for removing spots will erase scratches that do not go deeper than finish. Saturate a pad of medium-coarse steel wool with cleaning fluid, rub in direction of grain. Never rub across grain. When the finish is off, smooth the surface with pad of fine steel wool.

Deep scratches. Use plastic wood filler if scratch goes deeper than finish. After removing finish, smooth wood with sandpaper. Then fill scratch above floor surface. Remove excess with the straight edge of a wide scraper. When dry, sand flush with floor. Clean with rag and cleaning fluid. Filler is made in various wood tones, so try and match filler to floor.

Re-finishing. In both cases it is necessary to re-finish the marred areas. If floor is varnished, re-finish with varnish. Apply with brush, dry overnight. If spot is glossier than rest of the floor, dull it with fine steel wool. If floor is waxed, then rub wax into the scratched area until it matches the rest of the floor. Holes made by heels cannot be filled. You have to live with them or sand the floor right off.

How to silence floor squeaks

There is no need to worry about squeaks and groans from floor and stairs —your home is not about to collapse.

But such noises are annoying and, in some cases, can be cured in a very short time.

Squeaks are caused by boards that rub against each other or against nails. They may be caused by age, changes in weather, or unseasoned timber, or by a joist working loose.

To silence squeaks permanently, the loose boards must be fixed—but this is easier said than done. There are several temporary measures you can take, and it may be a question of repeating them if it is not possible to get to the seat of the trouble.

Glue it down. Wood floors in your home may start to creak soon after you start your central heating. In such cases try filling cracks in the area with liquid glue thinned with an equal portion of water. After dripping the glue into cracks in the area, let it dry completely before you walk on the floor.

Or try lubrication. Fine powdered graphite will often eliminate floor squeaks. Puff the powder into floor cracks in the vicinity of the squeak. The idea is to get powdered graphite on the spot where floor boards rub each other or a nail. This can be done using an old plastic tube. Cut off tube, clean out, fill with graphite, fold and reseal with tape.

Here are some permanent ways of dealing with squeaks:

A wedge might do the trick if you can conveniently reach the under side of the floor. Tip the end of the wedge with glue, but do not drive it in too tightly because it might lift the nails above floor level, so damaging floorcoverings. You may need more than one wedge if boards or joists— or both—have warped.

Loose joists: If possible, brace the joist and pack it up, either on its sleeper wall or where it enters the main wall of the house. If the joist is sitting on the damp-proof course, be sure not to break it. If the damp-proof course has been damaged, insert a new section.

Loose or warped floorboards: These should be re-nailed to the joists. Drive nails in at an angle through the good wood. Alternatively, use existing holes and screw boards to joists. Warped boards can be fixed as above. Or lift the board, reverse it, and then nail or screw it down.

Another spot for squeaks is where a section of a board has been lifted and put back with the end of the cut board only just resting on the joist. Lift the board and nail a length of 2 × 1 to the side of the joist. This length of 2 × 1 should also be pinned tightly up to the under side of the floorboards and be wider than the width of the single board which is being re-fixed.

A badly damaged or split board should be lifted and renewed entirely.

Replace broken and damaged flooring this way

1 Before you begin repairs, assess the extent of the damage to the flooring. Locate position of floor joists and bore starter holes so boards can be cut flush with the joists. The holes will give entry for your keyhole saw or power sabre saw.

2 If boards are tongue and groove, avoid cutting off tongue of old board at edge of opening. Saw the boards flush with joists at each end of the opening. If the area to be renewed is large, stagger the new boards so that no more than one or two of the board ends will be flush.

3 Nail support pieces to joists at both ends of the opening. Coat the cleats and the underside and ends of the new floor board with a wood preservative. If you notice moisture under the floor, do not ignore it, but try and discover its source, or consult your builder.

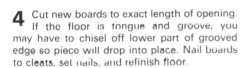

4 Cut new boards to exact length of opening. If the floor is tongue and groove, you may have to chisel off lower part of grooved edge so piece will drop into place. Nail boards to cleats, set nails, and refinish floor.

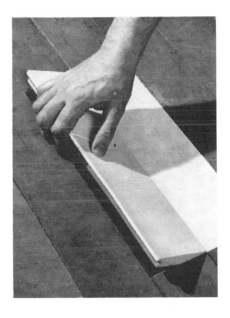

Ends of floorboards that go under the skirting can be tightened by inserting wedges between them and the skirting board. Each wedge should be as wide as possible so that the pressure is spread over a wide area.

Surface care. A block of wood used between hammer and floor surface will prevent hammer rings. It is also possible to locate the position of a joist by tapping the block with a hammer—a higher and more solid sound indicates its position.

Stair squeaks

1 Nail treads down, as most stair squeaks result from a tread rubbing against the riser below or against a stringer at one end. Drill pilot holes to form wide "V's" and drive nails into riser or stringer.

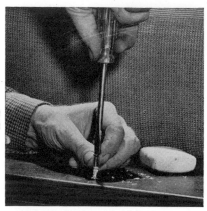

2 Or use screws—No. 8's 1½″ or 2″ flathead screws. Drill a hole for screw body just through the tread or top floor. Countersink the screwhead and fill with plastic wood. Sand smooth.

3 Hide screwheads with boat plugs, available at a marine supply shop, as they are better than dowels. Coat plug with glue, and tap it into place over sunken screw. Chisel flush, then sand and stain. The same method of fixing applies to dowels.

4 When the underside of a squeaking stairway is readily accessible, you can often stop squeaks by tightening loose wedges between treads or stringers. Coat wedges with glue, drive them into place, then nail.

Except for cure No. 4, you will need the help of another person. Your helper should stand on the offending stair while the cure is being carried out. The extra weight ensures that tread and riser are brought together as tightly as possible.

It is also possible to cure the squeak from the under side by screwing metal angle brackets to tread and riser. Once again you will need the weight of a second person on the offending tread to hold it down while you fix the brackets.

Hard-wearing floor tiles shown on the right are: (1) *thermoplastic* —for any room in the home, though some have limited resistance to grease and are therefore unsuitable for kitchens; (2) *linoleum*—easy to care for, suitable for any room; (3) *rubber*— warm and waterproof, can be used throughout the home (particularly in children's rooms because it is quiet underfoot); (4) *cork*—warm both to touch and in appearance, quiet, soft underfoot, some tiles impregnated with vinyl to give a grease and stain proof finish; (5) *vinyl*—easy to lay and clean, impervious to grease and damp, for use in any room where really sturdy floor-covering is needed.

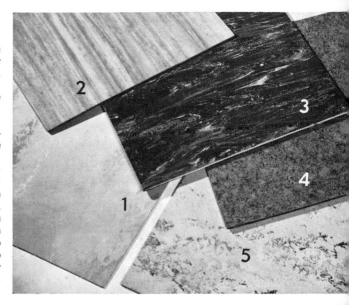

How to lay a tile floor

Before beginning to lay tiles or linoleum, consider the following points:

1. Wood Floors. Check that the floor is level; that there are no loose boards; and that all tacks and nails which project above floor level are removed or punched below the surface.

Replace any damaged boards; fill any wide cracks between boards, either with a strip of beading or cellulose filler—sand smooth afterwards. A slightly uneven floor can be levelled with a sanding machine— remember to keep machine moving or you will "cap" the floor. A badly pitted or cracked floor can be levelled by pinning down sheets of $\frac{1}{8}$" hardboard—use the special corrugated shank and nail because there is a tendency for hardboard sheets to "spring" when walked upon.

2. Concrete Floors. The floor should be level and any holes filled with a cement mix. Concrete should be dry— it takes about twelve weeks or more according to weather conditions for new floors to dry out. One of the brush-on cold bitumen proofing mixtures will curb the use of moisture. For cork tiles, it also acts as an adhesive.

Both types of floor should be as dust free as possible before you attempt to lay underfelt, linoleum tiles, or any other floor covering.

Any doors that open on to the proposed new floor should be taken off their hinges and re-hung after the floor has been laid. Do this because it is possible that you will raise the level of the floor which in turn will either stop the door opening or damage newly-laid flooring. It is also easier to work around the threshold when the door is removed.

Lay paper underfelt butt jointed, and allow no overlap. Cut strip to length, place in position on floor, roll back half-way. Spread adhesive and lay rolled-up half. Roll loose half back and repeat laying procedure.

Roll down underfelt with the special roller (the ends allow you to go right up to the skirting board) which can be hired at a small charge. The same roller is used to roll down tiles and lino, and its weight is adjustable.

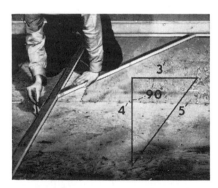

Work from the centre of the room by marking middle of the "master" wall. Nail long string to floor on mark. Use home-made king-size square to guide string to opposite wall; nail here. Cross string centre with second string stretched to centres of end walls.

Start your pattern by laying loose tiles along strings that are stretched across the floor. The centre point of the strings can have a whole tile laid over it, or be intersection of four tiles. For even border, centre of field may have to be moved.

Useful data on tiles:
* Vinyl: Measure 9″ × 9″ and $\frac{1}{16}$″-$\frac{1}{8}$″ thick
* Rubber: Measure 9″ × 9″ and $\frac{1}{8}$″-$\frac{3}{16}$″ thick
  Lino: Measure 9″ × 9″ and $\frac{1}{8}$″ thick
* Cork: Measure 12″ × 12″ and $\frac{1}{4}$″-$\frac{1}{2}$″ thick
  Thermoplastic: Measure 9″ × 9″ and $\frac{1}{8}$″ thick

    Some plastic and linoleum tiles are self-adhesive—they need only to be immersed in water before laying.

* Larger sizes available.

An easy way to plan a design for your floors is on squared paper with coloured pencils.

Generally, a small room looks best with a one-colour field and a border of the same tile. If you have a large room, you can use designs, checkerboard effects, and so on.

Basically, all the tiles are laid the same way, except asphalt. However, you should always use the adhesive recommended by the manufacturer for the particular type of flooring material and its condition of use.

Thermoplastic tiles are not rolled as are other resilient tiles, and generally you must wait until the adhesive dries before you lay tiles.

Lay tiles (or lino) in an even temperature of 65°-70°F—it is easier to work tiles (or lino) when they are warm.

To fit the border, lay the tile to be cut on top of adjacent already-laid tile. Lay a third tile over it, snug against the wall, to use as a guide. Score along edge of guide tile. Cut border tile along that mark. Thermoplastic tile breaks along a scored line; the others can be cut

Start laying tile by spreading adhesive along one string. Put down a single row, guided by the string. Continue in a pyramid until all *whole* tiles are down on half of room. Then lay the other half of the room, leaving the border to do last.

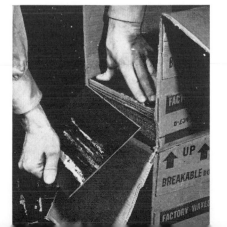

Breaking a tile is the easiest way to get it trimmed when you are fitting borders. Score surface where it is to be broken and break along this line by clamping it between other tiles in a carton. Jar the end sharply with the heel of your hand. This technique works, too, on the edge of a table if you use a board to clamp tile. Cork tiles should be cut right through.

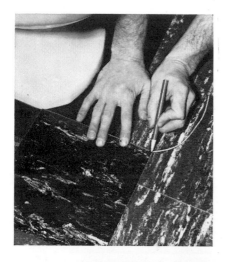

Cutting the tiles: A linoleum knife, or even household scissors follow a curve cutting linoleum, cork, plastic, or rubber tile. Tiles are easier when warm.

To fit around fixtures, place tile to be cut precisely over adjacently laid tile. Use whole tile to mark curves, point by point. Join points; cut tile along line. For how to make templates see page 40.

Lay diagonal field on 45-degree angle. Establish width of border by laying row of tiles along string. If space at walls is less than half a tile, slide entire row $4\frac{1}{2}$ inches back on diagonal. Now field will automatically centre itself evenly. Cut triangles to fill in saw-tooth edges of field.

Squared up with triangles, the diagonal field now needs only a border, and it is finished. Then carefully re-nail the base shoe over the outside edge of the border. Thermoplastic tile will lie better if it is warmed slightly after it has been set. This can be done with an electric hair dryer.

How to lay sheet flooring

Resilient flooring materials, including linoleum, are available in widths of six feet.

Since resilient flooring tends to conform to irregularities of the surface beneath, the condition of the floor over which you lay the material is extremely important. Whether it is concrete or wood, it should be smooth, sound and level.

A mastic can be used to level over rough concrete. Wood floors need board-type underlay.

Sheets of $\frac{1}{8}$ inch hardboard are frequently used to level off an old floor, because they do not build up the floor height excessively. Plywood is equally good.

Joints of the underlay should not fall directly over joints of the floor; the former should be either diagonal to the floor or placed in a staggered pattern. Use coated or ring-grooved nails on 6-inch centres each way or staples on 4-inch centres each way to secure underlayment.

Sweep the floor. If the floor is in good shape, you may not need underlay—only the felt lining sometimes called for. However, small irregularities tend to show through, so you will probably want underlay. Fill all nail holes or knotholes, sand all joints and places where you used filler. Then follow steps shown in this section.

In addition to your choice of floor covering you'll need chalk line, scribers, linoleum knife, trowel, 100-pound roller, adhesive, and paper felt (if installation directions call for it).

Paper felt is cut to length first. Paper felt adds quietness, more resilience to most flooring-covering materials.

Use notched floor trowel to spread adhesive over floor in uniform, thin coating. Roll felt back to centre of strip, apply paste, then do other half of strip.

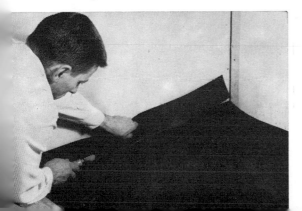

Scribe marks for special fittings. Here, material will extend to metal strip in centre of doorway. Set scribe to distance flooring will extend into the doorway, allowing overlap for fitting at trim strip.

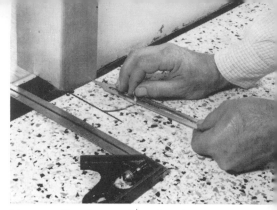

Move scribe along wall so that sharp point (under thumb) marks cutting line on floor covering. Scribe will mark the exact outline of door-frame and other irregularities. The fit at trim pieces should be as close as possible.

Remainder of wall outline is scribed onto the material so that proper amount can be cut off. This cutting and fitting is done before adhesive is applied over felt lining.

Underscribe marks the floor covering for close fit along metal trim strip, after other cutting (previous steps) has been finished. Felt butts against metal, does not overlap it.

Cut-room length strips of flooring slightly oversize. Butt far end against wall, other end against baseboard or lower part of wall. Mark line on floor covering and floor.

Draw floor covering back from wall, and note distance between lines. Transfer this measurement to end of strip and mark for cutting. Materials will fit from wall to wall.

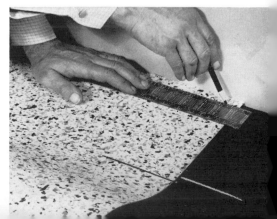

Spread adhesive over felt after flooring strip is cut and trimmed to fit. Chalk line across room will help keep strips straight and shows a boundary for spreading the adhesive. Spread adhesive for just one strip at a time.

Use 100-pound roller (this will have to be hired) to smooth newly laid covering. Flooring strips in this series of photographs are 6 feet wide. The strips are butt-jointed; be sure to press seam between strips carefully.

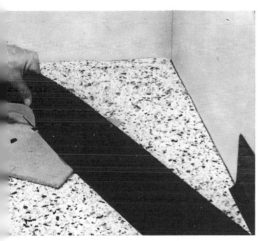

Cove base is being applied to finish this job. With 90-degree notch cut from coved portion, it bends around the inside corners. Preformed pieces fit over the outside corner.

Or you can cove the covering to add a neat finish to the job. If you try this, cut strips long enough for height of material on wall. Mitre corners.

Care of tools

The knife: Keep sharp by honing at regular intervals on stone or cloth.

Adhesive spreader. Keep clean. Do not allow adhesive to harden on blade—it will give an uneven spread of glue.

Rollers: Always carry rollers to the job and make sure they are free of all pieces of grit before use. Grit adhering to the roller will mark the new floor.

Cutting: Always have a square of hardboard or ply handy to cut upon. Cut with point and curve of blade.

How to lay plastic laminate

Plastic laminate is one of the most popular unit top coverings used today. One of its biggest advantages over the softer coverings of the past is ease of maintenance and longer life. Laminated plastic is highly resistant to impact, scuffing, and staining.

It must be remembered that plastic laminate has entirely different characteristics from the flexible materials often used for the same purposes. First of all, it is an extremely hard material. Ordinary wood-working tools are not made to handle plastic laminate. If you think of its properties as being more like thin cast iron, you will have a better idea of the necessary tools to use.

Although it is a very tough material, observe caution in the handling of plastic laminate—it can be broken, and once broken, you will have to design a smaller project or purchase a new piece.

Contact adhesive is normally used to bond laminated plastic to a unit top. The top itself should be quite strong— usually at least $\frac{3}{4}$-inch chipboard or plywood to assure a minimum of bending under heavy objects.

Cut the laminated plastic to exact size before bonding it to the counter top. Before actually doing the cementing, practice your technique with the slip-sheet of paper, until you can remove the paper (see next page) without edging the laminated plastic out of position.

Check laminate for fit. Then spread the contact adhesive evenly over it and the counter top, using a standard notched applicator. Recoat any dry spots. Remember to follow manufacturer's instructions on the adhesive container. This type of bonding operation is tricky; once the plastic laminate has touched the top it cannot be moved. By taking your time to "dry" fit the laminate and planning each step for its application, your job will be perfect. You are now ready to carry out the actual bonding of materials.

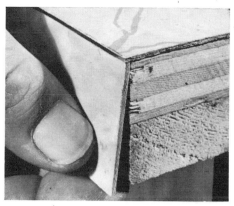

When cement is ready (15-20 minutes) cover the top with a large piece of wrapping paper, which serves as a slip sheet. Then position the laminate over the counter. Lift the laminate slightly, and slowly pull the paper out from under it—an inch or so at a time. As you do, press the laminate down with the tips of your fingers. Work carefully—do not forsake accuracy for speed. When all paper is out, go over the top with a roller to seat laminate firmly.

If you chose to apply edging strips last, you should have left an $\frac{1}{8}$-inch overlap around the edges (you can put edging strips on before marking top). Cut strips of plastic laminate so each piece matches perfectly. Sand edges of counter to remove any roughness, paint, glue, grease, and so forth. Then apply contact cement to edges of counter and to backs of strips. When the cement is ready to use, press the laminate in position to make the bond. Use a roller to seat strips.

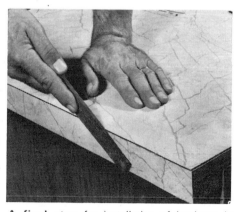

To install a basin in the surface, mark the exact opening size in the desired location. Use a sabre saw with a very fine-tooth blade to make the cut. You may have to bore a hole to get started. If you use a keyhole saw, bore a $\frac{1}{2}$-inch diameter hole at each corner to start the saw. Keep the holes within the cut-out line. When you make the cuts, saw away the scribed line. This will give you a slightly loose fit so you will not have to enlarge the hole. However, edges of the hole should be smoothed slightly with a file.

A final step for installation of laminate is to remove any roughness or unevenness from the edges and corners. Use a fine-toothed file. Work very cautiously to avoid chipping any of the material. If your unit calls for a splash back, you should mark and trim it the same way as the unit top. It can be mounted direct onto the wall or to a piece of plywood and fastened to the wall after the counter has been firmly anchored. You can get special plastic mouldings to trim the top edge, ends, and joint between counter and splash back.

How to cut in a door

Cutting an opening in a lath and plaster wall is not as difficult as it sounds, but it does require a lot of common sense and attention to detail.

First, you must find out if the wall is load-bearing in any way—some lath and plaster walls are. How do you tell? If a wall follows through from one floor to another, then it can be said to be load-bearing. But this does not necessarily mean that others are not, so check whether they are supporting half-floors (landings, etc.) or ceilings.

Choose with care the position of the new opening. Will the new door clash with others? Will it involve complicated cleaning and furniture arrangement? Will it mean alteration to electrical wiring or plumbing? Would it be better to have a sliding door (remember a sliding door needs somewhere to slide)?

Standard doors come in the following sizes, and can be hardboard or plywood faced with a glued block interior, or a solid panel door: internal 6' 6" high by 2' 0": 2' 3": 2' 6" and 2' 9". External 6' 6" high by 2' 6" or 2' 9". Glazed, 6' 6" high by 2' 6": 2' 9" or 3' 10".
Doors can also be made up to your own specifications but the extra cost is quite considerable.

How to cut the wall: First, measure and mark out on the wall the position of the door—remember to add thickness of door frame (2 sides and top) and clearance between frame and door. Cut away plaster and laths and then study the make-up of the wall before cutting the studs. The photographs on the following pages will show you how to go about the job.

Before starting a new opening, check the measurements

Chip away plaster along an outline of the door opening. Use your level to help you mark the door's position on the wall, and then open the wall as pictured. Cut back the other side of the wall to install jambs. When the plaster is out, saw through the lath along the edge of the studs, and remove the plaster and lath in the opening.

Saw off studs in the door opening, first at the bottom, then top. To avoid nails, make the bottom cuts about two inches above the sole. Use a square to mark guidelines at the top, and make the cuts accurately. The stud ends should fit squarely against the headers.

In load-bearing walls, use double headers set on edge. Nail them between the studs on both sides of opening. Pack out the headers so they are flush with stud edges, then nail them in place. Also, toe nail through short studs into header. This gives extra strength.

Supporting studs go on both sides of the opening. When the wall is not opened to double ceiling plate, the header should be extended to next existing stud and support block—or a short stud nailed under header. Double studs go under header next to jamb.

Cut off the sole on both sides of opening, next to supporting studs, after you have completely framed in door. If finish floor is already in, use a chisel and hammer to complete cut. Pry out piece; be careful not to damage floor. Finish flooring fills the space.

Side jambs fasten to head jamb, and unit is set in opening. Head jamb must be horizontal —side jambs plumb. To adjust and nail, add wedges between jambs and framing. Nails go through jambs and wedges.

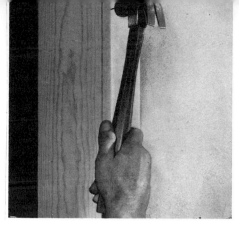

Extensive plaster repairs? Then you had better call a professional plasterer. When plaster dries, fasten on door mouldings, spacing nails 12 to 15 inches apart. When door is hung, stop bead is fastened on as final step.

Cutting openings in brick or breeze walls

Follow the instructions on page 263 up to and including cutting away the plaster which covers the brick or breeze.

Cut away two courses of bricks or one course of breeze, overlapping the width of the proposed new opening by at least the length of a brick. Now fix a lintel into position before cutting the rest of the opening—this will take the weight of the wall above the door opening. But, before fixing lintel, check that enough space is left for door, frame and opening space between door and frame.

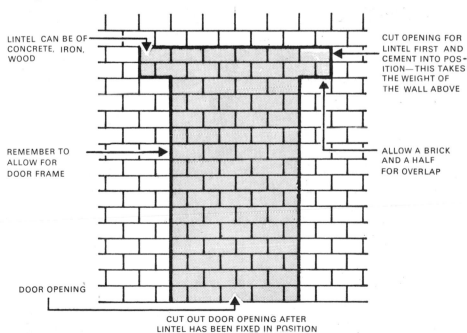

LINTEL CAN BE OF CONCRETE, IRON, WOOD

CUT OPENING FOR LINTEL FIRST AND CEMENT INTO POS-ITION—THIS TAKES THE WEIGHT OF THE WALL ABOVE

REMEMBER TO ALLOW FOR DOOR FRAME

ALLOW A BRICK AND A HALF FOR OVERLAP

DOOR OPENING

CUT OUT DOOR OPENING AFTER LINTEL HAS BEEN FIXED IN POSITION

How to close up a door opening

Like the majority of do-it-yourself jobs, closing up a door opening must be done to a plan.

Before you start to work, estimate and buy the necessary materials. This saves a lot of time running back and forth to the do-it-yourself shop and timberyard for supplies.

Salvage all the timber possible—jambs, headers, mouldings, and other pieces that you remove. You can use these "leftovers" for other jobs.

A claw hammer and a wide, flat chisel will enable you to do the work. A nail puller and crowbar may also be helpful.

The door comes off first—then you remove the moulding

Prise off the moulding—using a wide, flat chisel (as in picture) to avoid damaging the walls—after you have removed the door from the opening. Nail-heads will usually pull through the wood as you prise off the moulding. You can remove them when you are finished. Work carefully so you can salvage as much timber as possible.

Use a nail puller to remove stubborn nails. Only as a last resort should these nails be hammered into the woodwork. They may be rusty and would spoil future decorations. Do not forget to remove door stops and lock keep.

If the threshold is shaped, it will have to be removed. To do this, it may be necessary to saw through at each end where it joins the uprights of the door frame. Removal will make matching and fitting of the new length of skirting board much easier.

The next stage is the fixing of the support battens (or studs). Their thickness will depend on the material you intend using to "fill" the opening. For example, if the depth of the opening is 4" and ½" plasterboard is going to be used, then the support batten should be of 2" × 3".

Check all calculations and measurements because a mistake at this stage will give a bad join between the old and new walls which will be difficult to erase.

Nail lengths of 2" × 3" to the inside of the opening—top, sides and bottom—and then to a central support. Toe nail this support to top and bottom battens. Fix any insulating material now before fixing plasterboard to 2" × 3" battens.

Fill in opening with new material. After it is in place, fasten it to all three upright battens as well as the horizontal ones. Use galvanised nails if you use plasterboard.

Nail on new skirting board after filling in opening with new material (left). New skirting board should match old. Plastic wood fills the cracks and nail holes. Fill crack between new plasterboard and old wall—and sand surface smooth.

How to make doors and windows work

Doors and windows must open and close smoothly and easily, and keep out wind, rain, and dirt. When they do not, they become a nuisance—and sometimes even a liability.

Fortunately, it is not at all difficult to keep doors and windows in working order.

When a door is hard to open, or when a window refuses to close, when either rattles in the wind or lets in rain, you can quickly track down the trouble. It may be necessary only to tighten some hinge screws.

There is just one precaution. Remember that wood contracts in summer, and swells in winter. So do not be too free with your plane.

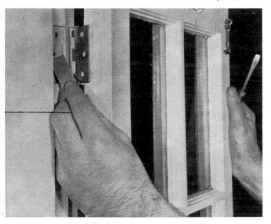

Shims close gaps. You can cure many door and casement window ailments with cardboard shims. If shrinkage prevents the latch from catching, or leaves a gap on the latch side, loosen hinge screws on the wall side. Insert a piece of cardboard behind each hinge, shifting the whole door over. Then replace the screws. Check the results; if the door has not been shifted sufficiently, use thicker cardboard or give hinge leaves on the door side the same treatment. If the gap is on hinge side, try half-width shims in wall-side mortise, placing them along edge of hinge farthest from hinge pin.

Sandpaper cure. If hinges are tight, yet swollen door still sticks near a latch-side corner, reach for the sanding block. Find spot of contact by running piece of cardboard between closed door and frame. Sand the spot with the grain.

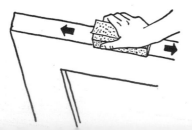

Tips for door repair

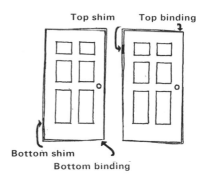

Top shim · Top binding

Bottom shim · Bottom binding

Shims end binding. You can often cure a door that binds by shimming out a hinge with cardboard—bottom shim for bottom bind, and a top shim for a top bind. Do not overdo shims, however, as door may bind elsewhere.

Loose hinges. If loose hinge screws will not hold, try longer screws. Or plug oversize screw holes with wooden pegs dipped in glue (above) or fibre wall plug and reset the screws.

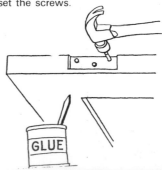

GLUE

Planing. Use a plane only if door is actually too wide or too high for the opening. If it is too wide, plane down hinge end and reset hinges (see below). Plane latch edge only if binding is above or below latch. Top edge can be planed without removing door; plane toward middle of door to avoid splintering. Use coarse sandpaper or rasp if plane will not fit.

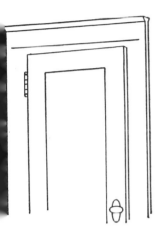

Shrinking whole door. A tightly fitted door may swell considerably in wet weather, becoming too large for the opening (left). To repair a door that is too large, it is necessary to take the door down since it must be planed on the hinge edge. Suggestions on how to take down a door easily are given on the opposite page. After door is down, follow steps shown below.

Removing a door If you need to plane the bottom edge of a door, or work on hinges, you will have to take the door down. It is easy; doors weigh 20 to 40 pounds, rarely more. Open the door and block up the bottom corner on the latch side with old magazines. Then use a stick of wood and a hammer, as is sketched, to tap out the two hinge pins. Remove bottom pin first, then top one, and door is free. When you re-hang it, replace top pin first. The older type of hinge will have to be unscrewed. Renew rusty screws when re-hanging door, also renew hinges if worn.

Remove door. Shrinking the whole door calls for planing hinge edge. Remove door, draw line on sides to show wood to be removed, unscrew hinges.

Plane. Then plane edge down to pencil line (that should be from $\frac{1}{16}$ to $\frac{1}{8}$ inch of wood). Keep edge square with face. Planing from hinge edge is easier than planing front and having to reset latch.

Chisel. Remove wood in hinge mortises with chisel to same depth as before. Replace the hinges flush with the edge of the door. Hang door in place again.

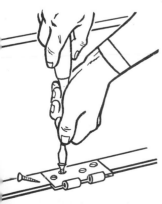

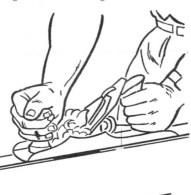

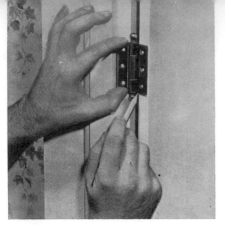

Hinge-edge warp. For a hinge-edge warp, add a third hinge between the top and bottom hinges. Open new hinge across crack, and mark its position. Cut mortises, force door into line, and attach.

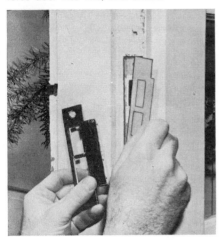

Filing opening. If lock tongue and opening in the strike plate do not line up, you can enlarge opening. See where latch is rubbing, and enlarge opening with a file. You may have to chisel the wood, too.

Strike plate shim. A strike plate can be shimmed out more easily than hinges if door latch does not engage the plate. Remove plate and trace outline of it on cardboard. Cut out shim; fit it into mortise.

Moving a strike plate. If the scratches on strike plate indicate that it has to be moved $\frac{1}{4}$ inch or more to match the latch tongue, move plate. Extend mortise in indicated direction (above); replace plate. Chisel out wood behind the plate opening (below), fill exposed part of mortise with plastic wood.

To silence rattle. If a door rattles, remove strike plate and extend the mortise toward stop bead. To make a smooth mortise, score the wood at $\frac{1}{8}$-inch intervals with shallow cuts; scrape out chips.

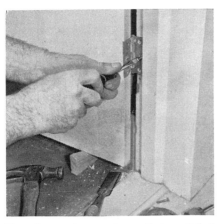

To raise or lower door. If door strikes head jamb or scrapes the floor, you may want to raise or lower it instead of trimming it down. If you do, remove hinges from jamb and extend mortises up or down as you find necessary. Put the wedges under door to hold it in its new position. Screw hinges in place, fill exposed mortises with filler, and touch up with paint.

Silence that loose door knob. If you have a doorknob that fits so loosely it rattles in use, you can easily silence it. Remove the retaining screw, pull off the knob, and drop a pellet of putty or weatherstripping compound inside the knob. When you re-assemble the unit on the door, the pellet of putty will form a cushion and take up the space that has caused the rattle.

Binding stop beads. If windows are hard to operate, check to see if the stop beads are binding. If that is the case, pry up the stop beads carefully, and move them slightly away from the sash. To avoid scarring visible wood, pry from the inside, as pictured. Pull old finishing nails through the stop beads, point first, with pliers. After re-nailing, countersink the nails and fill the holes and retouch with paint.

Breaking paint seal. A paint seal often keeps a sash window from moving up and down. Break this seal by running the point of a sharp knife around the sash. Do not use too much force; the knife might slip and scar the paint. If this fails, drive blade of putty knife between sash and frame. On a long-neglected window, you may have to drive wedges between lower sash and the sill from the outside.

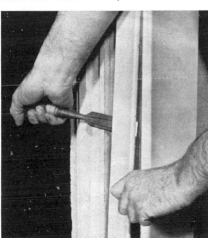

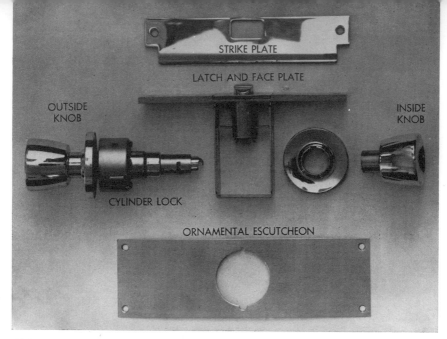

STRIKE PLATE

LATCH AND FACE PLATE

OUTSIDE KNOB

INSIDE KNOB

CYLINDER LOCK

ORNAMENTAL ESCUTCHEON

This "exploded" view shows the various parts of the typical replacement lock kit. Kits are available in a wide range of styles, and in most metallic finishes, for either inside or outside doors, plus bathroom and storm doors.

Install a new lock

Replacing a worn out or broken lock is comparatively easy because it is possible to buy a new lock which will fit into the door in exactly the same way as the old one.

Before you throw away a "broken" lock, check the inside mechanism for a broken spring. If this is the cause of the trouble, then it can be rectified quickly and cheaply by fitting a new spring. If it is too long, it can be cut with the help of pliers.

Remove old mortise, and strike plate, plus all old furniture. It is usually an easy job with just a screwdriver and pliers. Be careful with old, soft-metal screws—if corroded, they may twist off. Remove all screws and hardware before lock to avoid damaging wood.

Fitting the new latch may require some additional mortising or alteration of the existing mortise. Use a sharp wood chisel, cutting out wood where needed, and building up low spots with wood strips. When latch fits correctly inside mortise, mark for new cylinder.

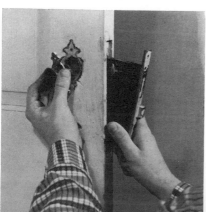

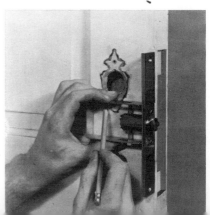

Use an expansion bit to drill hole for the cylinder. The unit shown required a $2\frac{1}{8}$-inch hole. Be careful not to splinter thin, old wood when the bit spur breaks through. Another easy way to make the cylinder hole is to use a sharp hole saw of correct size in your electric drill.

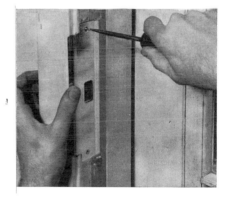

Install the new latch and face plate assembly, trying the cylinder to be sure it will pass through the hole. Shim or fill behind the face plate until it is flush with the edge of the door. Screw heads should be flush with the new face plate.

Remove the old strike plate from the door jamb and replace. Locate the plate so the latch fits in the recess. Fill in behind and around the plate as needed with wood putty, touch up with paint.

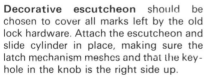

Decorative escutcheon should be chosen to cover all marks left by the old lock hardware. Attach the escutcheon and slide cylinder in place, making sure the latch mechanism meshes and that the keyhole in the knob is the right side up.

The inside knob and locking button snap easily over the end of the cylinder as shown below. Test the lock with keys to make sure it works properly. On door shown, escutcheons were used on both sides.

Mortise lock: This type of lock fits into a mortise cut into the centre rail of the door between the tenons—although in most cases, the mortise will cut into them. Check centre rail for tightness before fitting lock. Re-glue and wedge if necessary.

If the door has not previously been fitted with a mortise lock, the following diagrams and instructions will help you:

Draw a line down the centre of the door edge, and from this mark out a rectangular area the size of the forend of the lock. Using a chisel, cut out the depth of the thickness of the forend plus 1/16" (for clearance when opening and shutting the door).

The bit used to drill the holes in the centre rail should be 1/16" larger in diameter than the thickness of the lock case. Boring of the holes must be accurate, or you will find it difficult to make the key, spindle and door knobs work smoothly. Avoid under or over drilling by marking the shank of the bit with a small rubber band twisted on it at the required depth—that is, the length of the lock. Drill the top and bottom holes as near to the pencilled rectangle as possible to save a lot of cutting out with a chisel later. Drill remaining holes as close to each other as possible. Cut away the wood between the holes—a mortise lock chisel would help to cut the end grain of wood. Then check that the case will fit the hole—do not push the lock right home or you will have difficulty in removing it.

To make the key and spindle holes, place the lock on the side of the door and mark the centre of the holes on the door. Next, measure the thickness of the forend. Move key and spindle hole marks on the door towards the centre of the door the distance of the thickness of the forend. Repeat on the other side of the door and drill the key and spindle holes from each side into the mortise. Now shape the keyhole with a pad saw. Check that the lock fits correctly and that the key and spindle work quite freely. If adjustments are needed, remove the lock with a screwdriver inserted through the spindle hole into the lock follower.

When fitting the striking plate, close the door slowly so that the catch bolt marks the door frame—this gives the line for the top of the latch hole in the striking plate. To find the horizontal position of the plate, measure the distance from the slamming strip to the front edge of the latch bolt. Mark positions, hold the striking plate to them and mark out its area on the door frame. Then mark the holes to receive the bolts. Cut these out and, before screwing the plate to the frame, slightly bend the lip of the plate to enable the spring latch bolt to engage smoothly.

Rim locks: This type of lock is fixed on either side of the door. A shallow mortise is cut to house the forend, and holes drilled out for key and spindle. The lock does not have to be fixed to the centre rail of the door—it can be placed quite high out of the reach of young children.

To fix, hold the lock against the door and, on the door edge, mark where it is to be cut away to take the face plate. Cut away using a sharp chisel. Hold lock to the door again with the face plate in the notch cut for it. Now mark on the door the positions of door knob, spindle and keyhole. Drill out—keep the drill straight or you will find that the knob and spindle bind, and therefore the key will only fit the door from one side. Hold lock to door again, check that knob, spindle hole and keyhole are in correct positions.

Mark positions of fixing screws, drill starting holes for screws, and fix lock to door. Temporarily insert handles, close door, and mark on the door frame the position of the keep. It may be necessary either to sink the keep into the frame to get a tight fit, or to pack up the keep. Packing can be of thick cardboard, 3 ply, or $\frac{1}{8}$" hardboard.

Cylinder rim lock: This is fitted in the same way as a rim lock, except that a hole $1\frac{1}{4}$" in diameter is drilled through the door $2\frac{3}{8}$" from the door edge—this distance may vary according to the make of lock. It is important that the cylinder and latch case are in correct alignment. Cut the connecting bar to fit, but not more than $\frac{3}{4}$" of it should project through the wood. On the other hand, it should not be less than $\frac{1}{2}$" or you will find it difficult to connect the bar into the latch case. If it is longer than $\frac{3}{4}$" it will foul the knob mechanism in the latch case.

The connecting screws are then shortened as required. They go through the back plate into the cylinder body—four or five turns are sufficient to hold the cylinder body in place.

Screw latch case to door, set staple or keep into door frame, and screw into position.

How to lubricate doors and windows

Doors that stick or squeak will not close unless you use force a source of irritation that you can easily eliminate if you use the simple and inexpensive methods shown on these pages.

The moving parts of your house need lubrication. Once done, the job may not need redoing for a year or more. But do not tackle the task with too much enthusiasm; a little lubricant foes a long way. Too much will only gather dust or come off on clothes.

Lubrication of your house can be done with these tools: An oilcan (1) preferably with a flexible spout (2) a cork or wooden sanding block (3); a jar of petroleum jelly (4); puffer container of powdered graphite (5); a grease stick (6)

Do not lubricate the friction hinges that are found on metal window frames. Otherwise they will not stay open by themselves and the wind could damage both hinges and frame. Be very sparing with the oil when attending to window catches—some catches would be very easy to open from the outside if too much oil were used.

Sash pulleys need oiling from time to time and sash chains need rubbing over with an oily rag. A rub with a grease stick will help sash windows to move up and down easily and quietly. If the door hinge has a removable spindle, this should be taken out, cleaned and rubbed with a little petroleum jelly (see photographs below). On fixed hinges, oil should be worked into the hinge by moving the door backwards and forwards. With a soft duster, remove all surplus oil from hinges, locks, latches, sliding tracks etc. This will stop fluff and dust sticking to these moving parts.

Turn handle until latch is right in, then puff powdered graphite into works of lock and latch. Next, puff a tiny bit of graphite between stationary collar and shaft of knob on each side of door. (Or put drop of oil at same spot; remove excess.)

An unworkable latch should be replaced. Simply take off knobs, remove faceplates, and finally latch. (Take old one along to shop to get same size.) For loose knobs, remove set-screw that holds knob on, fill the shank hole in knob with putty.

Lubricate lock with thumb-pressure latch lever by puffing graphite into crevice where lever enters lock body. To puff it in latch, depress lever until latch tongue is in. Warning: Never oil a cylinder lock—the kind with keyhole and mechanism in cylindrical case. Oil gums the tumblers.

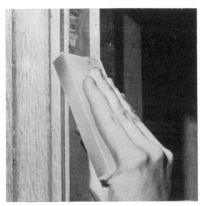

If door rubs against frame yet does not stick enough to require planning or rehanging, rub sanding block hard on surface showing signs of friction. At same time, rub lightly over face of strike plate (on frame); also clean any paint from surface of latch.

Friction catches on doors will operate more smoothly if you touch them with the grease stick or light oil from time to time. Do not try it on a squeaky oven door, however, since the oven heat would quickly melt the lubricant. Instead, rub point of a very soft lead pencil (which consists largely of graphite) on meeting surfaces of oven doors. Also puff graphite into openings around hinges of oven door.

Sliding doors of the type that hang from metal sheaves (cased-in wheels or steel balls) on metal tracks can be lubricated by putting a drop of oil on bearings of rollers and a light smear of petroleum jelly along the top of the metal track. For the type of sliding door which rolls on sheaves mortised in the bottom of door, lift the door off the track and turn it upside down to oil, as shown in the picture.

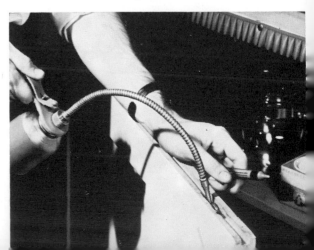

Sliding door that cannot be removed from its track can be treated by rubbing petroleum jelly lightly onto metal or wood track. Slide door back and forth until sheaves have taken up sufficient lubricant. Wipe off excess jelly so that it will not become a dirt collector later on. For doors that slide in grooved wooden tracks without metal rolling parts, ease ways by rubbing them with wax.

Metal windows: The hinges on the non-friction type of window need regular oiling to protect them against the weather. Friction windows (those that stay open without a support stay) need no oiling. But check that they do not get clogged when re-painting.

Metal doors: The open bolt fittings on these doors should have a little grease rubbed on the back of the bolt. It can be removed by releasing the retaining screw in the front of the bolt—but watch carefully for the small ball-bearing situated between the bolt and door.

For windows whose sliding surfaces are painted or varnished, use a grease stick or paraffin wax to lubricate. On sash windows, pull down upper half to expose pulleys. If you can reach spot where pulleys revolve, place a drop of oil on each side. Or puff in graphite.

Metal sash cords, metal window slides give smooth, silent operation when you wipe them with a light machine oil about every six months or so. Clean off all old paint and gummy oil from cords and slides with fine steel wool before you re-oil.

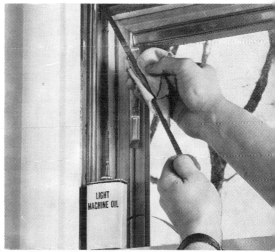

Your garage doors and tracks need grease and oil

Garage-door tracks are easy to lubricate by putting several spots of multi-purpose grease on the track. Let the wheels spread it out for you. Oil wheels (arrow) lightly. Lubricate both these places twice a year.

Handles and hinges on your garage doors should be lubricated two or three times a year. If your door locks with a key, puff a little powdered graphite into it in the same way as you do into your house and car locks.

Draught proofing

Your home may be well insulated, but you can probably cut your heating bill still more (often as much as 20 per cent) by draught proofing all the doors and windows. Besides keeping out wind and cold, draught proofing helps block the entry of dust and noise into your home.

You can buy draught proofing materials by the foot, yard, or in kits—with everything you will need to seal one door or window. Here are some of the best materials available, plus tips on their installation. Whatever method you use, make sure that it fits—badly fitted draught proofing does nothing, least of all stops draughts.

Installation is a job that is easy for the average handyman to do. All kits and most of the materials come with complete instructions.

Vinyl types: From left—friction-holding seal for metal sash; a gasket type for doors or windows; a sheath type for metal sash (requires adhesive); thin strip for inner edge of door; and wood-vinyl foam strip.

Urethane foam types: From left—an adhesive-backed foam strip $\frac{1}{2}$-inch wide; a vinyl tube gasket with foam inside; and a $\frac{1}{4}$-inch extra-thick foam with adhesive back. Several colours are available.

Felt and cloth types: From left—hair felt; wool and cotton felt; and a gasket type made of water-repellent fabric sewn around a core of rubber.

Door bottom types: At left is a metal and felt strip which is simply fixed to the door so it compresses against the sill. Centre is a metal threshold with a vinyl inset. It replaces old threshold; the vinyl compresses against the bottom of the door. Right is an automatic sealer with a heavy-duty felt strip that makes the seal. When door is opened the strip rises above carpeting inside house

Metal threshold is installed by removing the vinyl seal and cutting the threshold to fit between the door jambs. Then fasten it to the floor with the screws included in the package. Cut the vinyl seal the same length as the threshold and snap it into the grooves. The strip covers the screws and will take a lot of hard wear. Pack up with a strip of hardboard or cardboard if door does not meet pad.

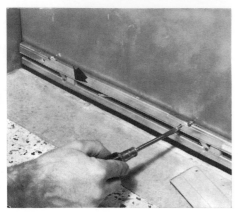

Automatic draught excluder consists of mechanical and covering shield. Both can be trimmed to fit any door. The mechanism is attached to the door first. It goes on the side of the door opposite the direction the door swings. Wood blocks (arrow) hold felt strip down during installation and are removed before the shield is added. Felt strip fits snugly against door threshold.

Shield is mounted on the door to cover the mechanism. Bumper plate goes on the door stop (on the hinge side) and engages the bumper when the door is closed. The bumper forces the felt strip down as the door is closed, lets it spring up out of the way when the door is opened. This type of excluder is the answer when an ordinary excluder will not clear carpeting or rug inside the house.

Combination strip of wood or aluminium and vinyl is added to existing door or window stop. Vinyl should compress when door or window is closed, Finish strips to match.

All gasket types are installed on the stops of either the doors or windows. Here the cloth gasket is stapled to the door stop. Or, it can be tacked on. This must be done carefully so that it fits tightly without holding door open.

Felt strip is tacked to window stops so that the edge of felt rubs against window. This one has metal reinforcement which also makes installation easier. When you work from the roll, you can cut length to fit exactly.

Adhesive-backed types do a good job on casement windows. Install on the window edge that overlaps the frame. Cut-as-you-go idea helps you fit exactly with no measuring. This type of self adhesive foam strip is ideal for use on cars to stop draughts and rattles.

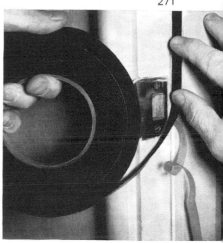

Dark coloured foam type is pressed on the edge of the door stop as paper backing is removed to uncover the adhesive. It is a good idea to install a small piece first and try closing the door to be sure it will not interfere.

This door kit has enough material to seal a door all the way around. Kits offer a variety of metals—and are sold by size of door. Small metal strip bridges the gap needed for the latch plate. The five strips seal the sides and top. This kit has locking threshold for bottom of door.

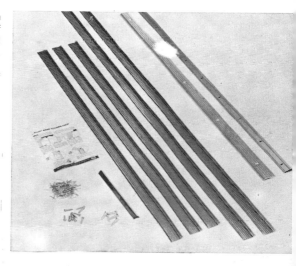

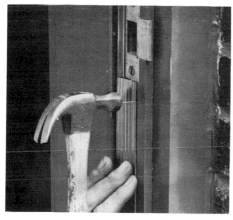

Copper strips are cut with shears, tacked on with small nails. When the door is closed, springy strips compress against the edge of the door to form a seal. The small, narrow strip is nailed to the stop behind latch plate.

An aluminium type attaches to the door jambs at the sides and top, and to the door itself at the bottom to fit against sill. It is easily adjusted with screws to maintain a tight seal if the door swells, shrinks or warps.

The Lock-keep needs draught proofing to complete job of sealing door. This is a thin strip just behind the lock's strike plate. It stops air leaks at the door lock, where a gap must be left in the metal draught proofing. Sides and tops of doors are stripped just as windows are.

Door bottom is often sealed with a special metal-and-felt piece of draught proofing instead of ordinary stripping. The clearance between door and threshold determines whether this piece is screwed to inside or inside of the door. Usually you get tighter seal by putting it on the inside of door. You buy it complete with screws.

Metal drip cap, nailed to the outside face at the bottom of the door, will correct a situation where your door lets water into the house. Used with a door-bottom draught excluder on the inside of the door, the drip cap gives you complete protection from water and draught. You might also want to attach drip cap to the bottom of your garage door to keep water from seeping underneath when it is closed.

Do not forget your garage doors

Draught proofing installed over paint or wood-preservative sealer, helps keep out elements. Tube-type stripping nails to bottom edge; heavy door seals it against concrete.

Paint bottom edge of wooden outside doors even if you apply draught proofing. Weather is biggest enemy of this type door; paint helps keep moisture from rotting wood.

How to replace a broken window

Broken windows are inevitable where there are children around. Your builders merchant will cut to size a replacement pane while you wait—plate glass has to be ordered.

With the few hand tools and materials shown in these photographs, you can replace the pane yourself in 20 or 30 minutes. Let the glazing putty form a "skin" before you paint it. When you paint, be sure to seal joint between glass and the putty with paint. Large plate glass window panes should be installed by a professional.

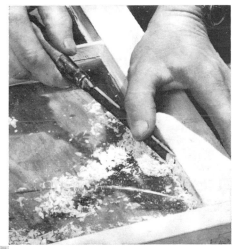

Remove old putty around cracked pane with an old chisel, jack-knife, or a glazier's knife. If pane is *broken*, remove glass first before you take out putty. As you work around, remove the glazier's sprigs that hold in the glass. Gloves protect your hands when you remove broken glass. To prevent splitting the wood, dig and chip out old putty a little at a time. Hot soldering iron will help soften the old putty.

Remove all the old putty so that the new glazing putty will stick to the wood. One way to remove it quickly is to place a small wood rasp in the grooves and "file", as shown in the photograph. The sharp teeth of the rasp cut away excess putty that is especially difficult to remove with a knife or chisel. The rasp leaves wood slightly scored so that the new glazing putty will bond properly.

Paint with undercoat or a wood preservative the wood that will be covered with glazing putty. This coating seals the wood from moisture. Let the wood preservative or undercoat dry thoroughly before you continue with job.

For an airtight seal, apply a thin bed of glazing putty in grooves (rabbets) that glass will rest against. Putty helps stop air leakage around new glass and also helps to cushion it. To apply putty, string it between thumb and forefinger, "wiping" it into rabbets. Use just tip of putty knife to smooth it. Thin layer is best; too much tends to force the glass out of square in the window frame.

Cut new glass to size with a jig like this, or buy the glass precut at a builders' merchant. To make a jig, tack straight-edge to a sheet of plywood. Place the square edge of glass against straight-edge and use edge of square as a guide for the cut-off. Score the glass, slide it over so cut-off line aligns with the edge of the plywood jig, and break it with the handle of the cutter.

Place the glass in frame and drive glazier's sprigs into wood. To help prevent future breakage, insert glass so its concave side is in. Sight edge to determine the right side. Then, apply putty, and bevel it with tip of your knife. Let putty set several days before you paint it. Make sure that the joint between glass and putty is thoroughly covered with paint for a weather seal.

For metal windows, remove broken glass, putty, and clean off any rust spots. Coat the bare spots with metal primer, let it dry, and apply bed of putty for seal and cushion. Set in new glass, and place the end of spring clip in hole in frame. Then press it into position. Apply putty evenly around metal frame, and bevel it with a glazier's knife. Then, paint the frame.

How to cut glass

These instructions are for cutting everything but safety glass, which you are not likely to break anyway. The trick is in getting a smooth, even cut (score) with a glass cutter. Scoring weakens the glass equally on one line, focusing all breaking tendencies on that single path.

Do not wait long to snap scored glass. Glass tends to heal itself, so it may not break clean if you delay.

Plate glass is heavier and thicker than ordinary window glass, and needs more pressure in the breaking. It is also slightly softer and tougher, is less likely to break unevenly. A sharp cutter just right for window glass may be too "hot" for plate glass.

Grinding and polishing glass edges by hand is possible, but tedious. The same job can be done in minutes on a belt grinder by your builders' merchant.

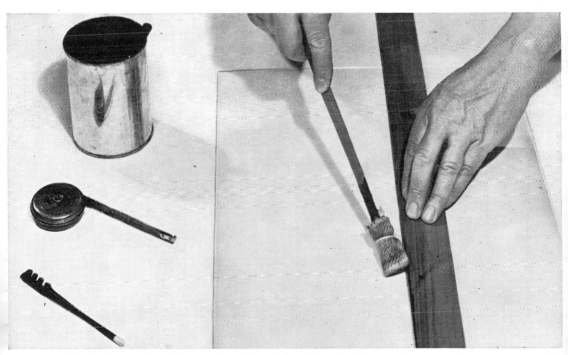

Tools for cutting glass are shown here. You will need an inexpensive cutter (lower left); a steel measuring rule (left centre); some fine lubricating oil, penetrating oil, paraffin, or turpentine (upper left); and a strip of hardwood about $\frac{1}{4}'' \times 3'' \times 4'$. A yardstick is too narrow to use as a straight-edge for cutting glass; you cannot get a good enough grip to hold it steady. The inexpensive cutter is just about the same as one a professional uses. The first step when preparing to cut glass is to find one large, flat working surface like a kitchen table, and pad it with old carpeting or layers of newspaper. Before making the cut, wipe a film of oil or turpentine on the glass, as illustrated. This oil on the surface helps prevent chipping and popping. Some glaziers only dip the cutter, but wiping the surface is advisable for the amateur.

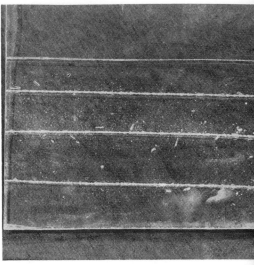

Score cut. Picture shows how to cut circle with ruler attached to a suction cup. For straight cut, cut marks to indicate each end of stroke. Line up straight-edge, wipe on oil, and draw cutter toward you in one stroke. Do not retrace clean cut; retrace only spots that the cutter has missed.

"Burned cuts"—like these—result from too heavy a hand; too light a hand will not score glass. Smooth stroke, even pressure, produce best results. Burned cut (glaziers say cutter's wheel is "too hot") is too deep, leaving chipped flakes.

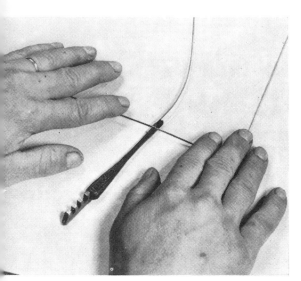

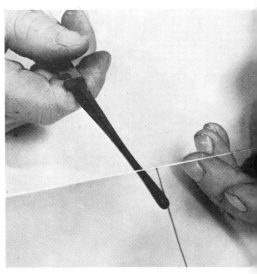

Free-hand curves are possible. Mark curve on paper, and use it under glass as guide when you score. After score is made, start break as shown, by laying glass on the cutter handle (or use a pencil) with scored line directly above. Then press down with both hands sharply and firmly.

Another way to start break on straight or curved cut is to hold glass off the table a few inches, and tap underside of score with knob end of cutter. Never tap the glass on scored side; it will not work and it may ruin the entire sheet.

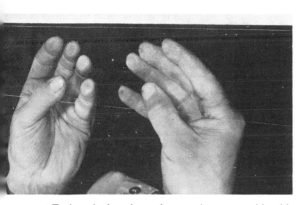

To break the glass after you have scored it with a cutter, shift it to the edge of the table so the score on the surface is past table edge and waste portion of glass extends into space. Hold the waste firmly with both hands and snap quickly downward. The break should then come clean.

Another way to make the break is to slip a straight-edge under the scored glass so it supports the pane just behind the score. Then, with one palm firmly on good portion, slap the other palm down and away from the score.

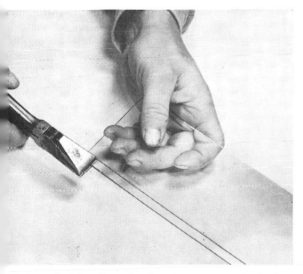

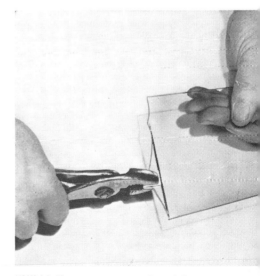

A strip of waste glass too narrow to be broken off with the usual methods can be broken free in one piece with a pair of pliers, preferably the large-surface type glaziers use (shown in the photograph). Hold pliers next to score at one end and twist downward and away from score.

"Nibble" away uneven edges left on waste side of score with pliers. To reduce chipping, fold piece of paper into small pad to give pliers more even grip. You can also do nibbling job with teeth in head of the glass cutter.

All about doors

How to flush panel a door: This is a comparatively simple conversion. Hardboard panels are made in standard sizes to fit most sizes of door. The panels are glued and pinned direct to the existing door.

First, remove all door furniture and any beading which may project from the door surface. Check that the hinges are in good order—you will add weight to the door when the panels are fixed. The job is simple if the panels fit on the door just within the area of the door stops. In this way, the door will not have to be re-hung.

Bevel the edges of the hardboard panels before fixing. Fix panel to door and cut opening for door knob and spindle and keyhole. If the lock is flush fitting then cut the hardboard to fit tightly around it (this will save re-siting the lock and keep). Guide holes drilled from the other side of the door will give you their position—repeat process for the other side of the door.

If you want an all-over flush appearance, then you must re-site the hinges, door stops and lock keep and—in the case of flush locks —the lock as well. This is necessary to take up the extra thickness you will be adding to the door.

Warped doors: Badly fitting or warped doors not only look ugly but let in draughts.

A gap may be due to a badly fitting lock. This can be checked by first closing the door and then pushing it a little harder to see if there is any play between lock and keep. If the door is fitted with a rim lock (a lock that is visible), any play will be seen immediately and can be taken up by setting the keep further into the door frame. It is necessary to do this in stages, checking at each stage until you reach the correct setting.

If the door has a mortise lock (only the door knobs or handles show), then the adjustment is a little more difficult because the keep is situated on the inside of the door frame where you cannot see the gap between it and the lock. Remove the keep, close the door, and insert a piece of thin cardboard between the frame and the door until it reaches the lock. Now press the door tightly shut, still keeping the cardboard against the lock. Mark in pencil the position of the edge of the door frame on the cardboard. Use this as a guide to reset the keep. After cutting the new mortise for the keep, the existing screw holes must be plugged and fresh holes drilled. Do not attempt to use old screw holes even if they need moving only 1/16"—if you do, the keep will eventually drop back into its old position.

A modern door sometimes develops a warp due either to unseasoned timbers being used in manufacture, or the door being hung incorrectly when the house was built. Providing the warp is not too bad, it can be corrected in one of the following ways:

Lock-side warp. To make a door with lock-side warp close more easily, prise up the stop bead (wood strip on the door-frame). Close door and draw line on jamb along inside edge of door. Re-nail bead on line.

1. Adjust the hinges. This is a tricky job as, in some cases, it means moving one hinge only 1/16 inch. To achieve this, the door must be taken down, the original screwholes carefully plugged, the hinge re-fixed, and the door re-hung.

2. Spring the door back into position. For example, if the warp is at the top, open the door so that it is nearly at right angles to the frame. Now fix a piece of 2 × 1 inch batten to the floor in front of the door and, at the top, wedge a length of 2 × 1 batten between the door and the wall—this length should be an inch or so longer than the distance from the wall to the batten which you have fixed to the floor. Before knocking this batten into position, place odd scraps of hardboard or ply at each end to protect the door and wall. When this wedge is in position, the door should be left for three or four days before the wedge is removed.

3. Another method is to remove the door-stops and re-site them following the line of the warp. Remove door-stops, close door to required position, mark position on door frame, and re-fix door stops following this line. The door stops could also be cut to shape so that the original straight edge is retained.

4. It is also possible to fill the gap caused by slight warps by fixing one of the self-adhesive plastic foam strips to the doorstop.

Rising butts: These hinges lift a door as it opens to give it the necessary clearance over a carpet.

Hinges come in right or left-hand fittings. Each hinge is in two parts, and is fitted in the same way as a normal hinge, except that each half is screwed to the door and frame separately.

To hang, open the door to an angle of 90 degrees and then lift it on to spindle half of the hinge which is fitted to the door frame. You may find it necessary to shave off the top corner (hinge side) because the door binds on the framework.

How to fix a torn-out hinge

Of all the malicious tricks of winter weather, none is worse than that gust of wind which snatches a door and wrenches off a chunk of wood, along with a hinge.

Except for painting, the whole repair job need not take you more than an hour. Briefly, here are the steps to follow: Saw away the splintered part, cut a patch from a piece of good timber, fasten it in with screws and waterproof glue. Then rehang the door.

Use saw first. Remove damaged door. Saw out section with splintered wood, leaving a square, sound edge. If necessary, true up the edge with chisel and block plane, then sand it smooth.

Make patch. Cut a piece of wood to right size and thickness (if possible, V-joint patch into door) and bore holes for screws. Coat edges with waterproof glue, tack replacement piece in position with a nail, then drill starter holes for the screws in the door, as shown.

Attach patch. Countersink the holes so screwheads will be drawn well below surface. Then drive the screws through patch and into door edge. Roundhead screws were used here because the flat base of head gives stronger grip.

Replace hinge. True up patch with plane and sandpaper, so it matches door exactly. Then mark the hinge mortise and cut it with chisel and mallet.

In cases where screws have pulled out and not splintered or damaged the surrounding wood, remove hinges and, if necessary, replace. Drive wooden pegs, dowels or fibre wall plugs into holes and cut off level. Replace hinges, fixing them with slightly longer screws.

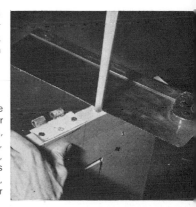

Sliding door gear

Before attempting to convert an existing swing door into a sliding door, make sure that it will be an asset. Remember that a sliding door must have somewhere to slide! In addition, because of the door's position on the wall, it may not give you the extra space you had hoped for. Approximately $2\frac{1}{2}$" are needed above the door opening in which to fix the gear.

If you decide that it is not possible to fit a sliding door, then consider the possibility of fitting a folding door. They come in various sizes and are complete with all fixtures and fittings. Folding doors fit inside the existing framework of the door opening.

If you convert the door from swing to sliding, the following alterations should be done before attempting to fix the gear:

Remove hinges and make good notches,

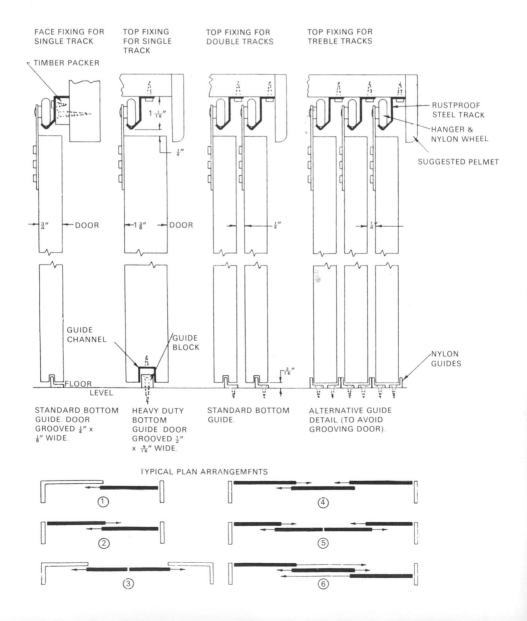

FACE FIXING FOR SINGLE TRACK

TIMBER PACKER

TOP FIXING FOR SINGLE TRACK

TOP FIXING FOR DOUBLE TRACKS

TOP FIXING FOR TREBLE TRACKS

RUSTPROOF STEEL TRACK

HANGER & NYLON WHEEL

SUGGESTED PELMET

DOOR

NYLON GUIDES

GUIDE CHANNEL

GUIDE BLOCK

FLOOR LEVEL

STANDARD BOTTOM GUIDE. DOOR GROOVED $\frac{1}{4}$" x $\frac{1}{8}$" WIDE.

HEAVY DUTY BOTTOM GUIDE DOOR GROOVED $\frac{1}{2}$" x $\frac{9}{16}$" WIDE.

STANDARD BOTTOM GUIDE.

ALTERNATIVE GUIDE DETAIL (TO AVOID GROOVING DOOR).

TYPICAL PLAN ARRANGEMENTS

both in door and frame. Take off all locks and bolts—this includes the lock keep in the door frame. Remove the beading around the door frame on the side on which the door is to be hung. Fill any holes between frame and plaster. Fit a door stop in place of the beading on the catch side of the door.

Fitting the gear: This depends on the make and type of gear you select. Detailed plans are issued with all gears, so follow these carefully. Do not tighten fully the adjustment nuts and screws until you are satisfied that the door is hanging perfectly straight. These nuts give about $\frac{3}{8}''$ up or down. There are several types of catch to choose from, and also various kinds of draught proofing strips.

Gears can be made up in double and treble tracks for wardrobes and floor-to-ceiling cupboards, but they are top fixing only—see diagram. An allowance of $\frac{1}{4}''$ is the minimum space between doors so that they slide without catching each other.

Sliding door gear is built to carry certain weights—do not overload, otherwise it will not work satisfactorily.

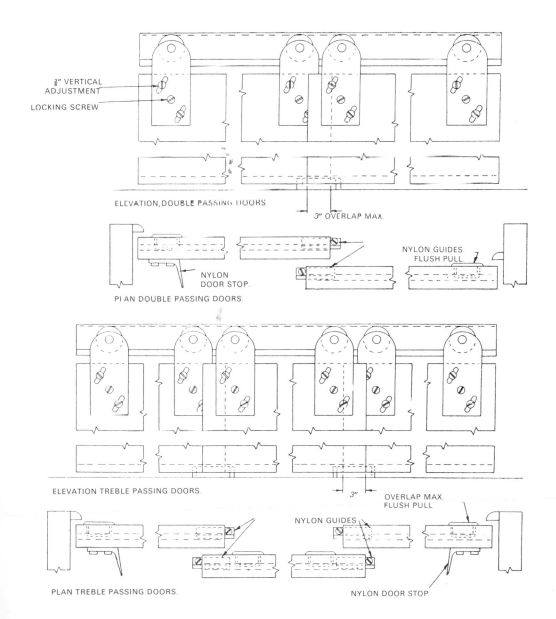

$\frac{3}{8}''$ VERTICAL ADJUSTMENT

LOCKING SCREW

ELEVATION, DOUBLE PASSING DOORS

3" OVERLAP MAX.

NYLON DOOR STOP.

NYLON GUIDES. FLUSH PULL

PLAN DOUBLE PASSING DOORS.

ELEVATION TREBLE PASSING DOORS.

3" OVERLAP MAX. FLUSH PULL

NYLON GUIDES

PLAN TREBLE PASSING DOORS.

NYLON DOOR STOP.

How to be safe on a ladder

When you have to climb a ladder to do a maintenance job on the house, be sure that the ladder and your methods of using it are safe.

Follow the steps pictured here to raise the ladder. Then climb it slowly, holding on with both hands. If you want to take tools along, tie them to a rope which is looped around your wrist, and hoist them up when you are safely situated.

While working, hang on with one hand. If you must use both hands on a job, hook a leg over a rung.

Set base against house and walk ladder up, hand over hand, as rapidly as you can. Keep arms fairly straight. Ladder seems to grow heavier at first, then light as it becomes vertical.

Hips between rails is the rule when reaching out from ladder. Never reach more than one arm's length. Hold on with other hand, to something other than ladder so you will not topple sideways.

Set bottom of ladder out a distance equal to a quarter of its extended height. This is optimum distance for the most strength and safety. The average person can raise a 24- to 30-foot ladder single-handed.

Never paint a new ladder. It may develop defects beneath paint where you cannot see them. For protection, give it a coat or two of linseed oil or a good clear varnish that does not hide wood.

Make your roof watertight

Water seeping into your home over a period of time can cause serious damage anywhere from attic to basement.

Damaged walls and foundations let in their share of water, but those faults are generally easy to locate. Tiny leaks in the roof, mud- and leaf-clogged gutters, ill-fitting downpipes and loose and crumbling mortar joints in the chimney may not be so apparent until water spots appear on your ceilings or walls.

A careful inspection of the loft and the under side of the roof will reveal where the water comes in. Make this inspection on a wet day because the position of the water stain on the ceiling may not indicate the entry point. Water can and often does enter through the tiles or slates at one point, and then runs down a rafter or tile batten to enter the ceiling at an entirely different spot. Mark the faulty slate or tile and leave the actual repair for a dry warm day. It is easier to work and handle materials in warmer weather. On flat roofs, you will find a crack or split in the roofing material more or less above the spot where the leak shows in the ceiling.

Water spots which appear at ceiling level on chimney breast walls could be the result of a crack on the flashings between tiles and stack. Small openings can be sealed by brushing on a liquid bitumen sealer—this also applies to small cracks or splits on flat roofs.

Repairs with sealing strip

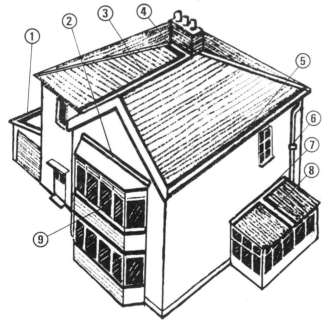

1. For sealing all joints and repairs to guttering and downpipes on garages. Also for waterproof flashing on roof joints and walls constructed with concrete and asbestos sheeting both flat and corrugated.
2. For flashings and aprons to both bay and dormer windows.
3. For waterproofing and repairing roof ridges, particularly suitable for a hip and ridge constructed of wood shingles. (Also for lining and repairing box and valley gutters between sloping roofs).
4. For flashing gutters and aprons on chimney stacks and repairs to existing flashing work.
5. For repairs to all house guttering, waterproofing and sealing under eaves.
6. For sealing joins and repairs to downpipes.
7. For flashing where lean-to roofing abuts onto the main wall.
8. Flashing and sealing glazed roofs, or capped sheets of corrugated plastic roofing material or asbestos.
9. For protecting window heads and sills; repairs to zinc, lead or copper weathering strip and sealing apron below window sills.

PREPARATION
Ensure that the surface to be covered is clean, dry and free from dust. Remove all flaking paint, putty, surface rust, etc., with a wire brush.

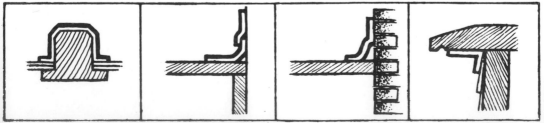

Check mortar joints in the chimney for water damage

1 Caulking seals cracks between roof, flues, chimney caps and keeps water out. Caulk top joint inside where flue sections butt together.

2 Broken or loose chimney cap lets water seep into mortar joints below. Chip, clean out old mortar. Then wet break with water, trowel in fresh cement.

3 To re-point, clean, wire brush, and wet joint. Insert cement, then smooth. Loose or cracked bricks in the stack should be replaced.

How to replace a damaged or broken shingle

1 If composition shingle is damaged, you should replace it. Loosen nails in shingle above damaged one. Flat spade slips under shingle without damaging it, while sharp edge lifts nails. Replace shingles on warm day when material is pliable. If necessary, use cold liquid bitumen to stick shingles down.

2 Insert new shingle, re-nail shingle above. Try to use same nail holes; cover nailheads with roofing cement. Use galvanised nails to fix new shingles, seal with liquid bitumen.

3 Stop leaking of split wooden shingle by driving prefitted square of aluminium or galvanised sheet under it. Metal should be big enough to fit under upper, centre shingles. Nail if necessary.

Gutters, downpipes need attention every six months

A twice-yearly inspection and repair of gutters and downpipes will double or triple the life of your roof drainage system.

It is best to inspect in the spring and autumn.

Standing water causes most gutter troubles. All gutters must be pitched slightly towards downpipe openings; water fails to run off when the pitch is lost. Check gutters by pouring water in them and observing speed and direction of flow. Control pitch by adjusting or replacing clips.

Standing water may also be the result of leaves or other debris clogging gutters and downpipes. A brush or glazier's knife will generally take care of that problem. If a downpipe is clogged, the chances are you will find wet leaves trapped in an elbow joint. Remove the elbow and clean it. Forcing leaves down the drain may only cause worse stoppage.

1 Keep gutters clean. Mud and rotting leaves clog downpipes and rust gutters. Small broom cleans away leaves and twigs; glazier's knife removes mud and other debris.

2 With liquid bitumen, coat inside of gutters to prolong their life. Re-coat every two years, or when gutter appears rusty. Aluminium, asbestos or plastic gutters do not need coating.

3 Wire strainers that you can buy fit into tops of downpipes to prevent clogging of your roof drainage system. Install strainers at each point where the gutters are connected with downpipes.

When you replace a gutter, use a fine toothed hacksaw to cut the sections to the required length. Mark a line around the gutter before you start sawing so cut edges will be exactly square.

Place a strip of sealing compound between the two pieces of guttering to be joined together. Then bolt the joint together to complete seal. Give the joint a coat of liquid bitumen as a second seal.

1 Temporary repair for holes in gutters is easy with plastic cement for metal. Clean gutter around hole and pre-fit fibre glass patch. Apply cement to metal. Spread cement out fairly thin.

2 Press the patch into place over hole. Spread excess cement over edges of patch to form watertight seal between metal and patch. Finish job by coating patch with cement. Patch will last for a very long time.

How to caulk

Cracks, inevitably, become a part of every home, even a well-built one.

Uncorrected, these openings let in moisture, draughts, insects, dust, and dirt. Generally, they can be sealed shut with caulking compound, a sticky, putty-like substance. It will expand and contract with the weather but the seal it forms remains unbroken.

Preventive caulking keeps a house new by sealing up cracks; curative caulking involves filling larger openings, or, sometimes replacing boards. Caulking should be an annual job.

In a corner, angle the gun at 45 degrees in the direction of movement. You will get a smooth, coved fillet that tightly seals the joint.

On the flat, maintain the 45-degree angle with the bevelled tip of the gun straddling the crack. Use enough pressure to fill the crack, not just enough to coat it.

Tiny cracks between tread and riser on outside steps should be sealed. Time to caulk is when the cracks first appear—do this before the winter frosts.

Wide cracks in masonry should be filled with mortar before any caulking is done. About $\frac{3}{8}$ inch is the maximum width for cracks that are safe to caulk; if they are wider, fill them with mortar first.

Inside caulking double-seals windows and frames against cold winter air, summer's humidity. If you plan to paint over the caulk, wait a few days after application for skin to form on surface.

Caulking around door-frame will keep workshop dust and dirt confined. Rough framing without caulk invites insects, dust and dirt.

Like toothpaste, caulking compound can be bought in roll-up tube with built-in nozzle. Tube has key that helps you roll it up easily. Here caulking is placed around bottom of column where it joins porch floor. Caulking helps to stop rot and decay.

Cartridges of caulk with their own nozzles can be slipped quickly into "side-loading" guns, and disposal of empty cartridges is as easy as getting rid of empty tomato cans. Check your home each year; cracks can open up frequently where wood meets wall or other kinds of masonry.

Guns for bulk caulk are made in size that will accommodate cartridges (shown) as well as caulk from big cans. The advantage of bulk caulk is that it is generally cheaper. There is also heavier grade for application with a putty knife.

Rope-form caulk comes in coiled strands, so you can unroll and use quantity you need. This material can be handled with fingers, but sticks well when formed into place.

Guard against rot

A wood preservative serves to curb rot. With any preservative, you get greatest protection when the largest possible amount of preservative penetrates the wood to the greatest possible depth.

Creosote is excellent for outdoor structures. Around your home you will probably prefer such preservatives as water-soluble chemicals (zinc chloride, for example) and organic-solvent types, which are essentially a solution of pentachlorophenol or copper naphthenate in a petroleum solvent, such as paraffin.

The best protected timber is that which has been pressure- or vacuum-treated at the mill. The best home treatment is "cold soaking" it in a tank of preservative. Preservative may also be brushed or sprayed on.

If mixed with a light, volatile solvent, preservatives may be painted over. Frequently the organic-solvent preservatives have waxes added to retard moisture penetration.

Apply preservatives to clean, dry wood. If timber will be exposed below or at ground line, soak 24 to 48 hours.

Apply preservative liberally with a brush before repainting your home. Be especially careful you soak places where moisture gathers or where wood is near or at ground line. Doorsills, bottom edge of siding, window frames, and virtually all framing members of your home need the protection of a preservative.

Turn the page for steps to take if you are too late with the preservative.

Mildew, a fungus, makes dark, rashlike spots where there is little sunlight, high humidity. Wash with warm water and soapsuds or trisodium phosphate solution.

Wood preservative solutions are protection against decay, termites. Use wherever moisture is a problem. Apply to new and old lumber, brushing it liberally.

Damaged or rotting window sill is easy to replace

To replace damaged sill and renew beading as necessary. Saw through sill. Pry out pieces without damaging side jambs. New sill should extend under side jambs.

Cut new sill to length; notch it to extend beyond frame. Apply knotting and primer to sill. In fitting, cut into frame if necessary to get snug joint. Wedges hold sill for nailing.

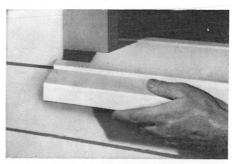

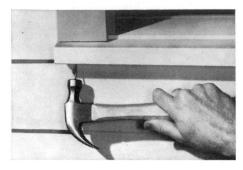

Nail new sill either from underneath or through side frames. Sill must be level and side frames plumb. Use oval nails. Use putty to fill nail holes.

Openings in joints should be sealed with calking to prevent recurrence of moisture damage. Replace all beadings. Try sash to be sure it works before re-painting.

Repairs to boarded walls

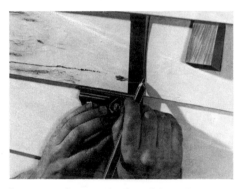

Use wide chisel to loosen strip above damaged board. Tap strip back, pull nails. Remove nails from damaged piece same way. Or, drive nails through siding with nail punch.

Insert wedges under board just above one you are removing. Work carefully to avoid splitting. Use square to mark vertical guidelines for saw cut. New board must fit tightly.

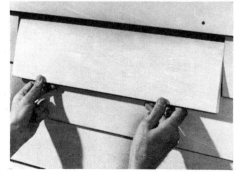

With wedges in place, cut out damaged board. Cut back to edge of studs or wall battens on both sides of damage. Nail cleats to studs to support new siding.

Cut and fit new piece of siding. Prime new board and exposed edges of old siding. Nail piece in place with rust-proof nails. Caulking compound fills holes and open joints.

Hose ages fast in summer sun, whether it is rubber or plastic. So hang it up when it is not in use. A circle of cans or an old bucket screwed to garage or tool house wall makes a good hanger, and holds small tools.

Try this short cut to coiling a hose. Pull hose out straight to eliminate kinks, and lay it in a figure 8 like this. Then fold into a circle for storing. When used, hose uncoils freely without the usual kinking or twisting.

How to care for a garden hose

Clamp, gripper fastenings speed hose repairs

When break appears near end, cut off damaged section and trim end square. Insert replacement coupling—either male or female, as necessary. Soap hose to make joining easier. Tap grippers down around hose.

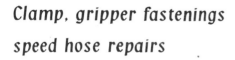

Screw clips are used to fasten simple couplings. For snug fit, inside diameter of closed band should be slightly smaller than outside diameter of hose. Tighten screw, and band will fasten hose securely to coupling.

To splice hose, cut out damaged section and square off ends. Band of tape around hose makes good guide for squaring up ends. Tap grippers before inserting second half of hose. Do not fasten grippers so tight they cut hose.

Patches will repair small breaks in plastic hose-pipe

Small breaks in plastic hose can be repaired with materials in a small kit that you can buy. The kit contains patches and adhesive. Clean pipe and cut a patch to cover the leak. Remove backing from patch and apply adhesive. Observe "set-off" time before bringing patch and pipe together. Press patch firmly in place and let dry.

To repair plastic hose, cut out damaged section and square up ends. Square ends are necessary for a watertight union, since plastic has less flexibility than a rubber hose. Use a straight-edged block as a guide when you make the cut. Block also helps steady hose.

Before attaching the repair coupling, soften the plastic. One method is shown above. Dip end of hose in hot water, near boiling, for about 20 seconds. Soften only first half inch of the hose this way. If more is softened, the hose may buckle behind the coupling.

A candle provides another effective way to soften the end of a plastic hose for repairs. Hold the cut end over candle flame and twirl it to heat it evenly. Just soften the plastic—do not heat until it sags. As in the hot-water method, soften only half an inch on the end. While the plastic is still soft, insert the metal coupling. .These couplers may vary in detail, but the basic principle of all makes is similar.

Building with blocks

Any garage, shed or lean-to which you plan to build will grow more quickly if you use building blocks instead of bricks. Every time you lay an 18″ × 9″ block, you are building the equivalent of six bricks, so the wall grows faster and uses less mortar.

There are several types of block which can be roughly classified as:

SOLID (dense concrete and clinker)

HOLLOW (concrete, clinker and clay)

LIGHTWEIGHT (concrete aggregate, clinker. And there is a special lightweight thermal block).

Only the dense concrete blocks can be used for external walls without further treatment against the weather. They are load-bearing but have poor thermal insulating value so need to be backed with a suitable insulating material. Walls made from other types of block need to be rendered, clad or protected by some other means to make them weather-proof.

When planning your garage or shed, the walls should—if possible—be multiples of the standard block size. This saves cutting, bad joints and waste.

Footings (foundation) for even the lightest of walls must be of concrete and twice the width of the wall being built. They should be 6″ thick and built on a strong sub-soil.

Remember that your building must conform to the new building regulations for size, position and materials. For example, a 4″ wall must not exceed 10′ in height. If the height or the length exceeds 8′, then piers 8″ square must be built at intervals of not more than 10′.

A final point—planning permission from the local authority is needed before you start to build a garage or outbuilding

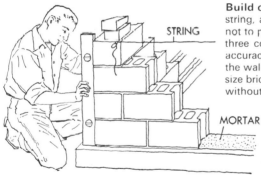

Build corners first, checking with level Stretch string, as guide for straight courses, taking care not to push the string out of line. The first two or three courses of blocks must be laid with great accuracy, because it is from these courses that the wall takes its shape. Remember that standard size bricks can be worked in with building blocks without any awkward cutting-in to do.

Use level often. Light taps with trowel handle help jiggle the block into position, as hand holding level exerts gentle pressure in desired direction. Once the block is in place, true and level, do not move it, or the bond of mortar will be destroyed.

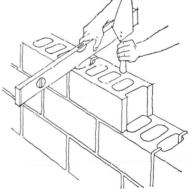

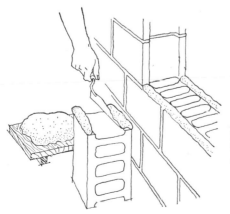

Butter edges of laid course for two or three block lengths. Then butter ends of block, slide them into position. Mortar must be continuous. Avoid letting mortar spread across blocks.

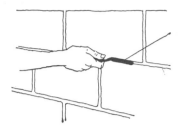

Strike joints after mortar has set slightly, to harden them, increase tightness to weather. Use a regular joint tool, or improvise with a $\frac{1}{2}$-inch steel rod.

Side wall piers

The best way, from the point of view of appearance, to construct the side wall pier is to form a set-back half way along the wall, using a 9″ square block. Thereafter a 9″ square block should be used at the pier in every other course, alternating with two full-size blocks (18″ by 9″ by $4\frac{1}{2}$″) overlapping for half their length.

The cavities of the pier blocks should be filled with 1:$2\frac{1}{2}$:4 concrete as the work proceeds. If additional strength is required, a steel reinforcing rod may be inserted into the cavity.

Special blocks fit in around door, window openings. After sill is mortared in, brace frame in place, then lay block up to them on both sides in frames at the same time. Lintel is mortared across the top, if masonry goes above it.

A brick for the un-handyman

Inca bricks are made. from a special formula plastic, and just slot together. They come in three sizes and are assembled dry; need no painting or plastering; and a full cavity wall can be set with one thickness of brick. The cavity can be used to hide or run in electricity cables or pipes.

The bricks are self-aligning and featherweight—13 ounces against 14 pounds for a comparable brick—so handling is easy, and there need be no messy cement inside the house. For extra insulation, they can be filled with sand, foam or loose fill.

The bricks are secured to the floor by 5/16th inch tie rods. These are first anchored by eye screws in a timber floor strip, then pass up through the cavities in the bricks to the top of the partition. Some of them are taken through a timber wall plate (at the top of the wall) and bolted down to tension the wall. The rest tie down the first three courses with metal plates which are seated inside the brick.

The illustrations here show some of the things that the un-handy man can do with this type of brick. For the experienced handyman, these bricks are also load bearing and can be used to build workshops, garages, greenhouses, etc.

Double bedroom into two singles. Opaque bricks up to 6 feet, then, if you wish, translucent bricks above for 'borrowed light'. Door jambs either held to bricks with one of the proprietary cavity fixing pins, or a timber insert —suit yourself! Put up permanently or take down tomorrow. Store bricks outdoors in neat cubes. Cavity bricks provide excellent sound insulation.

'Ingle nook' room divider. Brick solidity without all the weight—assembled dry and without any dirt! Polished hardwood top dropped on, fixed with locating brackets or adhesive. Hide electric cables inside.

Shower partition. Put up a shower screen in minutes! Use Inca-Mastik to seal bricks. Solvent-weld plastic fittings. Fix shower pipes in position with high heat resistant polypropylene clips.

Draught-free porch. Use Inca Daylight bricks to let in all the light, keep out all the draughts. Bricks easily cut with a fine saw to fit the awkward corners. Fix outer door jambs to Inca Bricks with a timber insert—easy!

Cement chart

JOB	MIXTURE			
	CEMENT	LIME	SAND	COARSE AGGREGATE
BEDDING FOR PAVING SLABS	–	1	3	–
DRIVES, GARAGE AND SHED BASES FOUNDATIONS FOR BRICK WALLS, ETC.	1	–	$2\frac{1}{2}$	4
MAKING WALL BLOCKS	1	–	2	4
GARDEN PATHS, REINFORCED CONCRETE FOR SILL, LINTELS, ETC.	1	–	2	3
POINTING BRICKWORK	1	2	8	–
COLD WEATHER MIX FOR EXTERNAL WALLS	1	1	5	–
FINE WEATHER MIX FOR EXTERNAL WALLS				
MIX FOR INTERNAL WALLS	1	1	4	–
DAMP RESISTANT MIX	1	–	3	–
FLOORING SCREEDS	1	–	3	–

Types of mortar joints

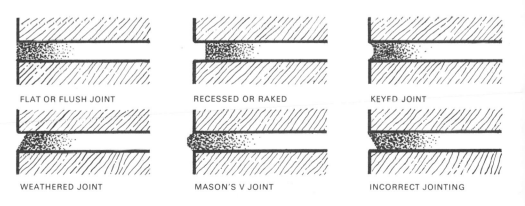

FLAT OR FLUSH JOINT   RECESSED OR RAKED   KEYED JOINT

WEATHERED JOINT   MASON'S V JOINT   INCORRECT JOINTING

How to lay bricks

If you want to make bricklaying as simple as it looks, take these important preliminary steps.

1. Select the right brick for the job. Many different colours, types, and sizes are available. For most work, you will probably be satisfied with the $8\frac{3}{4} \times 4\frac{3}{16} \times 2\frac{7}{8}$-inch common brick. But there may be times when you will want fire brick, paving brick, a rough-textured brick, or some other type.

2. Decide which mortar to use. Some of the formulas are stronger than others; some are lighter in colour. A good one is a cement and lime mortar made of 1 part Portland cement, 1 part hydrated lime, 6 parts sand (or in place of lime add a plasticing agent).

This is recommended for all kinds of brickwork that is exposed to weathering.

3. Determine the pattern in which you will lay the brick. The design of the brickwork is the "bond", and there are many of them.

4. Choose the type of mortar joint to make between the bricks. See diagram of various mortar joints.

5. Decide on thickness. For a wall not over 2 feet high, you can manage with a single tier of brick. Higher walls should be 2 bricks wide. Whether the wall is of single or double construction give it strength by adding a pier every 8-10 feet.

6. Get the right tools—a good mason's trowel, cold chisel, hammer, rule, steel square for laying out corners, spirit level, mortar box, bucket, a strong white cotton line, and a piece of pipe for tooling joints.

7. If the wall is to be only six bricks high and purely decorative the founda-tions need be only a 2" layer of concrete on consolidated hardcore. For other walls, it should be of concrete 18" wide × 9" deep on consolidated hardcore. In both cases the foundation level should be one brick below the earth level.

8. Finally, wet the bricks down thoroughly. Let the fine spray of a hose play on them for an hour or so.

1 Mortar mixture given in step 2, left, makes a good mix. Sand should be dry, cement and lime free of lumps. Mix dry ingredients to a uniform colour. Then pour in water a little at a time; mix until it looks like a smooth plastic. The mortar should be mixed on a solid flat surface such as a concrete drive or path, but the area must be washed down with water before the "left-overs" from the mix set hard. If such a surface is not available, then mortar should be mixed up on 1 inch boards fixed together to give a suitable working area. Flat galvanised iron sheets give a good mixing surface.

2 First, stretch a line between stakes. To make sure that you cut no more bricks than necessary, lay out the bricks experimentally. Start the corner leads (shown in photograph) between which the rest of bricks will be laid later.

3 Use spirit level often. Hardest job is keeping brickwork straight. Use level to check vertical and horizontal lines, particularly on corner leads. Always keep leads higher than intervening brickwork.

4 When corner leads are established, drive a nail into end of each lead and stretch a cord between them. This guide-line should mark top and outside edge of next course to be laid between the leads.

5 Pick up a trowel of mortar and spread it with a smooth sweep over one or two of the bricks of the course. Then, with the point of the trowel, make a shallow furrow down the centre of the mortar bed.

6 To fill the joint between the ends of two bricks, butter the ends of the brick to be laid with mortar. Do not try to lay the bricks first and then slush the mortar into the crack between them.

7 Shove brick down into mortar bed and against the last brick until mortar oozes out at top and joint is the right size. If brick is too high, tap it with trowel. Cut off excess mortar flush with brick.

8 To lay the closure brick (last brick in a course), put mortar on both ends of the bricks and on the ends of the two bricks that are already in place. Once a brick is laid, do not shift its position.

9 When you lay a wall of two or more tiers, work a thin soupy mortar down into the centre joint with a trowel. The bed of mortar for each course should extend from front to back of the wall so the joint between tiers is never more than one brick deep. When you finish a day's work, cover the top of the exposed brickwork with boards, tar paper, or tarpaulin. Lay header course every fifth, sixth, or seventh course of wall to tie the two tiers of stretcher bricks firmly together.

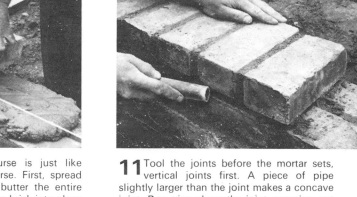

10 Laying a header course is just like laying a stretcher course. First, spread a good mortar bed. Then butter the entire side of header brick and force brick into place until mortar oozes out.

11 Tool the joints before the mortar sets, vertical joints first. A piece of pipe slightly larger than the joint makes a concave joint. Run pipe along the joint, scraping out and compressing the mortar.

12 A week or two after the bricks are laid, scrub them with a solution of 1 part hydrochloric acid and 10 parts water. Rinse them immediately and thoroughly with water to remove all traces of the acid.

13 Use a brick bolster to cut a brick to fit a small space. Set brick on edge on a firm surface, and rap the chisel sharply with a hammer. Scoring all sides of the brick first will help assure a square cut.

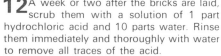

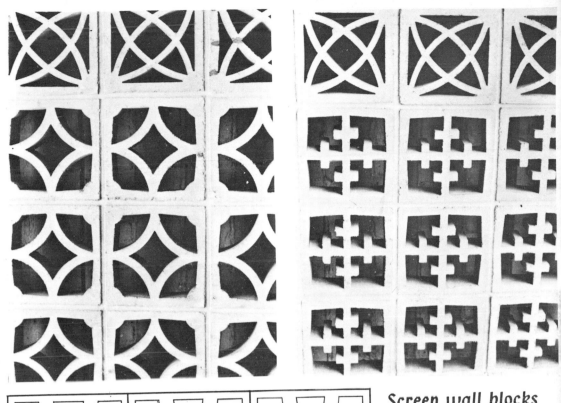

Screen wall blocks

Screen blocks are very popular and can be used to build ornamental garden walls in a great variety of designs. The blocks come in many sizes and colours and can be used in conjunction with the standard brick. Footings required are as for brick.

Cutting the units should be avoided as far as possible, so wall dimensions should be chosen to suit unit sizes. Below are a few of the attractive wall screens available.

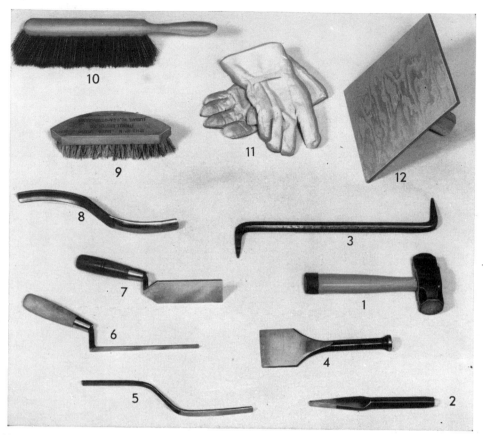

Here are the tools for masonry repair jobs: club hammer (1); cross-cut chisel (2); mortar rake (3); brick bolster (4). These tools are used for cleaning out old mortar. Other tools are: double-bladed joint filler (5); single (6); square-ended marginal trowel (7); striking tool to match joint surface (8); soft-bristled wet brush (9); stiff-bristled dry brush (10). Canvas work gloves are a good idea; they will protect your hands during the rough work of removing the old mortar. Make pointing hawk (12) from plywood.

Mortar joint repairs

It is not often that brickwork needs repairing. Well-laid walls will last a lifetime, but re-pointing and minor repairs can be done by the handyman.

On the following pages are some useful hints and suggestions. And on pages 293-

300 there are step-by-step instructions for building a wall.

In addition to the tools shown above, you will need a bucket and a shovel to make the mortar mix.

On a joint that is cracked down one side, loosen the mortar by breaking away the un-cracked side with a brick bolster. Strike sharply enough to break the mortar, but not so hard that the chisel becomes wedged. Loosen and break the mortar this way, then remove the pieces with the rake or the point of a chisel. Widen narrow joints the same way. The same method will work on sound joints that must be removed, but it is better to use a flat chisel.

Chisel out the harder spots with the cross-cut chisel, which should be smaller than the joint's width. Take the mortar out in "bites" of an inch or so, cutting inward to a depth of at least $\frac{3}{4}$ inch. Always work in bites with the chisel angled toward the open joint, or you will chip edges of the bricks. Avoid wedging the chisel, but if you do, work it out gently. The point of this type of chisel should always be "swedged" slightly (widest at the cutting edge) and should be kept sharp for cutting.

Cracks that run through a brick may be left alone if not over $\frac{1}{32}$ inch wide. If crack is wider, the brick should be removed and replaced. Where appearance is not important, or if a replacement brick is not available, cut a joint through the brick with the wide chisel. Angle the chisel toward the crack and tap gently to avoid wedging the chisel. Another method is to cut and point a joint through the cracked brick, then paint it to match the brick after the mortar has dried thoroughly.

Old, soft mortar or joints loosened with a wide chisel are best cleaned out with a mortar rake as shown. Pull the point down the edge of the joint to remove all of the old mortar. Clean all edges this way to give the new mortar a clean edge to bond with. The mortar rake is also handy for removing old caulking compound from around windows and doors. Joints too hard or too narrow to rake out should be chiselled out or cut with a portable electric saw.

Mortar mix is 1 part cement, 1 part lime and 6 parts sand or instead of lime add a plasticing agent. Add waterproofing mixture if desired. Small amounts of mortar can be mixed in a bucket, as shown; larger amounts in a mortar box. Colour can be added to the mix to match the existing mortar. Wet a sample of the old mortar, then mix the new a few shades darker—it will become lighter as it dries.

Add water to the dry mortar mix until it is the consistency of thick paste and stands on your trowel as shown above. Use no more water than necessary—it is easy to smear the wall with too wet a mix. If the mortar becomes too wet, add a small amount of dry mix or let it stand until it thickens. Do not mix more than you can use in an hour. Dampen the pointing hawk before using—it will help keep the mortar from sliding off. Be sure the joint is clean and damp before you begin pointing; use wet brush or fine spray.

Here is the easy way to fill a horizontal joint —simply push the mortar off the hawk and into the joint with a joint filler. Use several strokes, taking off a small amount of mortar each time to avoid smearing mortar outside the joint. Pack mortar tightly, then cut off excess with a trowel. Keep joint—entire wall if possible—damp while working. If it dries moisten with wet brush or fine spray from garden hose, but be careful not to wash fresh mortar out of new joints onto bricks.

For vertical or hard-to-reach joints, scoop up a bit of mortar on end of joint filler as shown. With practice, you will be able to slide it off the hawk and into the joint in one continuous motion. If your mortar is the right pasty consistency, it will stick to the tool long enough to reach the joint. It helps if you tilt the front edge of the hawk upward as you slide the mortar off and up into joint. If the mortar becomes too dry, add some water and re-mix. Keep mortar out of the sun.

Mixtures figured out for you

PART EMENT   **2 PARTS SAND**   **3 PARTS GRAVEL**

Mix it yourself for patching or construction. Use 1 part cement, 2 parts sand, and 3 parts gravel. First mix cement and aggregate (sand and gravel) to uniform colour. Add water—a little at a time. Too much weakens mixture; never use over 6 gallons to 1 sack of cement. See also chart on mixes—see page 297.

Ready mixed cements are easy for the handyman to use. They come sacked with right proportions of cement, sand, and gravel. You add water according to directions. Job determines type of mixture. Mortar mix (1) is for pointing and bricklaying; medium mix (2) is for walks and concrete floors; heavy mix (3) is for driveways, curbings. Small quantities can be mixed; entire sack need not be used.

How to use concrete

Equipment which you will need is pictured here: (1) a wood float, which you can make, (2) steel trowel, (3) 10-foot rule, (4) edger, (5) bucket, (6) hammer, (7) nails, (8) level to check the forms, (9) shovel, (10) saw, (11) straight-edged board, and (12) measuring box. Box is 3 feet long, 1 foot wide, and 1 foot deep.

With a few inexpensive tools, you can do such jobs with concrete as laying a path or drive, or laying paving stones.

You can get a good concrete mix by using materials in the proportions shown in the upper left-hand photograph. Mix cement and sand first to uniform colour, then stir in coarse aggregate. Make a depression in the middle of the dry pile, and add water gradually, mixing until concrete reaches the right consistency.

However, if you do a large job, like a driveway, tell a ready-mix contractor the width, length, and depth of the area to be filled. He will estimate your needs, and a truck will deliver mixed concrete to you.

Many jobs can be done with ready-to-mix formulas that come packaged in correct proportions (see upper right-hand photograph).

You can lay the concrete directly onto the ground but take the necessary precautions—see pages 306-9.

Build form, held with stakes on outside. Pitch surface slightly for drainage. On soft ground use a hardcore base. If new concrete butts against fixed object, insert expansion joint. Coat form with oil so new concrete will not stick.

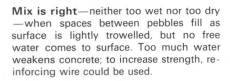

Mix is right—neither too wet nor too dry —when spaces between pebbles fill as surface is lightly trowelled, but no free water comes to surface. Too much water weakens concrete; to increase strength, reinforcing wire could be used.

Use concrete within 30 minutes of mixing it. Spade well as it is laid to make it dense. Then screed it off level with a straight-edged board (shown). Now there should be only a faint film of water on surface. Slide board along top edge of forms so concrete surface is smooth and level.

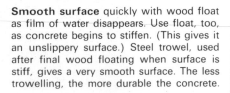

Smooth surface quickly with wood float as film of water disappears. Use float, too, as concrete begins to stiffen. (This gives it an unslippery surface.) Steel trowel, used after final wood floating when surface is stiff, gives a very smooth surface. The less trowelling, the more durable the concrete.

Edging tools give job professional look; use them immediately after surface has been trowelled. Edging gives neat roundness to grooves between sections and to edges. Divide walk into sections by cutting a groove with trowel one-third thickness of slab. Finish groove as shown.

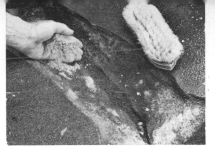

To patch broken concrete, clean and dampen break. Do not leave water standing on surface, though. Put form in place, if necessary, then scatter pure cement right out of sack into break (centre). Scrub cement in with brush as primer for patch.

To assure firm bond, place concrete in break before primer dries. Place patch (right) within half an hour after concrete is mixed. For dense concrete, tamp with shovel or trowel while placing. When break is full, level patch.

How to lay paving slabs and stones

A garden path should be decorative as well as useful, so you may want to surface it with stone, tile, or brick.

Heavy materials can be laid directly on a sand base but strength is added to less sturdy ones by laying them on a mortar base.

In addition to allowing the use of thinner surfacing materials, a solid mortar base eliminates weeding between cracks and resists frost damage.

The procedure shown here with stone is the same one used with brick, tile, and other paving materials.

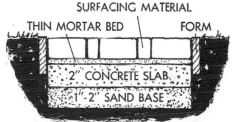

SURFACING MATERIAL
THIN MORTAR BED FORM
2" CONCRETE SLAB
1"-2" SAND BASE

Typical mortar base cross section shows concrete slab placed over sand base. On slab is a thin layer of mortar in which the paving materials are laid. Bricks are shown here, but stone (photograph below) or other such materials may be used.

Spread a 1" layer of concrete on firm base and level off. Lay slabs or crazy paving direct on to this mortar mix. Tamp down slabs, etc. with wooden mallet and use spirit level often.

When paving is placed, fill cracks with same sand-cement mix you embed materials in. Leave no air pockets. Stiff mortar is easiest to work with at this stage. Brush with broom to improve texture.

How to lay paving materials directly on a sand base

A good sand base is a surprisingly solid foundation for outdoor paving. If sand is well soaked and tamped before you lay paving, you will have only a minimum of settling.

Bricks, tile, stones and concrete slabs can be placed directly on the sand base.

If you pave beneath trees, sand base may be preferred because it lets water and air down to roots. Maintenance is greater than with mortar-base paving. You will have to weed between cracks and level bricks occasionally.

Secret of good sand-base paving is careful tamping and fitting. Tamp sand under each paving unit as you lay it. Sand base provides drainage, simplifies laying, and reduces frost heaving. Soak the sand thoroughly first.

Many patterns can be worked out with most paving materials. To save time, experiment on grass or drive first. Here, 8-inch tiles in staggered pattern are used with standard bricks of same colour. (Bricks fill 4-inch gaps.)

Tamp to settle and smooth the surface as you finish each row of paving. Do not tamp directly on paving itself or you may crack it. Check the edges of the paving often to see that they line up with the edges of the form.

When you have finished laying the paving, brush sand between cracks. Dry sand will sift better. Do a good job of filling cracks, and you will have less rocking and shifting of the tiles or whatever paving material you use.

After brushing in all the sand that you can, spread more sand and wash it between cracks with a hose. Repeat until cracks are filled. Remove forms and replace sod around outside of paving, or leave forms as a border.

How to make forms and grids for concrete paths

Simple paths or terraces with rectangular or square divisions usually need no further elaboration to be attractive. Squares are sometimes left open for planting flowering shrubs, etc. The thickness of concrete recommended is 2'' on normal ground, and 3'' on soft ground.

Clear the site of grass and loose stones and pack the earth thoroughly by rolling or ramming. Soft earth, rubble (hardcore) or clinker should be rammed into the ground before laying concrete.

Lay forms made up of wood of the same depth as the thickness of the concrete to be laid. All pegs should be on the outside of the forms. Concreting can either be done continuously or in bays. Either way it is wise to keep to a maximum workable distance of 5'. In continuous concreting, thin softwood laths should be placed every 5' and left permanently in place—these and other joints prevent concrete from cracking through frost, etc.

The first step is to level off ground. Frame area to be concreted, using pegs on outside of frame to secure it. Now add cross-pieces to form desired pattern of path or terrace.

Check form to see that it is level when finished. Prop up sections that sag; remove earth or hardcore from those that ride high. If terrace adjoins the house or garage, give it a slight pitch so surface water will drain away. To get uniform pitch easily, pack with same size pieces of scrap wood along one side of the form.

Make a curved border by driving stakes at 3 foot intervals on desired arc. For removable border form, use 4'' strips of $\frac{1}{8}$'' or $\frac{1}{4}$'' hardboard. This is ideal material for the purpose as it will not crack or split when in contact with water.

How to handle pre-mixed concrete

When the forms are in and the hardcore base has been laid, you are ready to take delivery of the concrete. If the area to be concreted is a big one, have only half of the concrete delivered at a time.

By filling every other form, you can work on all four sides of each square, so the job will be much easier and quicker.

Be certain everything is ready for the arrival of the concrete. Check the forms again—have surfacing tools on hand. You will need a shovel, a concrete trowel, and a straight edge. As concrete is poured, tamp it in corners.

Each form should be slightly over-filled. Remove surplus and level the surface by using a heavy board, a foot or so longer than the form. Work this back and forth with a sawing motion. Do not attempt to get surface smooth at this time—just level.

After levelling, take a break. Allow the concrete to go off. Begin checking it with a trowel after 20 or 30 minutes. When trowelling no longer brings water to the surface, give concrete its final finish. Use a steel trowel for smooth surface, wood for a rough one, or you can leave the rough surface left by the levelling board.

An attractive fence like this can be constructed by a handyman. The lath screen effectively partitions areas in the garden. Sink 2 × 4s as support first, bolstering the foundation with concrete to offset high wind resistance offered by the fence. Add a slotted 1 × 6 for baseboard; cover lath and baseboard junction with quarter-round moulding. Two 2 × 3s, nailed to the uprights near top, support the 3 × 1 inch slatts. In addition, they give another horizontal line to fence's predominately vertical appearance. You can modify the design with colour variations or with changes in spacing between the slender lath uprights

How to build a fence

A fence can do several things for you: mark property lines, give privacy, help control wind, provide a background for flowers, keep children and pets in or out of the garden.

A handyman can build virtually any type of fence. The most intricate will generally have three simple parts: posts, rails, and screening. In some cases, the rails may actually screen.

Post-and-rail fence has many variations

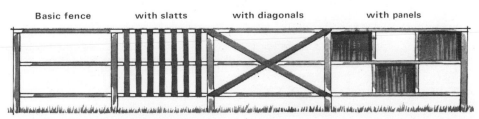

Basic fence   with slatts   with diagonals   with panels

Post-and-rail fence quickly changes its character when you start adding extras. Just which screening material you add depends on what you want the fence to do. A general rule: make pattern evolve from material and way it is used. Do not tack on unneeded trim.

Set corner posts first, then connect the tops with a taut cord. When the end posts are even, the other posts can be levelled easily.

First, set the posts ...

Before beginning to erect or even buy fencing materials, check with your local authority about regulations regarding fences. On some boundaries, fences may not exceed a certain height, and in other cases the type of fence is stipulated.

Stake out position of fence and run guide lines between stakes. Next place stake at each post position—these should be between 6 feet and 8 feet apart, 8 feet being the maximum.

Posts which are to carry heavy fencework should be buried one-third of their length or to a depth of 2 feet if anchored in concrete. This does not, of course, apply if you are using concrete spurs.

To lengthen the life of posts, set each on a pocket of gravel or sand for drainage. If the posts are not pre-treated, coat the parts to be buried with a chemical preservative.

As you set posts, brace with outrigger stakes and check alignment. Do not tamp soil around posts until alignment and height are correct.

When setting posts in concrete, mound top to shed water away from post. Let the mortar set about 4 or 5 days before continuing work.

... then add the rails and screening

The basic post-and-rail fence is easy to build, and needs no adornment. Every joint, however, will show, so workmanship is important—unless materials are rustic so that minor imperfections do not detract.

You can build a basic post-and-rail fence now, and add panels or slats later. Choose joints that will carry weight of screening material.

The method of fastening depends on size of timber and weight that rails will carry. A butt joint is usually unsatisfactory unless it is supported by a cleat, made of wood or metal. (Metal ones are less conspicuous.)

There are many ways to make screening that will help control wind, sight, and even noise. *Vertical slats* may be made of 2 or 3 ×1, or dowels; *diagonal braces*, of 4 or 5 ×1 timber; *panels*, of wood, plastic, asbestos, wire mesh or plywood.

Add top rail first. Use it as a guide for lining up other rails. Coat wood at joints with preservative before nailing. When posts are spaced accurately, pre-cut the rails and save fitting time.

These basic joints can be modified according to your experience and equipment. Butt joint on left is substitute for mortise joint on right. Lap joint, centre, is common fence type—also used often for attaching rails to side of post.

Mark the position for the bottom rail by measuring from the top rail—not by reference to the ground level. Use nails which are at least three times longer than the thickness of the wood.

Ideal for the unhandyman

Here are two outside constructional jobs that can be made from the plastic bricks described on page 295. Full instructions on how to lay the concrete foundations are supplied by the manufacturers. The wooden cross beams of the rose trellis piers can be purchased from timber yards or do-it-yourself shops. The door to the greenhouse is a stock item obtainable from any builders' merchant.

With rose trellis piers you can build an ornamental rose walk with a handsome brick finish, which will not rot or fall down. Use alternating colours for patterned effects, either random or in courses. Top garden wall with flowers.

Garden greenhouse can be rotproof. Use Inca Bricks for base walls and Inca Daylights above. These are translucent, letting in the light but protecting tender plants. Cavity in bricks provides excellent insulation too.

Turn a terrace into an attractive patio with this pre machined and easy-to-erect loggia kit. Made from rot-resistant red cedar, it comes in two sizes complete with nails and screws. All uprights and roof timbers are notched and tapered ready for erection. The unhandyman (or for that matter the handyman) should have no difficulty in making a professional job from these kits—and they can be added to at a later date.

Another kit for the unhandyman is this pergola. Once again this is made from red cedar and all posts, cross and side timbers are notched ready for erection. The kits (there are two sizes) include plastic covered wires and rust proof screw eyes, so no maintenance is required and therefore climbers need not be disturbed. The avenue between posts can be 5 ft. 4 ins. or 3 ft. 6 ins.

Retaining wall-fence in wood

Use retaining wall-fences like the one shown below to create unusual terrace or patio designs.

The type of wall you build will depend on the height needed and on the materials available. Before starting the job, make a detailed plan of the design you have in mind.

Construction of the simplest and smallest retaining wall will mean the moving of some soil and some digging—both jobs are hard work—so design your wall-fence to cut labour to a minimum. On page 301, there are some ideas for brick walls and fences.

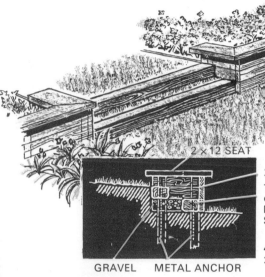

2 × 12 SEAT

2 × 6 BOARDS
TREE TRUNKS
or
RAILWAY
SLEEPERS

4 × 4 POSTS
30" IN SOIL

GRAVEL   METAL ANCHOR

This wall incorporates a flight of steps in a retaining wall, and uses hidden posts for support. When posts are placed in front of a wall, the soil forces the wall tightly against the posts. But, when the posts are behind the wall, the joints must carry the full pressure of the soil behind the wall. To carry this weight, fasten the face boards with 6-inch carriage bolts. This type of construction is not advised for walls higher than 30 inches.

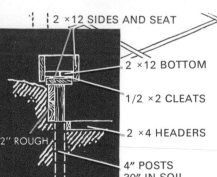

2 × 12 SIDES AND SEAT

2 × 12 BOTTOM

1/2 × 2 CLEATS

2 × 4 HEADERS

2" ROUGH

4" POSTS
30" IN SOIL

36" O.C.

Here is a simple method of combining a flower-box with a seat wall. The flower-box can be removed at any time; it gives you an opportunity to introduce more colour to your landscaping theme. Notice that the paving units coincide with intervals between posts.

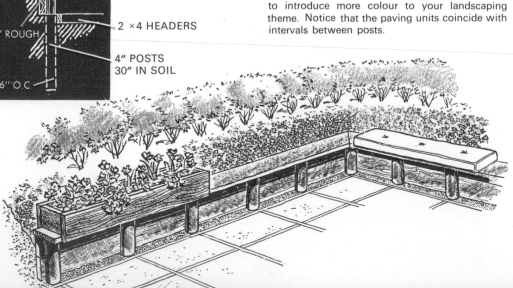

This design incorporates a seat, and the posts can be extended to support a trellis top. The seat support posts are set in concrete, and the others can be set direct into the earth. Instead of using chains to support the seat, legs could be added to the front corners.

In this design the wall is extended beyond the bank of earth and converted into a fence, which terminates in a corner and lamp-post. Alternate posts, inside-outside, for looks.

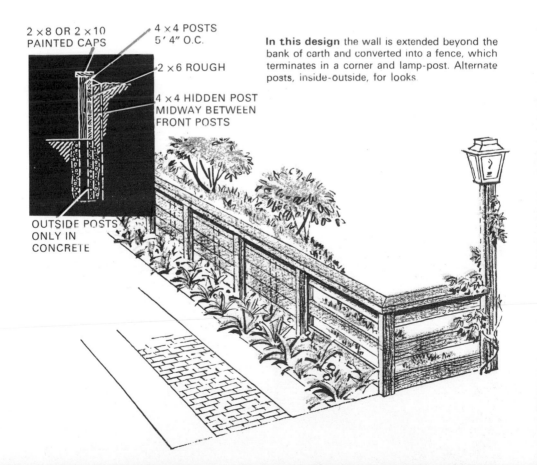

2 × 8 OR 2 × 10 PAINTED CAPS

4 × 4 POSTS 5′ 4″ O.C.

2 × 6 ROUGH

4 × 4 HIDDEN POST MIDWAY BETWEEN FRONT POSTS

OUTSIDE POSTS ONLY IN CONCRETE

Care of your garden tools

Scrape soil off a tool immediately after it is used, and before the dirt has a chance to harden. A small putty knife is just the thing to use to clean the surface of the tool.

Thoroughly rub down tool blade with coarse grade of steel wool or sandpaper if dirt has had a chance to harden on blade. Gloves protect hands against dirt and abrasions.

Sharpen a hoe (shown), shovel, grass clippers, and pruners regularly. Clamp in vice for filing. File only the face of a hoe, keeping the strokes at about a 30-degree angle.

Use a rust preventative after cleaning tool that you will not be using again right away. Here, the preventative is painted on with a brush. A light film of oil is effective, too.

Keep the handles of your tools as smooth as possible because it is friction, not hard work, that causes blisters on hands. Sand handles, winding up with fine grade of paper.

Rub down handles of tools with linseed oil after you uave removed any splinters and other roughness by sanding. The linseed oil seals out dirt, and helps to keep the wood smooth.

Low windows, too near the floor for furniture, allow you to stretch storage completely across one wall. And sliding doors do not infringe on the floor space for furniture. Added advantage: cabinets give you continuous work counter. This same idea can be used to line walls without windows.

Storage problems

Good storage is the result of careful planning that makes the most of even the smallest space. When you plan your new storage, keep this question in mind: Will it do the job I want it to do?

When possible, gain more storage space by incorporating a number of basic ideas into one unit.

On the next few pages there are some construction suggestions for increasing the storage space in your home. Use these ideas either on their own or combined to suit your needs.

Typical storage areas   Areas where storage can be added

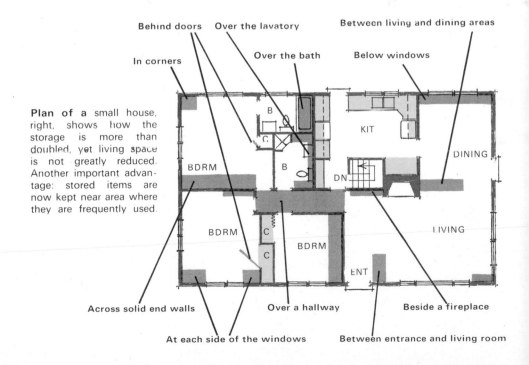

Plan of a small house, right, shows how the storage is more than doubled, yet living space is not greatly reduced. Another important advantage: stored items are now kept near area where they are frequently used.

Behind doors   Over the lavatory   Between living and dining areas

In corners   Over the bath   Below windows

Across solid end walls   Over a hallway   Beside a fireplace

At each side of the windows   Between entrance and living room

B   KIT   DINING

BDRM   B   DN   LIVING

BDRM   C   BDRM   ENT

C

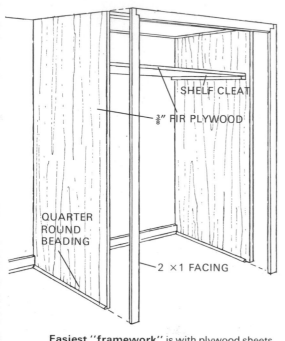

SHELF CLEAT

$\frac{3}{8}''$ FIR PLYWOOD

QUARTER ROUND BEADING

2 ×1 FACING

Cupboards to make...

Easiest "framework" is with plywood sheets cut to form storage unit to which you can add shelves, hanging poles, drawers, door, so on.

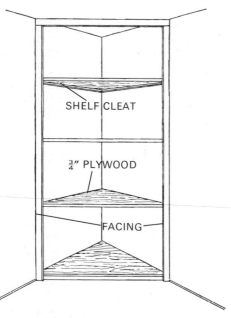

SHELF CLEAT

$\frac{3}{4}''$ PLYWOOD

FACING

Corner cabinets usually have plywood shelves. Shelves fit into supports fixed to walls at sides. Facing is made up of 2 ×1 battens. Doors fasten to frame. Edge shelf fronts with solid wood.

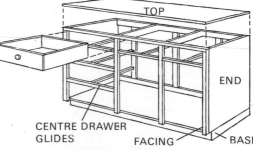

GROOVE FOR SHELF

RABBET JOINTS

Bookshelf parts consist of five pieces of wood—four pieces form "shell" in which shelf fastens. Add legs, back, doors or drawers, and unit becomes a cabinet.

TOP

END

CENTRE DRAWER GLIDES

FACING

BASE

Base cabinet is also wooden shell—with 1 ×2 batten frame with hardboard or 3 ply sides—in which drawers and the shelves are fitted. Width of 1 ×4 base, 3 inches narrower than cabinet width—allows "toe" room. Unit can be bolted to the wall or left unattached.

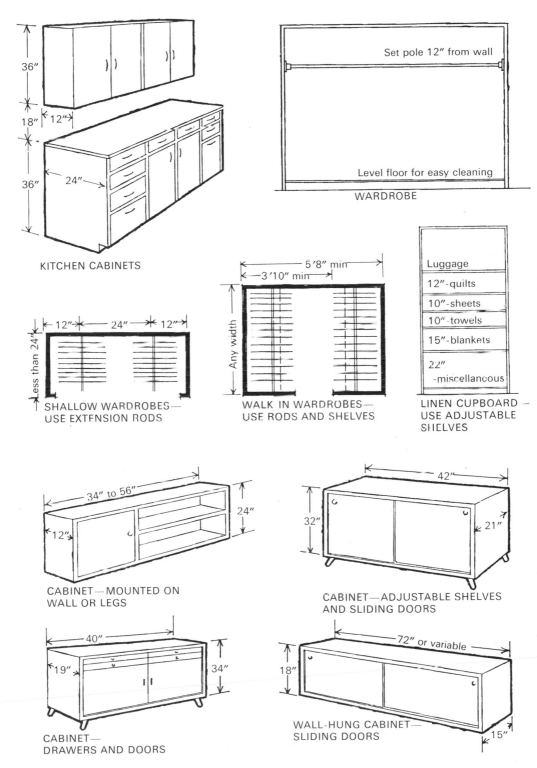

36″

18″ 12″

36″ 24″

KITCHEN CABINETS

Set pole 12″ from wall

Level floor for easy cleaning

WARDROBE

Less than 24″

12″ 24″ 12″

SHALLOW WARDROBES—
USE EXTENSION RODS

5′8″ min
3′10″ min

Any width

WALK IN WARDROBES—
USE RODS AND SHELVES

Luggage

12″-quilts

10″-sheets

10″-towels

15″-blankets

22″
-miscellaneous

LINEN CUPBOARD—
USE ADJUSTABLE
SHELVES

34″ to 56″

24″

12″

CABINET—MOUNTED ON
WALL OR LEGS

42″

32″ 21″

CABINET—ADJUSTABLE SHELVES
AND SLIDING DOORS

40″

19″ 34″

CABINET—
DRAWERS AND DOORS

72″ or variable

18″

15″

WALL-HUNG CABINET—
SLIDING DOORS

Quick index of cabinet joinery

Here is a brief survey of the kinds of joints you will be using in the construction of storage units described in this chapter.

More advice will be found in **Wood joinery methods,** page 125 and **How to use glue,** page 137.

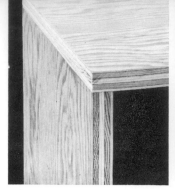

Butt joints (left) are the easiest to make, but they are weakest of joining techniques. Cut timber square and fasten with screws, nails, and glue. Rabbetted method (right) makes strong joint, especially if stress will be from top down. Width of cut is half thickness of timber; depth matches timber to be joined.

Mitred corners are more difficult, but stronger and neater than butt joints. Cut timber at 45 degrees; fasten with nails and glue.

Edge joints go together with glue; get support from dowels or splines. Locate and drill holes accurately. Put in dowels with glue, spread glue along edges, and clamp together.

Spline joint is made with a plywood strip glued and "wedged" in grooves. Cuts in edges of timber are glued and bar clamped.

Combination joint is good for joining sides of cabinets to bottoms. Fix with screws or nails and glue for extra strength.

Glue blocks will strengthen as well as add more glue surface to any joint. Push them into place with short, sliding motion so they seat tightly against both members.

Rabbet joint is good way to conceal cabinet back. Cut $\frac{1}{4}$-inch rabbets the thickness of back in sides, top, bottom framing pieces.

How to support "inside" shelves

Adjustable shelf brackets fasten to cabinet sides with screws. Tiny clips lock in holes to support shelves; clips can be re-positioned.

A groove for shelves gives maximum support against stress up or down. Fasten shelf in through side with screws or nails and glue.

Easy-to-make supports

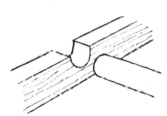 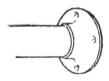 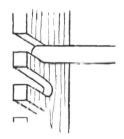

Support pieces fasten to the walls; pole fits into notch.

Insert poles in pipe flanges first; screw into cupboard walls.

For adjustable supports, cut a series of angled notches.

Cabinet doorstops

Most hinged doors need a stop to prevent them from being pushed into the cabinet, pulling screws out of their hinges or splitting wood to which hinges are screwed. Here are several ways to end this problem; each is effective.

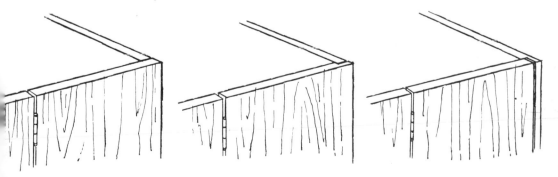

Butt stop (left) is really side of cabinet; door closes against it. Rabbet stop (centre) works on lipped door principle; the rabbet matches thickness of cabinet side. Side rabbet stop (right) is cut in the cabinet side. Other ways: door stops fixed inside cabinet or special combined door catch and step.

How to install cabinet hinges

Butt hinge is probably the quickest and easiest to install. It is screwed to facing edge and to door edge. To prevent splitting wood, drill or punch pilot holes for hinge screws.

Semi-concealed hinges are made for "lipped" (rabbetted edges) doors. To install, fasten hinge to cabinet face; hinge "plate" goes on back of the door. The screws need pilot holes.

Door catches should usually be installed near door pulls. This gives straight pull on catch when the door is opened. If catches are mounted at the top or bottom of door, hinges may be subjected to strain by uneven pull. Friction catch here is mounted under shelf.

Invisible hinge is mortised into edge of facing and door.

Pivot hinge screws to top and bottom of side and door.

H-hinge fastens to front of facing and to front of door.

Easy sliding-door construction

Double groove is the easy method for sliding doors. Make two cuts along front edge of cabinet top, bottom. Make cut $\frac{1}{16}$" wider than doors; depth: $\frac{1}{4}$" at bottom; $\frac{1}{2}$" along top. You buy plastic or wood runners already grooved.

Below is a slightly different method of runner. Make a groove with beading. Bead covers front edge of cabinet, and is fastened on with panel pins. Set pins, fill the holes, and sand them smooth.

Metal track is positioned, fastened to bottom, top of cabinet to accept metal rollers, which are mortised into top, bottom of door. Rollers are "grooved" to ride smoothly on track.

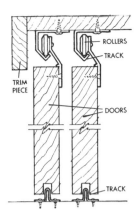

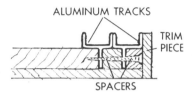

For heavy doors (above), track fastens to framing members. Door bottoms run on floor tracks. Aluminium (left) can be used for light doors. Screw it to top, bottom edges of cabinet, space with wood or hardboard strips. Pre-drill track and strips for screws; trim the edge.

How to build trouble-free drawers

A lipped front drawer front covers drawer opening when drawer is closed; it serves as a drawer stop. The size of the lip depends on the amount of frame there is to hide.

Rabbetted drawer front looks like this. The rabbets accept sides; drawer fits flush in the cabinet opening. To assemble drawer, use glue, finishing nails. Set nails, and fill holes.

Drawer bottoms should "float" in or on supports. This allows for expansion and contraction which can split drawer bottom apart if bottoms are fastened in. Support bottoms in grooves (left) or on beading. Cut grooves on a power saw.

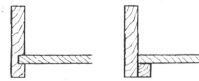

Rabbetted drawer back is neater, stronger than butt-joined back. Cut rabbet in side members to thickness of back. Use glue, screws or nails to fasten unit together.

Grooved back offers strongest construction; use for drawers that take a lot of heavy handling. To assemble any drawer, fasten back corners first, slip in bottom, then the front.

Drawer supports you can make

"**Three-point**" suspension is easiest way to support drawers. Front of the centre guide fastens to back of front facing strip; back fastens to cabinet back; centre it in opening.

"**Cleat**" **guides** fasten directly to sides of cabinet; grooved drawer sides ride on them. Cut grooves before assembling; flush drawers need 1/16 inch around drawer and opening.

Grooved drawer back accepts guide which is $\frac{1}{4}$ inch wider than front facing strip. Lipped drawer fronts hide guide. On backless cabinets, fit and nail guides in notched upright.

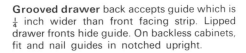

Metal drawer guides and channels for lipped drawers fasten to drawer sides and cabinet. To determine $\frac{1}{2}$-inch clearance needed, measure opening, drawer before assembly.

Grooved drawer-back technique can be used for drawer-divider frame supports. Guide is rabbeted and screwed to front, back of framing screwed to the cabinet side framing.

How to make cabinet doors

You do not need a cabinet maker's skill, expensive materials, or costly tools to build sturdy doors for cabinets and cupboards. With hand tools alone, you can make a variety of doors that will be strong, good-looking, and efficient. A power saw will speed the work and make it easier, however.

Simplicity is the secret of making good doors. Some small doors are merely rectangles of plywood, formed with a few saw cuts. Others are made from stock timbers, standard manufactured boards and simple joints.

Panels of $\frac{1}{4}$-inch plywood—natural or decorative—make good sliding doors. Cut with sharp fine-tooth saw. Apply bead to edges of large doors. Seal *both* sides with finish.

Hardboard panels slide smoothly and should not warp if finished on both sides. Drill holes for handles. Clamp and bore into block of wood to get clean edge.

Translucent doors of plastic sheet material show off shape of objects in cabinet. Keep door height under 6 inches. Cut plastic with tin shears; use silicon-carbide paper to smooth edges. Make stiffener-strip handles.

Glass sliding doors are easy—glass merchant does cutting and edge polishing. Use crystal sheet or plate, clear or obscure in variety of patterns. For handles, cement knobs to glass, or have finger holes drilled by glazier.

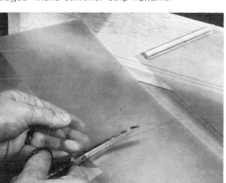

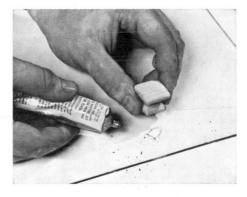

Small doors that close flush with the face of the cabinet can be made from $\frac{3}{8}$ inch ply. For stops use either edges of rabbets or strips fastened inside the opening at the correct depth. A neat and strong hinge (which also reinforces door against warp or shifting) is continuous, or "piano" type shown on door.

Make a stopped rabbet now in each side rail. Let each piece down onto saw blade, and groove it only from pencil mark to pencil mark. Use chisel to remove waste. This makes sharp inner corner to line with stile rabbet.

Medium-size doors, both sliding and hinged types, can be made with 1 x 2-inch frames and thin plywood or hardboard panels. Cut stiles and side rails to the correct length. Rabbet entire length of each piece on power saw. Lay pieces in position and mark side rails as shown here.

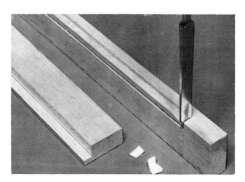

Lock rail and stile ends in clamp or vice to align surfaces. Drill through rail into stile for dowels. Centre holes on edge. After holes are drilled, smear glue on dowels, drive them into place. For interior doors, polyvinyl resin glue sets fast, requires medium pressure.

Let glue set, then trim off excess dowelling. Sand frame smooth, and finish. Cut plywood or hardboard panel to size and fit it into rabbet. Place mitred moulding strips over edges of panel. Drive brads diagonally into strips to hold the panel tight in frame.

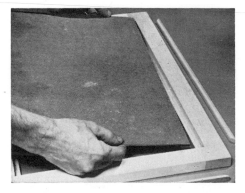

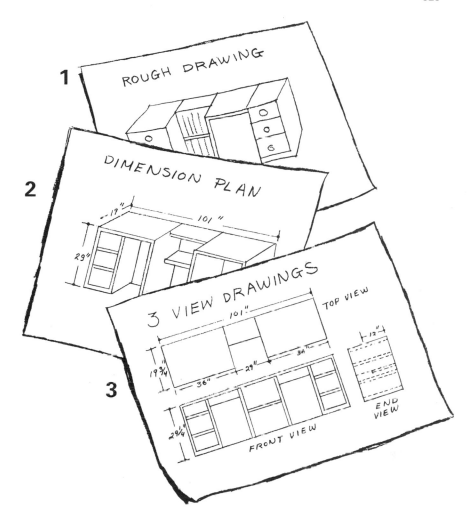

Plan projects on paper

Do not start a job with no more than a vague, half-formed idea in your head. Take an evening or two and plan the job so you will know exactly how it goes together and how much material will be needed.

The three drawings shown above are easy to make and they supply all the information you will need to plan your project to the last detail. (1) The *rough drawing* is for working out the basic design and general dimensions. (2) The *dimension plan* gives exact cut size of materials and a good idea of proportions. (3) The *three-view drawing* is called in, when necessary, to nail down every complicated detail of your project.

You need only the simplest of equipment; sheets of paper for sketching, and graph paper for the dimensional and three-view drawings. Keep to the same scale for each job. Sharp pencils, eraser, compass and ruler are basics; add T-square and set squares.

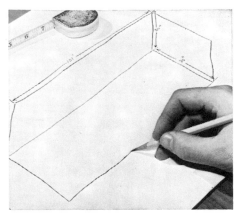

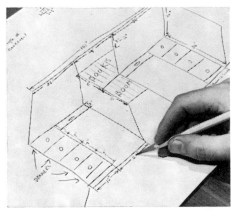

Practically any project you plan is limited in size and shape by its surroundings. The first step in planning is to determine the *limiting dimensions* and make a *rough drawing* to use as a design outline. This drawing need not be accurate in scale or proportion; all you need is the basic shape and the dimensions. Here, a three-dimensional box shows this information. A three-dimensional drawing, similar to this, not illustrating perspective, is called an isometric drawing.

The next planning step is to work out the basic design of your project to fit the space allowed exactly. If there are limiting dimensions in the design, work them out first and fill in the other details later. This double desk and bookcase unit was designed to hold a set of encyclopedias, so the books were measured and the bookcase section was designed first. Here again, scale, proportion, and thickness of materials are not as important as creating the needed design.

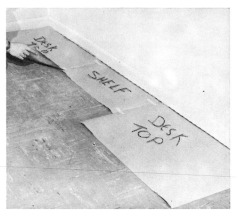

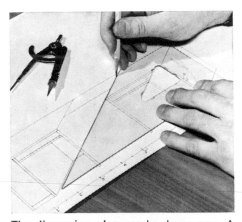

Before investing money in materials and more time on planning, it would be wise to find out if your project will fit the space and if it will be larger or smaller than needed. You will also want to know if the whole unit will be in good proportion and if it will project too far into the room. You can learn all these things and more by making full-size paper patterns and laying them in the space to be occupied by the finished project.

The dimension plan can be drawn now. A three-dimensional drawing is easy to make with a set square. Line up one side of the 30-degree angle with any convenient horizontal line on the graph paper and draw the slanted line along the other side of the angle. Make this drawing to scale, counting the squares for dimensions. Draw a scale at the bottom of the drawing and measure the slanted lines with a compass.

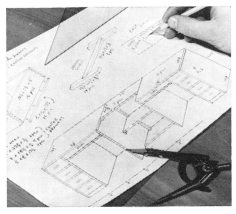

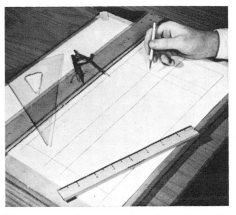

Elaborate on the dimension plan as much as necessary. Show material thickness to scale. Draw details in double scale. Make other small supplementary sketches to visualize problems. Write in the exact dimensions to let you measure and cut the material directly from your drawing. Indicate the material needed so you can make a buying list for all materials and hardware.

If your graph-paper dimension plan tells you everything you need to know, stop drawing and start building. It is sometimes necessary, however, especially for large, intricate projects, to make a *three-view drawing* with the help of a draughtsman's T-square and drawing board.

Put masking tape on a ruler, covering up the existing numbers. Using a scale of $\frac{1}{8}$-inch to the *inch* (or larger for smaller jobs) mark off the ruler in feet. Pick dimensions off the scale and transfer them to the drawing with your compass. Show hidden edges as dashed lines. Draw front view first, then side and top views. It is much easier to transfer dimensions from one view to another with the T-square and set square.

Make cutting diagrams for sheet material such as plywood and hardboard. First prepare some graph paper in a scale size of 4 × 8 feet. Then cut out sections of graph paper to scale for each piece needed in your project. Make these pieces slightly larger than scale size to allow for saw cut, but note the exact dimensions along each side. Arrange pieces on the 4 × 8 "plywood" graph paper for minimum waste. Mark real plywood same way.

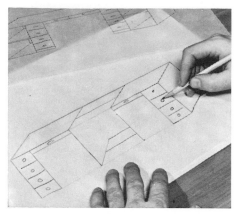

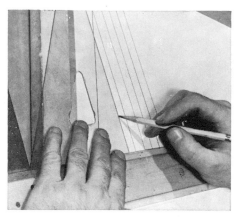

When working out the initial design for a project, draw the limiting dimensions on a piece of graph paper. Tape pieces of tracing paper over the graph paper, sketching in and working over designs until you hit on the one you want to build. By having the limiting dimensions on the graph paper beneath the tracing paper, you will not have to lay out the outline again for each new design idea. Do not be satisfied with your design until you have tried out all the possibilities for your project.

To draw a series of parallel slanted lines, place your set square on the paper at the correct angle. Then tilt the T-square to line up with the bottom edge of the set square as shown and hold it firm with the heel of your hand. By sliding the set square along the T-square with your fingers you can make any number of parallel lines. If you have a large number of these lines to make, it is a good idea to tape the T-square in the desired position to avoid its possible movement from the proper angle.

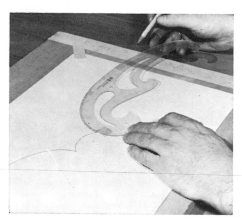

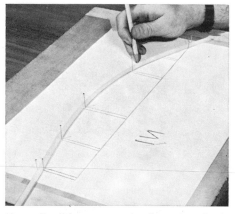

Drawing curved lines usually presents problems, but you can find almost any curve you may need on a French curve. Sketch in curve free-hand first; then line up French curve and draw the line in solid. Putting small bits of tape at both ends of curved segment you are using helps you re-locate it quickly when reproducing the same curve elsewhere. Use a compass for circular and semi-circular curves.

Use a flexible curve made of wood or plastic to help you draw long, gentle curves. Position it on the drawing board with pins as shown. You can measure the length of the curve you draw by marking the ends of the line on the flexible curve while it is in position, then laying it out flat when it is removed. Keep a good supply of sharpened 3H or 4H drawing pencils on hand—and a good eraser. Do your rough sketches with a soft pencil—B or 2B.

Garage storage

Many garages and lofts are overflowing with "indispensable" equipment necessary for maintaining a household. Homeowners find themselves moving pyramids of boxes, gardening tools, sporting equipment, and all kinds of odds and ends to get at one item—always at the bottom.

If your home has these problems, here is an ideal storage system. It provides neat, accessible places for everything, at low cost. And it takes only a minimum of work, tools, and skill.

These units were built in a garage, but you could adapt them to nearly any situation. You will end up with more and better storage space in the same floor area—in fact, it may be difficult to fill it up.

Before gathering materials together, you should, of course, decide where you want to put your storage units. A long, blank wall is best, but you can install it around windows or doors.

Take a tape measure and notebook, find out how much room is available, and work the project out on paper. Then you are ready to calculate the materials needed.

Rows of cardboard boxes give dust-free storage for small seasonal items. The floor space under the boxes is reserved for bulky items which are too heavy to lift. When building this type of storage rack in a garage, leave adequate space for opening the car doors.

Make the open framework for the boxes from 1 x2 battens. Nail the front framework together, then stand it upright against the wall and mark the walls for fixing positions. Make the 1 x2 uprights long enough to fasten to the ceiling. In loft areas fix uprights to joists.

Buy or collect boxes of a uniform size that will fit neatly between the studs—size of boxes determines the dimensions of the framework. When storing heavy objects in boxes, you should reinforce the bottom with an extra sheet of cardboard trimmed from another large box.

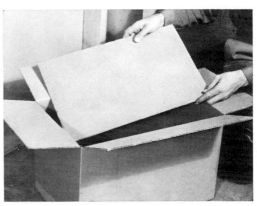

Give the boxes a wash coat of varnish. Your storage will be much more attractive if you also paint at least the exposed side of the boxes a bright colour. Almost any paint you happen to have on hand will do this job—water-base paint is best.

Make labels from pieces of white card and stick them to the boxes with rubber cement. If you use rubber cement, you will be able to peel off the old label easily and replace it with a new one whenever you wish to change contents of box.

Nail in shelf supports at heights convenient for things you plan to store. You can use 1 × 2, as shown, or go to 2 × 2 for heavier duty. Shelves can be either $\frac{3}{8}''$ plywood, blockboard, chipboard, or even hardboard, if light objects are to be stored.

Cut plywood, or other material chosen to make the shelves, to fit. There is no need to nail it down, because you might want to move it to another position as your storage needs change. Try to make all shelves pf the same dimensions as the cardboard boxes you have used so that the whole unit is interchangeable.

For garden tools, you will probably want to reserve some wall space near the door. Cut a series of notches in a piece of 1 × 2 and nail it to the wall for off-the-ground storage of shovels, hoes, and other long-handled tools. A length of 1 × 2 across the battens keeps other tools against the wall below. Make the hose reel from tin cans. Screw them to a scrap of plywood nailed to the wall. Put small hand tools in open ends of the cans.

This unit provides for many storage needs, but it occupies very little floor space. Experi-ment with a 2- by 8-foot piece of paper to see how it will fit.

A room divider to make

This storage divider wall contains ample storage space, a cabinet for record player and television, and a desk.

The wall was designed with four ideas in mind—ease of construction, economy of materials, ease of movement, and maximum storage capacity. Three sheets of faced plywood, three sheets of birch plywood, and a little hardwood are all the materials you need. This unit fastens together in four sections which can easily be taken apart if you ever want to move it.

The unit can also make an additional room in your living room. A track folding door covers the conveniently placed entry to the living room.

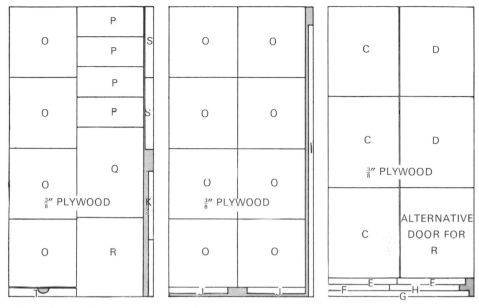

These three diagrams show you how to cut doors, shelves, and other small pieces for maximum economy. Cut the main panels (A, B, M and N) to the sizes shown on the drawing. Drawer front and other small pieces not shown on these diagrams are cut out of scraps left over from main panels. Note the alternate choice for door piece R.

Cut strips of beading $\frac{3}{8}$ inch × $\frac{3}{8}$ inch to edge the doors. Make mitred joints at the corners. Nail and glue strips to edges. Sand the doors to make the strips flush with the door veneer. The dimensions of the doors given on the drawing are for the size you should cut the plywood. When you add the $\frac{3}{8}$-inch edging strips, the doors will be the size needed for the finished unit.

You can cut mortises for the concealed door hinges with a radial arm saw as shown here, or in a similar manner on a table saw. You must also slightly bevel the door edge opposite the hinges to allow the doors to fit flush and still have clearance for opening. Make bevel with plane.

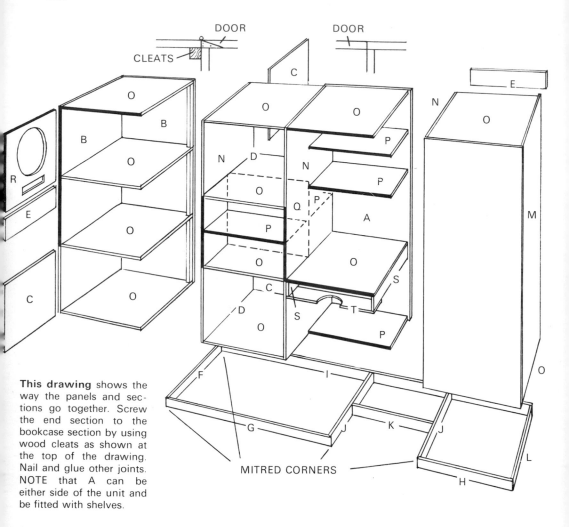

DOOR

CLEATS

DOOR

This drawing shows the way the panels and sections go together. Screw the end section to the bookcase section by using wood cleats as shown at the top of the drawing. Nail and glue other joints. NOTE that A can be either side of the unit and be fitted with shelves.

MITRED CORNERS

$\frac{3}{8}$" FACED PLYWOOD

A	$23\frac{3}{4}$" × 7'	2
B	23" × 7'	2
C	23" × 27"	DOOR 3
D	$23\frac{3}{4}$" × 27"	DOOR 2
E	$22\frac{1}{4}$" × $2\frac{1}{2}$"	2
* F	$1\frac{3}{4}$" × $20\frac{1}{2}$"	1
G	$1\frac{3}{4}$" × 44"	1
H	$1\frac{3}{4}$" × $28\frac{3}{4}$"	1

*** To avoid a lot of hand cutting, F, G, H, I, J, K, L can be of 1 ×2 battens.**

$\frac{3}{8}$" PLYWOOD

I	$1\frac{3}{4}$" × 7'6"	1
J	$1\frac{3}{4}$" × $19\frac{3}{4}$"	2
K	$1\frac{3}{4}$" × $22\frac{1}{4}$"	1
L	$1\frac{3}{4}$" × 19"	1
M	$23\frac{3}{4}$" × 7'	1
N	23" × 7'	3
O	$22\frac{1}{4}$" × 23"	12
P	$22\frac{1}{4}$" × $10\frac{3}{8}$"	5
Q	$22\frac{1}{4}$" × 28"	1
R	$22\frac{1}{4}$" × $25\frac{1}{2}$"	1
S	$23\frac{1}{4}$" × 3"	2
T	$22\frac{1}{4}$" × 3"	1

Fasten the hinges to the cabinet walls as shown. Drive screws in the elongated holes first, check door alignment, then drive in the remaining screws. The finished job leaves only a very small part of the hinge showing when the doors are closed. You can use magnetic door catches on the doors. No door knobs will be necessary because you can get good fingerholds on the edges of all the doors.

Build the drawer as shown here for the desk section. Cut $\frac{1}{2}" \times \frac{1}{2}"$ grooves in the drawer sides to receive the wood drawer guides (arrow). Groove sides, front, and back $\frac{1}{4}"$ from lower edge to set in a hardboard drawer bottom. Build the complete desk assembly, then screw it in place after the wall is assembled. Make a laminated plastic top for the desk. Cement top on last.

If you plan to have strip or other concealed or semi-concealed lights in the divider, then the wires for these must be run in as you build the unit. It is not advisable to wire these lights directly into the house circuit—run a fused plug to an existing power point. In this way, the divider can be moved from one position to another.

You can adapt the basic design of this unit to your own special needs very easily because of its construction technique. If you make the unit taller or shorter, be certain that you maintain the 30 inch desk height.

If you build the unit against a wall, only two sheets of faced plywood are required. Use $\frac{3}{8}$-inch plywood for the back. You might want to consider a section four feet wide to store a foldaway bed or card table and chairs.

When planning, try to use the standard size sheets of hardboard or plywood. It will be cheaper than having each piece cut separately at the wood shop. There is a chart giving the sizes of these boards on page 107.

Build your own kitchen island work centre

A kitchen island is an easy, inexpensive way of making use of wasted kitchen floor space and giving additional work surface, storage, and a snack bar.

Techniques that make for easy construction and best use of materials have been carefully worked into this design.

Use second grade plywood, since only one side of each piece will show when the island is assembled. After you have cut and assembled all the pieces, sand and prime the whole island before finishing. Aerosol spray enamel, applied in several thin coats, makes a good, smooth finish. It is especially easy if you finish the island in several decorative colours.

An inexpensive way to have plastic laminate doors and drawer fronts is to buy off-cuts. These are available from your d.i.y. shop. The off-cuts have plastic laminate already glued to plywood or blockboard. You will probably have to trim them up as shown. You can choose from several different colours for drawer fronts and doors.

Cut $\frac{3}{4}$ inch rabbet at the ends of the drawer fronts. Groove drawer sides as shown to ride $\frac{3}{4}$ inch $\times$ $\frac{1}{2}$ inch drawer slides. Cut the slides from hardwood and fasten them in the drawer openings with screws and glue. Make $\frac{1}{8}$ inch grooves in the drawer sides and the front, $\frac{1}{2}$ inch from the bottom edge to receive drawer bottoms of hardboard. Drawer back is fatened between the sides so its lower edge sits on the hardboard drawer bottom.

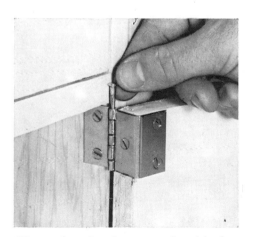

Hinges for the doors can be plain butt type, but these flush door hinges give better support when driving screws into plywood. Cut shallow mortises in the doors to receive the hinges. Since these are loose pin hinges, you can mount one leaf on the door and the other on the island, then hang the door by replacing the pins. Use a plane to bevel opposite edge of the door slightly to let it open.

Slide-out shelves are made as shown. Make slides from aluminium channel or wood. You can also buy ready-made slides. Some models have nylon rollers for extra ease. Put a $\frac{3}{8}$ inch shim behind the slide on the door side of the cabinet. This lets the shelf clear the door as it is pulled out. Rub paraffin wax on shelf edges and on the drawer slides to make them work more easily.

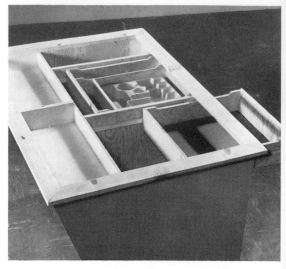

Assemble your island in the kitchen, since it is too big to go through most doorways. Put on the plastic laminate top last of all. The laminate should overlap the edges, so cut it about $\frac{1}{8}$ inch larger than the plywood top. Before finishing, cover all exposed plywood edges with edging. The shelf under counter is for place mats, etc.

Island looks like this before plywood top has been put on. Note the framework to make the top appear thicker. Nail the actual top to this frame before applying the plastic laminate top and edge strips. Notice how the drawer is divided into storage compartments.

How the island goes together

Main parts of the island are shown here. clamp centre dividers (B) together and cut slots for door frames (F). This assures that door openings will be square. Inset 2 × 4 base 2½ inches from front and sides for toe room. Make shelf of scrap for tray storage section at right.

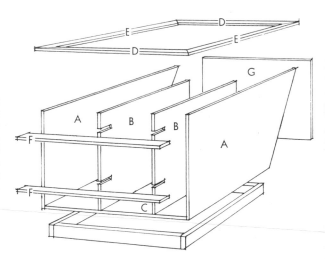

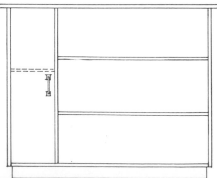

If you already have an eating area in your kitchen, you might want to alter the design on the eating side of the island to include open shelves and one additional door as shown in this drawing. Also, you may want to glue strips of felt to the bottom edges of the 2 × 4 base to prevent floor scratches.

Cutting diagrams for your kitchen island

These cutting diagrams show you how to get most pieces for construction of the kitchen island out of two sheets of $\frac{1}{2}$-inch and one sheet of $\frac{3}{8}$-inch plywood. In addition to the plywood, you will need a sheet of $\frac{1}{2}$-inch hardboard for drawer bottoms, a 12-foot 2 × 4 for base, and laminate plastic for top.

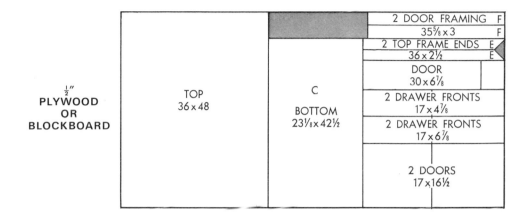

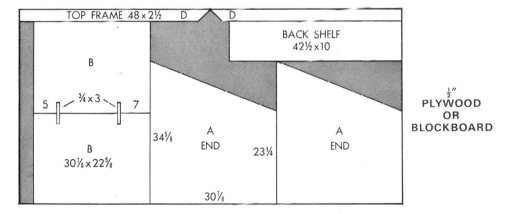

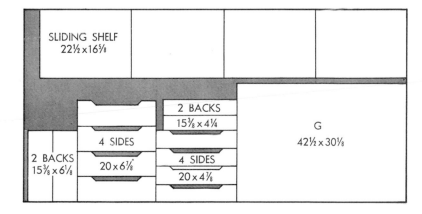

Metal refinishing—the right way

The most skilled handyman is often a dismal failure when it comes to proper metal refinishing. Usually, the mistakes are made at the start when not enough importance is given to careful application of metal primers—the surface-preparation agents.

Metal primers do two things that no other coating can do. They are made to form a surface on metal for other paints, and they set up a chemical barrier against rust and corrosion.

Metal rusts when exposed to moisture, air—and other rust. As rust forms, it creates an acid which speeds up the processes of rust and corrosion.

Primers lie in wait for the corrosion or rust to start. When this happens, the primer reacts chemically with the acid as it forms to neutralize the corrosive action of the acid.

Outdoor tools, furnishings and equipment obviously need periodic inspection and treatment for rust, but do not overlook metal equipment in the house—corrosion takes place there as well as outdoors. Any metal exposed to long periods of dampness and absence of daylight is fair game for rust and corrosion.

The table below lists some of the metal priming situations you will need around the home.

A quick guide for metal refinishing

Metal	Type of finish	Preparation	Primer	Finish coat
Iron and Steel	Ultra smooth—cars, bikes, appliances.	Sand away rust, feather edges of paint.	Zinc chromate, two or three coats. Sand.	Spray or brush enamel.
	Utility—outdoor furniture and equipment.	Remove old paint with a remover, wire brush or torch.	Zinc chromate, two or more coats—thickness counts.	Glossy enamel, and eggshell paint, exterior rubber base paint, gloss paint or other finish.
	Rough—badly rusted.	Scrape and wire-brush.	Red lead.	
	Galvanized iron.	Wash with detergent, or let weather.	Zinc dust—zinc oxide primer.	
Aluminium and Copper	Utility finish.	Clean with wire wool.	None.	Same as above.
	Clear finish.	Clean with wire wool—do not finger after cleaning.	None.	Spar varnish (copper). Acrylic or butyrate lacquer (aluminium).

The kind of finish you get depends on the preparation you give the surface. For critical work—and all work when feasible—clean away the rust right down to the bare metal, ready for primer. Feather the edges of original paint so they will not show under the new finish when it is applied. To sand large areas, use power sander with open coat sandpaper. When you do power sanding, you should still feather the edges of the paint by hand, using fine sandpaper. Aluminium oxide or garnet sandpaper works best, lasts longest.

Refinishing outdoor furniture is a job quite similar to refinishing wood furniture. Take off the old paint with paint remover, then sand away rust by hand or with a power sander. A propane blow-lamp takes off paint in a hurry. Use a flame-spreader attachment and scrape off the burned paint as you go. A wire brush in an electric drill is a fast way to spot clean ornamental ironwork which is hard to clean otherwise. With practice, you can remove all rust and partially feather edges of old paint in one operation.

On badly rusted pieces of equipment, scrape off loose rust with a putty knife and wire brush. Use one of the special rust primers, some of these seal the rust areas that cannot be cleaned away. Allow this type of primer to dry out before applying top coats. You can even leave this kind of primer exposed to the weather for several weeks before applying the finish paint.

Galvanized metal needs only a good scrubbing with detergent and water as preparation for primer. Do this even though the surface looks clean, because the oils used in the galvanizing process will be present. You need not etch galvanized metal with acid or vinegar as is popularly believed. Tests made by paint manufacturers show that this does more harm than good. Prime with metallic zinc paint or one of specially made galvanized metal primers.

Use zinc chromate primer on bare iron and steel, but never over rust. Brush it on evenly but heavily. Avoid touching the bare metal with your hands, and wash off the surface with turpentine before applying the primer. Do not permit zinc chromate-primed pieces to sit out in the weather before applying the finish coat. Although it is the best primer for iron and steel, it is not durable enough to hold up long without a good enamel top coat to repel moisture. Let zinc chromate dry overnight before applying the top coat, even if it seems dry.

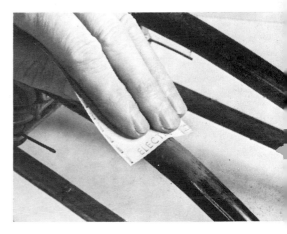

Sand the primer to make a smooth base for the top coat of enamel. Be careful not to sand the primer through at any point. Use wet or dry sandpaper. When finishing large areas, such as car body repairs, use water with the sandpaper to keep it from clogging. Also, sand area around primer to help the enamel coat stick when you spray it on. When spot-finishing surfaces that have been waxed, be sure to remove wax around the area with turpentine, *just sanding will not do the job.*

At corners, on edges, and other spots where wear will be heavy, double up the coverage by lapping over the edges with your brush as you go. However, don't let the primer sag into a "fat edge", which is not durable. Most vulnerable places are points of fabrication, where rust is most likely to start. Make sure coverage is good at joints. The finish wears off the bumps and rough places faster than elsewhere, so on pieces of welded construction, use a file or disc sander to smooth ridges of the welds.

Red lead primer with the proper base (labelled "moisture displacing") can be used in extremely damp situations. You can apply this primer over metal that has been simply wiped off with a cloth. Always prime dry when possible, but do not let water stop you. This type of primer also has excellent rust penetrating qualities, so it is the perfect one for maintenance of outdoor equipment. It comes in colours that blend with the finish paint.

348

The right kind of top-coat finishes the job

An extra smooth top coat is easy to obtain with an aerosol spray enamel. They come in a wide range of colours, and some are specially made for the treatment of rust. But the finished result still depends on the initial preparation.

When using an aerosol, remember to give it a good shake—both before you start spraying and periodically during spraying. Protect the surrounding area with sheets of newspaper, and do not hold the spray too close to the job.

A good quality gloss paint provides a good finish to wrought iron furniture, but again the finish is only as good as the preparation. Do not forget to prepare and paint those surfaces which are normally out of sight.

Some wrought iron pieces (such as door stops, hinges, letter-boxes, door-knockers) look better with a matt finish. This is achieved by brushing on flat black instead of gloss. Preparation is carried out in the same way as for gloss painting.

For downspouts and gutters

Gutters and downpipes are finished the same way as any other galvanized metal unless they are rusted—then you treat them like any other rusted iron and prime with a red lead primer to penetrate the rust. To make the gutters really last, give them a coat of liquid bitumen on the inside. This paint will fill pinhole leaks caused by rust. To paint the insides of downpipes, drop a weighted string through the downpipe and tie one end to a sponge. Soak the sponge with paint and then pull it through.

Stop rust and corrosion

Rust and other forms of corrosion cost money—and more money if left unchecked.

Right at this moment, some part of the metal in, on, or around your home is being quietly destroyed by corrosion. It may go unnoticed—until too late.

You can beat this ever-present enemy by taking a few minutes of your time to make a tour of your home, both inside and outside. Make a list of the metal parts that could rust or corrode. Then make periodic inspections, watching for the trouble signals listed below. When you discover damage caused by corrosion, follow the appropriate steps outlined here.

Watch for tell-tale signs of corrosion:

- Iron and steel develop the familiar reddish or brownish colour as they rust. (The term *rust* is commonly used only for corrosion of iron or steel.)
- Copper and bronze acquire a greenish patina or a dark brown colour. This form of corrosion is sometimes desired for decorative purposes.
- Aluminium takes on a chalky white appearance.

If rust has already taken over, remove the loose surface flakes with a scraper and a stiff wire brush. Sand the surface until bright metal shows, wipe clean. Some paints can be applied directly over coatings of corrosion.

Over the cleaned area apply a prime coat of red lead paint, then undercoat(s) and then top coat. On small jobs, an inexpensive aerosol spray paint works very well. They are available in a wide range of colours.

Check gutters and downpipes. Keeping them clean adds to their life by allowing them to dry quickly. Best rust preventive is a coat of liquid bitumen. You should brush evenly over inner surface.

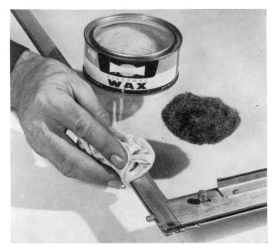

Aluminium windows and doors, outside trim, etc., tend to turn white with age. To preserve the new appearance longer, coat with paste wax or one of the new aerosol spray aluminium preservatives. If corrosion is already evident, give the surface a brisk rub with very fine steel wool to restore the shine. If you decide to paint, clean with aluminium preparation compound, then apply primer.

Galvanised steel garbage cans are almost sure to rust eventually. Paint inside with zinc chromate while can is new. Periodic cleaning and drying prevents rust. Prime and paint outside to protect base and bottom of can.

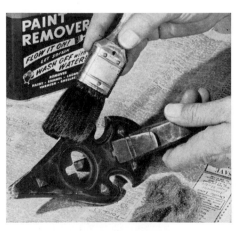

Brass outside hardware will tarnish after the original lacquer wears off. Remove the remaining lacquer with paint remover, clean with a good brass polish, then finish with a clear lacquer to preserve its appearance.

How to work with metal

For every metal-working job, there is a tool and technique that will reduce it to the proportions of your more familiar woodworking tasks. So do not be afraid to work with metal just because it is an unfamiliar material. In fact, if you have read this far through the book, you will already have seen how easily metal-working fits into your workshop, even if it is equipped primarily for wood-work.

The use of a hacksaw fits naturally into your hand-tool skills; knowledge of fastening with bolts, rivets and screws is as easy to come by as of other materials; tools for cutting some kinds of aluminium are the same as for wood cutting; soldering skill is an absolute necessity; and the ability to use files and grinding equipment properly is very useful.

Described here are the operations of drilling, threading, cutting, and forming various shapes and bends in metal. All of them just as useful to the handyman as the other skills that have been described in earlier pages of this book.

All your tools for simple metal-work are familiar to every handyman: drills, reamer, countersinks, cold chisel, ball-peen hammer, punches, tap-and-die sets, etc.

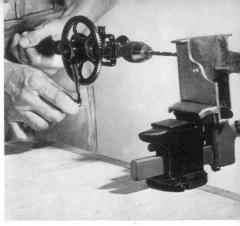

Centre punch is a must in metal drilling. Sharp tap from hammer produces a tiny indentation to mark exact point, preventing drill from wandering. Do not strike too hard, and keep punch sharpened.

Keep drills cutting in metal with a steady pressure, and they stay sharp longer. Hold drill steady, with work firm in vice. Go easy or drill may break.

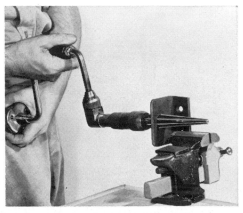

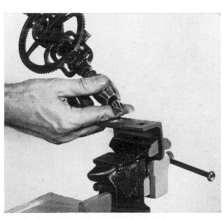

Reamers enlarge holes when you need an in-between size—or existing hole is too small. Do not push too hard, or reamer may bind— but keep it cutting. You will nick the reamer if you turn it backwards while you are working.

Countersink in metal as in wood for flat-head screws and bolts. Use tool in hand or an electric drill or brace. Specify "for metal" when you buy drill. A file used period-ically will keep its hardened edges sharp.

Cold chisels move metal fast when sheet is too thick for tin snips, too wide for hacksaw. Use them to cut rods quickly, to remove rivets and rusty nails, and to chip away excess metal. Shear-cut heavy sheet by clamping it in a vice as shown here, cutting close to the jaws. You can avoid jaw marks on your work by making a pair of soft-metal cushions for jaws.

To make cut-outs in metal, scribe hole, then centre-punch and drill series of over-lapping holes. Clean up the edges with cold chisel, using your file for the final dressing.

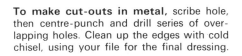

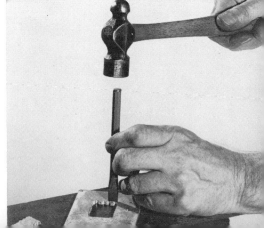

Punches are very useful for metal-working, since they can reach in where your hammer cannot go, and help direct the hammer's force to precise areas. Use them for such jobs as driving out pins, for loosening large, screw-fastened fittings, and for drawing holes together for position fastening metal to metal.

For screws in metal, taps, and dies

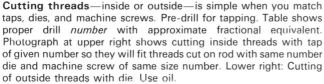

Cutting threads—inside or outside—is simple when you match taps, dies, and machine screws. Pre-drill for tapping. Table shows proper drill *number* with approximate fractional equivalent. Photograph at upper right shows cutting inside threads with tap of given number so they will fit threads cut on rod with same number die and machine screw of same size number. Lower right: Cutting of outside threads with die. Use oil.

Tap-drill sizes for common machine screws

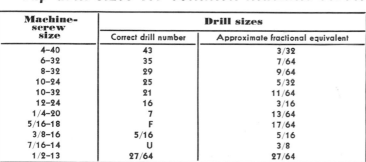

Machine-screw size	Drill sizes	
	Correct drill number	Approximate fractional equivalent
4–40	43	3/32
6–32	35	7/64
8–32	29	9/64
10–24	25	5/32
10–32	21	11/64
12–24	16	3/16
1/4–20	7	13/64
5/16–18	F	17/64
3/8–16	5/16	5/16
7/16–14	U	3/8
1/2–13	27/64	27/64

For a firm grip
a vice is your tool

Avoid jaw marks from vice on your work by making a pair of soft-metal cushions to fit over the jaws of the metal-working vice. Copper, aluminium, and so on are too soft to mark other metals and will let you clamp vice up tight without making tooth marks. Cut metal cushions as shown. Hammer snugly around jaws to make them stay in place.

For bending curves in metal, make jig by clamping two bolts in a vice, as shown. Slide the metal between the two bolts. Make the bends in several bites, moving the metal after each of the tiny bends. Small bites make tight bends, bigger bites give larger curves—for any combination.

To bend corners in metal, clamp the piece in a vice, strike sharp blows near jaws. Each right-angle bend "absorbs" half the thickness of the metal, so figure this "shrink" in computing the lengths when you cut. With soft metals, use a wood block as cushion to avoid marking surface.

To bend sheet metal, clamp it tightly between two pieces of hardwood in vice, with auxiliary clamp if needed, as shown here. Force the initial bend by pressure from the heel of your hand. The use a mallet against block to set the sharp corner of the metal at the exact angle you desire. A bevel on the block in back can help you gauge uniform repeat bends in the sheet.

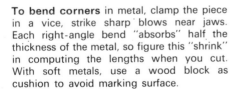

Easy picture framing

There are no quick methods or tricks for making picture frames. One of the biggest difficulties is cutting the mitre joints correctly so corners fit perfectly. It is a wise practice to make several trial cuts on scrap wood—2 x 1 or 1 x 1 will do—and gain experience before embarking on the job. Make a complete frame out of scrap to be sure you can get even joints at all four corners.

When you begin work on a picture-frame, make all measurements precisely and then double check before you start cutting. If the material has a design on it, plan cuts to make corner designs match.

Photographs or drawings should be mounted under glass to prevent curling. Prints can be mounted on the rough side of hardboard to simulate a canvas texture, or you can simply tape them to stiff cardboard. Varnish oil-painting prints, spray others with clear plastic.

You can buy picture-frame mouldings from an art supply store, either pre-finished or unfinished. They are all rather expensive.

Timber shops stock a wide variety of mouldings which you can use at a much lower cost than the ones shown above.

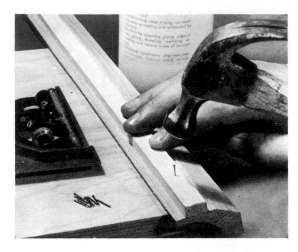

To **adapt** ordinary moulding for use in a picture frame, nail and glue a thin wood strip on the back, $\frac{1}{4}$-inch from the inside edge. This strip takes the place of the rabbet on standard picture frame moulding. Put this strip on before you cut the mitred corners, for a neater job. Set your combination square at $\frac{1}{4}$-inch, as shown far left, to space the strip uniformly.

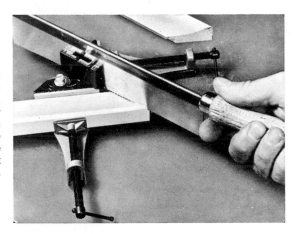

A mitre box corner clamp is an inexpensive tool that will help you cut exact 45-degree mitres easily. Use a dovetail saw or back saw for cutting. A complete set, consisting of three corner clamps and one mitre clamp, will take most of the squaring and cutting problems out of a picture-framing job for you.

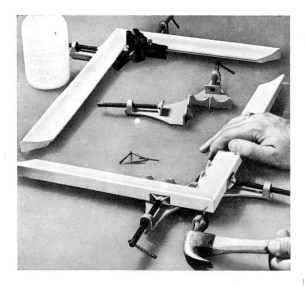

Clamp and glue the frame together as shown here, fitting two opposite corners first. If the joints do not come together well, clamp a folded piece of sandpaper in the joint and slide it back and forth to true the two mitres simultaneously. Small brads through the joints add strength. Drill pilot holes to prevent splitting.

Set the picture in the frame by driving small brads or glazier's points into the frame behind the picture mounting. If you do not wish to mount the print on hardboard, tape it to a stiff piece of card-board. When mounting pictures under glass, make sure both the picture and glass surfaces are perfectly clean.

Cutting a mount for picture mounting takes a steady hand. Buy picture mounting board. Cut the opening slightly smaller than your picture. Use a sharp knife and a straight edge, and cut a bevel about 30 degrees from the vertical. Tape the picture to the board, and tape the board to stiff card-board for mounting in frame.

On frames made from pre-finished moulding, make the mitres less obvious by rubbing the joint with paint of the same colour as the original finish. Mix some fine sanding dust with the paint to help fill in an imperfect mitre joint. For an easy finish on an ordinary moulding frame, rub paint on with a soft rag so the grain shows.

Here is your picture almost ready for hanging. Finish the job by putting screw eyes in the back of the frame about one-third of the distance down from the top. Attach the wire to the screw eyes with enough slack so the wire comes nearly to the top of the frame. Bend the screw eyes over so the frame hangs flat against wall.

Here is a way to mount prints of oil paintings so they have the canvas-textured surface of original oil paintings. Cut a piece of standard hardboard $\frac{1}{4}$ inch larger on all sides than the print you're going to mount. Brush a solution of $\frac{1}{4}$ white glue and $\frac{3}{4}$ water on the rough side of the hardboard. Scrub it well into the surface. Then soak the print in a large tray of water until it lies flat of its own weight.

Remove the print from the water, blot it thoroughly, and apply the same solution of glue and water to the back. Give the hardboard another coat too, then fit the print on the hardboard, spacing evenly on all sides. The print will probably stretch a little when you soak it, and should fit the hardboard almost exactly. Lay wax paper over the print and with a cloth rub from the centre toward the sides to remove all the excess glue solution.

Finally, lay several thicknesses of newspaper over the wax paper on the print and clamp the sandwich between two pieces of $\frac{1}{2}$- or $\frac{3}{4}$-inch plywood. The layer of newspaper serves as a pad to force the wet print into the rough surface of the hardboard. Be sure to clamp the sandwich tightly and evenly, or weight it with a big stack of heavy books. Let the print dry overnight, then remove the newspaper and wax paper. Now brush print with a coat of dull varnish.

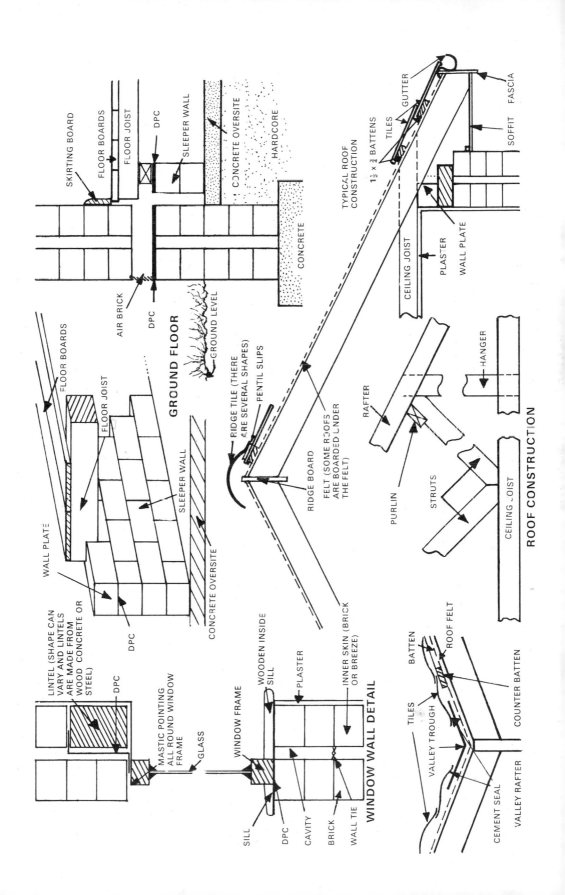

GROUND FLOOR

SKIRTING BOARD
FLOOR BOARDS
FLOOR JOIST
DPC
SLEEPER WALL
CONCRETE OVERSITE
HARDCORE
CONCRETE
AIR BRICK
DPC
GROUND LEVEL

WALL PLATE
FLOOR BOARDS
FLOOR JOIST
SLEEPER WALL
DPC
DPC
CONCRETE OVERSITE

LINTEL (SHAPE CAN VARY AND LINTELS ARE MADE FROM WOOD CONCRETE OR STEEL)
DPC
MASTIC POINTING ALL ROUND WINDOW FRAME
GLASS

WINDOW WALL DETAIL

WINDOW FRAME
WOODEN INSIDE SILL
PLASTER
INNER SKIN (BRICK OR BREEZE)
SILL
DPC
CAVITY
BRICK
WALL TIE

TYPICAL ROOF CONSTRUCTION
1½ x ¾ BATTENS
TILES
GUTTER
FASCIA
SOFFIT
CEILING JOIST
PLASTER
WALL PLATE

RIDGE TILE (THERE ARE SEVERAL SHAPES)
PENTIL SLIPS
RIDGE BOARD
FELT (SOME ROOFS ARE BOARDED UNDER THE FELT)

ROOF CONSTRUCTION

HANGER
RAFTER
PURLIN
STRUTS
CEILING JOIST

TILES
BATTEN
ROOF FELT
VALLEY TROUGH
COUNTER BATTEN
CEMENT SEAL
VALLEY RAFTER

Furniture measurements

Side chair

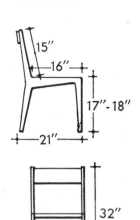

15"
16"
17"-18"
21"
32"
5"
16"
17"

Table & chairs

32" 15"-18"

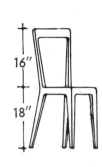

16"
18"

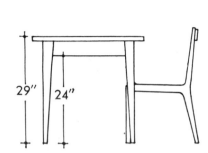

29" 24"

Low chair

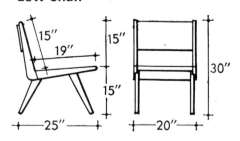

15"
19"
15"
15"
25"
30"
20"

Book heights

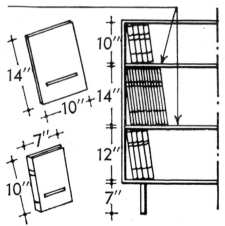

14"
10"
7"
10"
10"
14"
12"
7"

Desk or Host chair

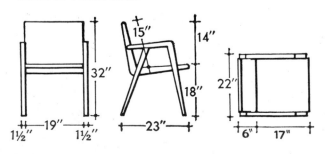

15"
14"
32"
18"
22"
19"
1½"
1½"
23"
6"
17"

Bookshelf

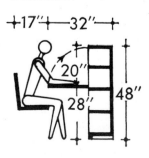

17" 32"
20"
28"
48"

Central heating

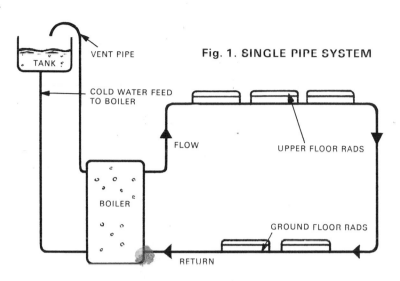

TANK

VENT PIPE

COLD WATER FEED
TO BOILER

Fig. 1. SINGLE PIPE SYSTEM

FLOW

UPPER FLOOR RADS

BOILER

GROUND FLOOR RADS

RETURN

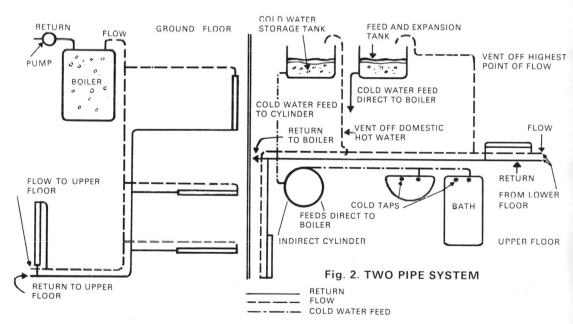

RETURN

FLOW

GROUND FLOOR

COLD WATER
STORAGE TANK

FEED AND EXPANSION
TANK

VENT OFF HIGHEST
POINT OF FLOW

PUMP

BOILER

COLD WATER FEED
DIRECT TO BOILER

COLD WATER FEED
TO CYLINDER

VENT OFF DOMESTIC
HOT WATER

RETURN
TO BOILER

FLOW

FLOW TO UPPER
FLOOR

COLD TAPS

BATH

RETURN

FROM LOWER
FLOOR

FEEDS DIRECT TO
BOILER

INDIRECT CYLINDER

UPPER FLOOR

RETURN TO UPPER
FLOOR

Fig. 2. TWO PIPE SYSTEM

——————— RETURN
– – – – – – FLOW
—·—·—·— COLD WATER FEED

Those who have had little or no experience of central heating installation can
save a considerable amount of money by
first consulting one of the many do-it-
yourself central heating manufacturers.

The manufacturer will design a system
to suit your particular needs. Before
doing so, the following information will
be required: Sizes of the rooms concerned;
temperatures required; how walls and
roof are constructed (heat loss has to be
taken into account); is the loft insulated?;

Fig. 3.
COMPRESSION FITTING

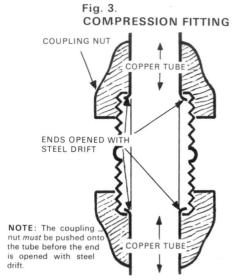

COUPLING NUT

COPPER TUBE

ENDS OPENED WITH STEEL DRIFT

NOTE: The coupling nut *must* be pushed onto the tube before the end is opened with steel drift.

COPPER TUBE

and are the windows double glazed? There are schemes whereby the home handyman does the majority of the work supervised by an expert. Under these schemes, the necessary specialist tools for the job can be hired.

The boiler must have a solid concrete base to stand on—not just a slab of concrete set on a wooden floor. You must also decide what type of fuel to use—gas, oil or solid fuel—and you should consider the following points about these fuels:

GAS—clean, needs no storage and is supplied at reasonable cost. But, if there is no gas already in the house, then the cost of running in supply pipes could be very high.

OIL—the important thing to consider is the storage tank which should be large enough to store at least four weeks' supply. Oil taken in small quantities is costly. The capital cost of an oil-fired boiler is greater than that for gas and so are maintenance costs, but the running costs are less providing supplies are bought in bulk.

A gas or oil-fired boiler must not be connected into a chimney built for use with solid fuel *unless it* has been fitted with a flexible asbestos liner. The gases from these boilers eat into ordinary flues, causing them to crumble and allowing gases to escape into the house.

SOLID FUEL— cheap to run but entails daily cleaning and carting of fuel from store to boiler. There is also the problem of disposing of the ash. Heat control is not so responsive as that in a gas or oil-fired boiler.

There are two types of central heating installation—the single pipe system and the double pipe system—and the difference between the two systems is shown in Figs. 1 and 2. The single pipe system is easier to install and requires less pipe (therefore less cost), but there is a difference of temperature between the first and last radiators in the circuit. With the double-pipe system, there is a constant temperature from each radiator even when one or more is out of service.

Remember when drilling holes for pipes in walls, etc. to allow space for expansion —a $\frac{3}{4}''$ pipe should pass through a 1" hole and a $\frac{1}{2}''$ pipe through a $\frac{3}{4}''$ hole.

To measure up the amount of pipe required, draw up a scale plan of the entire house showing the position of the radiators and the pipe runs. As you measure for pipes, make a note of the other fittings you will require, e.g. elbows, tees, reducing tees, check valves, drain plugs and couplers—all these come in compression or capillary fittings. Remember to allow for the insertion depth of the pipes in the fittings. You will also require copper spacing clips to hold the pipes to walls and skirting boards—they should be fixed one to approximately 4' of pipe. Pipes that pass through voids (lofts and under floors) should be lagged.

A compression fitting is screwed together while a capillary fitting is sweated together with a blow-lamp. Do not clean the fitting until you are ready to make the joint. A gas blow-lamp allows you to apply heat at all angles—protect walls and woodwork with an asbestos cloth. A newly-soldered joint should be allowed to cool before any further work is done on that particular section. Fig. 3 shows a typical compression fitting. Note that the ends of the pipes must be cut and fitted square or the joint is liable to leak.

Pipe bending is done with the aid of a

piece of softwood, about 30" long × 1" thick, and a bending spring. In the length of wood, drill 2 holes—one at $\frac{3}{4}$" for $\frac{1}{2}$" pipes and the other at 1" for $\frac{3}{4}$" pipes. Clean off any burr on the pipe after cutting.

When applying strands of hemp and jointing paste to the threaded fittings, ensure that there is no spill over into the bore. The fittings on the radiators nearly always need to be cleaned of paint—do this with a wire brush fitted to an electric drill, but do not allow any bits to fall into the radiators. Clean fittings with the aid of a vacuum cleaner and then screw the vent valve and plug into position. Dirt, flakes of paint, etc. in radiators or pipes will stop the flow of water very quickly.

The expansion tank should be fitted in an accessible position and it should have a tightly fitting lid to stop dirt filtering into the system. Leave a hole in the lid for the expansion pipe—this is the pipe which brings the water back into the system.

Circulating pumps should also be fitted in an accessible position. Most pumps need little or no maintenance. But if you drain the heating system for a period of days, then it is advisable to disconnect the pump and dry it well—otherwise rust could form on its internal parts. Any foreign bodies left in the system could damage the pump bearings.

Central heating painting problems

Here are some points to watch when painting radiators and pipes.

Radiators are generally made of pressed steel and therefore present no difficult painting problem. They may arrive already primed. But, when starting from bare metal, it is a wise precaution to avoid the use of lead-based primers because lead tends to become brittle, eventually cracking and damaging the finish. Other compositions are more flexible and lighter in colour. This is an additional advantage when finishing a radiator in a light colour, because primers gradually become deeper in colour under the influence of heat. Generally, glass paints are the best finishing paints because they withstand the expansion and contraction of the metal under temperature variations better than highly pigmented paints.

Hot water pipes will most likely be of copper, and a different technique should be followed. Rub down copper pipes with wire wool and paint thinners, and then apply gloss paint direct, without primer or undercoat. Alternatively, a heat resisting aluminium paint can be used. If you prefer unpainted copper pipes, they should first be cleaned. Then, after washing off the cleaning agent, coat at once with clear cellulose lacquer. The pipes will stay bright and clean for a long period without polishing.

There is often misunderstanding about the heat insulating effect of different finishes and colours suitable for radiator painting. The heat from a radiator is transmitted by convection and radiation, and colour has little or no effect on either. Nor does gloss or flat paint inhibit these processes. But if the paint contains metallic powders (for example, aluminium or bronze), then radiation will be considerably reduced. The best advice that can be given, therefore, is to use a good quality gloss finish.

Ways & means of double glazing

It is through the windows, each consisting of one piece of glass only, where maximum heat loss occurs—the larger the window, the larger the loss. Double glazing—two thicknesses of glass with still air between them for insulation—cuts heat loss by over half, cuts condensation, cuts noise and cuts fuel bills.

The cost of double glazing starts at about 3s. per square foot and, for the professionally installed systems, at 15s. per square foot. All forms of double glazing give similar thermal insulation, but performance is determined by the efficiency of the installation. In other words, you get only what you pay for.

Double glazing can be fitted into old or new buildings. If sealed units are used, they are cleaned as you would a normal window pane—two sides only. In some other installations, all four sides of the glass will need cleaning—the frequency will depend on the efficiency of the seal.

Basically, there are two methods of double glazing. The first consists of a window surround carrying two panes of glass individually glazed. This can be either in a wide rebate with the panes of glass separated by beading, or in separate rebates with one pane glazed from the inside and the other from the outside.

In the second method, the ordinary glazed window is converted by adding a second frame which is held in position by special surrounds or channels and clips or hinges and screws. This system is most suitable for do-it-yourself installations.

When adding a pane of glass, check that it does not foul window fittings, handles, etc.

A sealed unit is the most permanent form of double glazing that can be installed. It consists of two pieces of glass sealed together as a unit with an airstrip between. The unit is glazed into the window frame in the same way as a normal pane of glass and, when installed, is indistinguishable from an ordinary pane of glass.

The following diagrams show the various ways of double glazing:

The sealed unit for new buildings and conversions

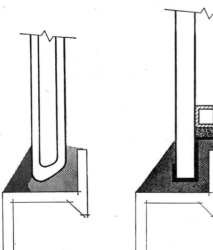

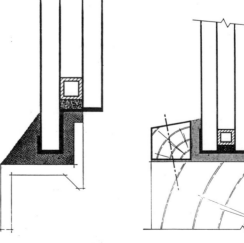

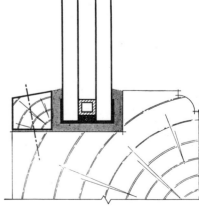

Sealed unit glazed into a metal frame, as here; or for wooden frames.

Stepped, sealed unit for use with frames with narrow rebates.

Sealed unit in a wooden frame; or for metal frames.

Adding a second pane of glass

	Using Wooden Moulding	*Using Plastic Extrusion*	*Frame to Frame First*

**FRAMING
METHODS**

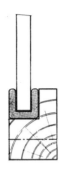 

Use a rebate moulding giving at least $\frac{1}{4}$-in edge cover to the glass, with a cushioning material between.

You have a wide choice now of plastic strips which fit neatly round the additional pane of glass.

With this type of extrusion which is adhesive backed you fix this to your window frame first.

**FIXING
METHODS**

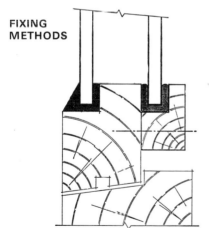 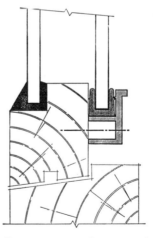 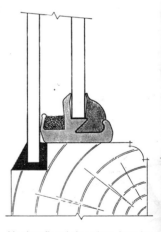

Secure the glass by screwing the moulding to the window frame. Use brass or plated screws to avoid rust.

One very convenient way of securing the additional frame is to use clips which enable the frame to be removed for cleaning.

Having fitted the glass into its channel, you retain it with the special fixing strip.

Conversion tables

Feet	Metres
1	0·30
2	0·61
3	0·91
4	1·22
5	1·52
6	1·83
7	2·13
8	2·44
9	2·74
10	3·05
11	3·35
12	3·66
13	3·96
14	4·27
15	4·57
16	4·87
17	5·18
18	5·48
19	5·79
20	6·09
21	6·40
22	6·70
23	7·01
24	7·31
25	7·62
26	7·92
27	8·23
28	8·53
29	8·83
30	9·14
31	9·45
32	9·75
33	10·06
34	10·36
35	10·67
36	10·97
37	11·28
38	11·58
39	11·88
40	12·19
41	12·49
42	12·80
43	13·10
44	13·41
45	13·71
46	14·02
47	14·32
48	14·63
49	14·93
50	15·24

Metres	Feet
1	3·28
2	6·56
3	9·84
4	13·12
5	16·40
6	19·68
7	22·96
8	26·24
9	29·53
10	32·81
11	36·09
12	39·37
13	42·65
14	45·93
15	49·21

Inches → Centimetres

Inches	1	2	3	4	5	6	7	8	9
0		2·54	5·08	7·62	10·16	12·70	15·24	17·78	20·32	22·86
10	25·40	27·94	30·48	33·02	35·56	38·10	40·64	43·18	45·72	48·26
20	50·80	53·34	55·88	58·42	60·96	63·50	66·04	68·58	71·12	73·66
30	76·20	78·74	81·28	83·82	86·36	88·90	91·44	93·98	96·52	99·06
40	101·60	104·14	106·68	109·22	111·76	114·30	116·84	119·38	121·92	124·46

Centimetres → Inches

Centimetres	1	2	3	4	5	6	7	8	9
0		0·39	0·79	1·18	1·57	1·97	2·36	2·75	3·15	3·54
10	3·94	4·33	4·72	5·12	5·51	5·90	6·30	6·69	7·09	7·48
20	7·87	8·27	8·66	9·05	9·45	9·84	10·23	10·63	11·02	11·42
30	11·81	12·20	12·60	12·99	13·38	13·78	14·17	14·56	14·96	15·35
40	15·75	16·14	16·53	16·93	17·32	17·72	18·11	18·50	18·90	19·29

Square Inches → Square Centimetres

Square Inches	1	2	3	4	5	6	7	8	9
0		6·45	12·90	19·35	25·80	32·26	38·71	45·16	51·61	58·06
10	64·51	70·97	77·42	83·87	90·32	96·77	103·22	109·67	116·13	122·58
20	129·03	135·48	141·93	148·38	154·84	161·29	167·74	174·19	180·64	187·09
30	193·55	200·00	206·45	212·90	219·35	225·80	232·26	238·71	245·16	251·61
40	258·06	264·51	270·96	277·42	283·87	290·32	296·77	303·22	309·67	316·13

Square Centimetres → Square Inches

Square Centimetres	1	2	3	4	5	6	7	8	9
0		0·15	0·31	0·46	0·62	0·77	0·93	1·08	1·24	1·39
10	1·55	1·70	1·86	2·01	2·17	2·32	2·48	2·63	2·79	2·94
20	3·10	3·25	3·41	3·56	3·72	3·87	4·03	4·18	4·34	4·49
30	4·65	4·80	4·96	5·11	5·27	5·42	5·58	5·73	5·89	6·04
40	6·20	6·35	6·51	6·66	6·82	6·97	7·13	7·28	7·44	7·59

Square Feet → Square Metres

Square Feet	1	2	3	4	5	6	7	8	9
0		0·09	0·18	0·28	0·37	0·46	0·55	0·65	0·74	0·83
10	0·93	1·02	1·11	1·22	1·30	1·39	1·48	1·58	1·67	1·76
20	1·86	1·95	2·04	2·13	2·23	2·32	2·41	2·51	2·60	2·69
30	2·78	2·88	2·97	3·06	3·16	3·25	3·34	3·43	3·53	3·62
40	3·71	3·81	3·90	3·99	4·09	4·18	4·27	4·36	4·46	4·55
50	4·64	4·74	4·83	4·92	6·01	5·11	5·20	5·29	5·39	5·48
60	5·57	5·66	5·76	5·85	5·94	6·04	6·13	6·22	6·31	6·41
70	6·50	6·59	6·69	6·78	6·87	6·97	7·06	7·15	7·24	7·34
80	7·43	7·52	7·62	7·71	7·80	7·89	7·99	8·08	8·17	8·27
90	8·36	8·45	8·54	8·64	8·73	8·82	8·92	9·01	9·10	9·19

Square Metres → Square Feet

Square Metres	1	2	3	4	5	6	7	8	9
0		10·76	21·53	32·29	43·05	53·82	64·58	75·35	86·11	96·87
10	107·64	118·40	129·17	139·93	150·69	161·46	172·22	182·98	193·75	204·51
20	215·28	226·04	236·80	247·57	258·33	269·10	279·86	290·62	301·39	312·15
30	322·91	333·68	344·44	355·21	365·97	376·73	387·50	398·26	409·03	419·79
40	430·55	441·32	452·08	462·85	473·61	484·37	495·14	505·90	516·67	527·43

Index

Bold type shows main entries